The Making of a
Royal Marines
Commando

The Making of a

ROYAL MARINES COMMANDO

Nigel Foster

PAN BOOKS

First published 1987 by Sidgwick & Jackson

This edition published 1998 by Pan Books
an imprint of Macmillan Publishers Ltd
25 Eccleston Place, London SW1W 9NF
and Basingstoke

Associated companies throughout the world

ISBN 0 330 35526 0

1 3 5 7 9 8 6 4 2

A CIP catalogue record for this book is available from
the British Library.

Typeset by SX Composing DTP, Rayleigh, Essex
Printed and bound in Great Britain by
Mackays of Chatham plc, Chatham, Kent

This edition is dedicated to all those fortunate enough to have worn the Green Beret.

Contents

Thanks and disclaimer

The author would like to thank all those former and present members of the Royal Marines Commandos and the United States Marine Corps for their help in producing this book. Except where otherwise indicated, all opinions and comment are solely the author's own.

'There is no progress without criticism . . . Curiosity leads to investigation – which opens discussion – which gives rise to opinion – which breeds criticism – which results in improvement.'

Colonel James C. Breckenridge, USMC, 1929

Preface

Major-General Julian Thompson CB OBE

Napoleon once said: 'The first quality of a soldier is fortitude in enduring fatigue and hardship: bravery but the second. Poverty, hardship, misery are the school of the good soldier.' He might have been talking about the Royal Marine Commandos, and describing the Commando Course. For, as I said in the preface to the previous edition of Nigel Foster's book, anyone reading it will learn there are no short cuts to the making of a Royal Marine Commando – only mud, toil, sweat and sometimes a few tears. Poverty, in the sense that softness and luxury are absent; hardship, the mental and physical testing; and misery, the sheer 'bloodiness' of it at times; all are necessary if one is to follow another famous soldier's dictum: 'train hard; fight easy.'

Nigel Foster is right to emphasize these aspects of Commando training, especially now. As this book goes to publication the 'bean counters', as he calls them, in the Ministry of Defence, including some in the upper ranks of the services who should know better, are questioning the need for the training to be so demanding. The latter include one officer who asked if the commando standards are set deliberately high in order to exclude women. The answer is that the standards are set to prepare men for the toughest kind of fighting in the world, foot soldiering, of which Royal Marines are the supreme exponents. Despite modern technology, foot soldiering is still, compared with other forms of combat, very low tech. As a parachute engineer in the Falklands observed, it usually involved attacking up a bare hillside with the aim of killing others before they killed you. Which should surprise no one who knows that the foot soldier's definition of a battle is an event that is fought uphill, often in the dark, and at the junction of two or more maps. It does surprise the 'bean counters', and the kind of people who ask the aforementioned question, because none of them have any experience of any kind of combat, let alone what Royal Marine Commandos are expected to achieve.

At the same time politicians have been spouting phrases such as the 'new caring army' (by extension the armed services), and 'equal opportunity employers'. The Army have introduced 'gender-free physical tests', a euphemism for lowering the standards; and there may be pressure on the Royal Marines to follow suit. As Nigel Foster points out:

> It is not enough that you want to do a thing so badly . . . This is the first harsh lesson taught by the Royal Marines – wanting is not enough, wanting *does not entitle* you to try. Only your own ability and real commitement can do that plus the pragmatic consideration that even if you do manage to pass the course, will you be of any *use* to the Corps? [my emphasis]

The Royal Marines have always cared, at least in my experience, but there is no room for sentimentality.

Equal opportunity to the Royal Marines means if you can 'hack it', your background, colour, and creed will be no bar to acceptance. Debased standards will result in lower performance in battle; the only test that counts. The latest social engineering ploy by the 'bean counters' is to suggest that young people who have been on the dole for a while should join the armed forces, or lose their dole money. Two hundred years ago, magistrates offered petty criminals the option of transportation as convicts to Australia or joining the Army or Navy. Is this really how our politicians view the services? Over the past ten years, out of 50,000 who have applied to join the Royal Marines, fewer than 3,750 have finished training. Experience over those ten years showed that the vast majority of those who joined because they had nothing better to do failed.

There are difficult times ahead. But there always have been for the Royal Marines, and I am sure they will overcome them.

CHAPTER ONE

Achievers, Please

Speed is the essence of war. Take advantage of the enemy's
unpreparedness; travel by unexpected routes and strike him
where he is defenceless.

The Royal Marines are the finest commando-trained
infantry in the world. Within the Corps exist sub-units
which are among the best special forces in the world –
and others that are totally unique, so that comparisons
are impossible. They are also trained to conduct
amphibious warfare.

Many would argue that the Royal Marines' amphibious role is the Corps's prime *raison d'etre*. But while
amphibious warfare has become one of the Royal
Navy's three main roles, limiting Royal Marines
Commandos to this type of operation would be a criminal waste of an extremely valuable asset, despite the fact
that amphibious warfare is as much art as science and
needs to be continually practised. As a Chinese sage
pointed out nearly two and half thousand years ago, all
war is an art, inasmuch as successful commanders and
their troops are marked by a high degree of initiative,
creativity, intuition, boldness and flexibility . . . which is

exactly what commando-style operations are supposed to be.

This invariably disturbs those traditional souls who insist that everything be done by the book and that there's a book for everything. Conjuring up, perhaps, the image of an old-fashioned sergeant-major determined that his lads will be as creative as the best of them: 'On the word of command, Parade will assume a dreamy expression and consider the meaning of life. Parade will commence intuitive thinking by twos. Para-a-a-de – think!'

Commandos don't need to be told to think for themselves. Or to be told the value of initiative, creativity, intuition, boldness and flexibility. Without these qualities, no commando will live long enough to regret lacking them. The Royal Marines are professional commandos before they are anything else.

Why commando?

In his commentary on Sun Tzu's *The Art of War*, General Tao Hanzhang quotes Marshal Liu Bocheng (President of the Chinese Military Academy in the 1950s): 'Generally speaking, forces which fight in a regular way according to usual tactical principles are normal forces. Forces which fight otherwise, move stealthily and attack the enemy by surprise are extraordinary ones.' This stems from Sun Tzu's use of the expression 'extraordinary and normal forces', which scholars are still arguing about, but seems to refer to how normal troops are used, rather than specially trained soldiers. None the less, Marshal Liu's description sums up commando troops extremely well. And whereas in Sun Tzu's time any well-trained and led force could be used in an extraordinary way, for a long time now the commando role has required both special training and special men.

The word 'commando' first appeared in South Africa around 1830. It was used by Boer settlers to describe a group of civilians called out at a moment's notice for military duties. The 'command' came down and the 'commando' obeyed. By the time of the Boer War (1899), the initial concept had been refined through countless actions against the Zulu and Ndebele peoples – who often employed similar hit-and-run tactics themselves. So it was that British generals, who appeared to have forgotten everything that Wellington and the Spanish guerrillas had proved against Napoleon during the Peninsular Campaign, were faced with extremely mobile, highly trained groups of well-armed farmers who inconsiderately refused to fight the kind of large-scale battle that might end in their own defeat. Groups, or 'commandos' of men who operated over as wide an area as possible . . . and didn't seem to understand the concept of a front line. Good God, there had to be a front line – how else could one possibly know where to place one's troops? If this seems a little unfair on the then British military establishment, it's worth remembering that it had also appeared to have forgotten – or never known – those lessons learned more recently from the North-West Frontier. But then, the Imperial Indian Army always was a little more switched-on than its big brother . . . and had long understood how to best use both time and tempo, both of which are crucial to any successful military operation – and both of which are tailor made to be exploited by commando-trained troops.

Speed is the essence

In terms of achieving a politico-military objective, time is either open-ended or vanishes with alarming and indecent haste. Open-ended in terms of, say, accepting that while the optimum military outcome might never be achieved, it should be possible to keep things reasonably under control for the foreseeable future . . . or until it all becomes too messy and expensive. Examples include the North-West Frontier (again) and Northern Ireland.

Time vanished with alarming haste for British paratroops during the Battle of Arnhem in the Second World War, as it had done for the Confederacy during the American Civil War . . . and as it threatened to do during the Falklands War, for then time was definitely on the Argentinian side. No commander can ever control time, but the most professional can either effectively slow it down or speed it up to his advantage. Some of the more surprising outcomes have occurred when two opposing sides have been following different timetables, often because they actually have different aims. For example, the then Secretary of Defence Robert Macnamara, possibly in accordance with President Kennedy's political objectives, saw the Vietnam War as something to be won in the field and then as quickly as possible. This resulted in the Pentagon attempting to fight a classical campaign that called for set-piece battles and body-counts. But Hanoi had no such timetable and never sought to impose one until victory was in sight. Like the Boers over sixty years beforehand, neither the Vietcong nor the North Vietnamese Army saw the need to play by their enemy's rules. Interestingly enough, this seems to have been well understood by the Australian forces fighting in Vietnam who used commando and special forces tactics to deny Hanoi the one thing it always needed, which was control of the South Vietnamese countryside.

He who deliberately hesitates may end up winning

This leads to tempo, in this case referring to the speed or rate a specific commander fights a particular battle or campaign. All battles are a clash of tempo; the trick is to disrupt the enemy's and/or make him subject to your own. As General Gray, USMC, has said: 'Tempo is a significant weapon, because it is through a faster tempo that we seize the initiative and dictate the terms of war . . . it is the ability consistently to shift quickly from one tactical action to another . . . it is not in absolute terms that tempo matters, but in terms relative to the enemy.'

Tempo is created in four main ways.

First, by multiple and simultaneous tactical operations.

Second, by anticipating how best to exploit successful results before they occur.

Third, by decentralized decision-making, as witness

Field Marshal Slim's comments about the Burma Campaign in the Second World War: 'Commanders at all levels had to act more on their own . . . in time they developed to a marked degree a flexibility of mind and a firmness of decision that enabled them to act swiftly to take advantage of sudden information or changing circumstances without reference to their superiors.'

And fourth, tempo is maintained by avoiding unnecessary combat, giving the example of the German blitzkrieg through France in 1940 which was characterized by the deliberate avoidance of pitched battle. As Basil Liddell Hart said: 'The French commanders, trained in the slow motion methods of 1918, were mentally unfitted to cope with the panzer pace and it produced a spreading paralysis among them.' Those French commanders were also committed to the idea of deliberate and methodical battle, as more recently occurred in the Iran/Iraq War, and with about as much success as the trench carnage produced in the First World War. Battles, campaigns and wars are won by the side displaying the greatest initiative, creativity, intuition, boldness and flexibility, given a local parity in troops and weapon systems. The USMC refers to this philosophy as maneuver (*sic*) warfare: '[it] . . . seeks to shatter the enemy's cohesion through a series of rapid, violent and unexpected actions which create a turbulent and rapidly deteriorating situation with which he cannot cope.'

It's to be remembered that the United States Marines are not commandos. How much more effective, then, in carrying out this particular approach will be troops who are commando-trained. The philosophy, by the way, is spot on. It works. When applied to tanks, it's called a *blitzkrieg*.

Nor is there any apology made for quoting so extensively from an American manual. For many years now, America's strategic thinking – especially as it relates to amphibiosity and political power projection – has been streets ahead of Britain's. They also experiment with different concepts whenever possible, something to be borne in mind as and when American forces appear to be doing something a tad unusual. The Pentagon knew full well, for example, that it could have probably sorted out the problems in Grenada by borrowing a dozen or so downtown Detroit homicide cops. But how often do you get the opportunity to exercise on such a large scale with a real enemy?

(See Annex A: United States Marine Corps Military Doctrine.)

Amphibiosity

'An amphibious force provides a balanced, self-sustaining and autonomous intervention and reinforcement capability with strategic reach.'

Take a look at the map of the world. Search out Denver . . . Ulan Bator . . . Ayers Rock . . . Timbuktu . . . Novosibirsk . . . and Lhasa. Those are the only major cities and tourist attractions geographically immune to a sea or water-borne invasion. Perhaps they should form some sort of club. Simple facts: over seventy per cent of the world's surface is covered by sea. The vast majority of the world's population lives within three hundred miles of the coast. 3 Commando Brigade can operate over six hundred nautical miles inshore from the point of landing. With good, navigable rivers or lakes, even more.

Be afraid. Be very afraid . . .

In 1949 Chairman of the US Joint Chiefs of Staff General Omar Bradley stated: 'I predict that large scale amphibious operations will never occur again.'

In July 1950 the North Korean offensive all but pushed the American United Nations forces into the sea. Conventional wisdom dictated either dropping an atomic bomb on P'yongyang, or a slow reinforcement of Pusan – the only South Korean port still in UN/ American hands. And while that happened, the North Korean forces would consolidate their hold on South Korea. In other words, the possibility of another world war, or the attempt to find some face-saving settlement. General Douglas MacArthur decided otherwise. On 15 September the 1st Marine Division USMC, plus a Royal Marines Commando unit, landed at Inchon just west of Seoul. They were soon reinforced by a US Army Corps, Seoul was recaptured, the North Korean lines of communication cut, UN/American forces broke out of Pusan and North Korea eventually retreated back to the 38th Parallel. It was one of the greatest strategic successes of the twentieth century and very nearly didn't happen: the US Navy considered Inchon to be totally unsuitable for a landing, since the tides and beaches were all wrong. Which was exactly MacArthur's point: Inchon was the last place the North Koreans would expect an invasion to take place.

In fairness to the US Navy, it has to be remembered

that until Inchon, Second World War amphibious warfare had mostly seen either small, almost piratical, operations with limited strategic objectives, often purely diversionary, or full-scale invasions and as such, relatively inflexible: because so many men and so much equipment have to be landed, you must use the best possible beachhead. Those operations that fell somewhere between the two, like Dieppe or the battle for Betio island in the Pacific, were at best Pyrrhic victories, at worst unmitigated disasters. MacArthur wanted to mount a full-scale invasion using a bad beachhead. Bad beachhead, bad operation: it was as simple as that. That said, once the US Navy had been convinced, they assembled the necessary ships in record time.

Captain, art tha' sleepin' there below?

The obvious lesson of Inchon was that an amphibious force can outflank a larger enemy army at the time and place of its choosing. Also that flexibility and surprise always succeed. Historians who remembered Wolfe's victory at Quebec, or the capture of Gibraltar from the Spaniards, quietly laughed. Once again the lessons learned centuries ago were being re-learned. There was another more subtle lesson, that some admirals still have problems understanding: overall command of an amphibious operation must lie from the very beginning with those responsible for achieving the ultimate military objective. In operations that will result in the poor bloody infantry or grunt-squashing armour achieving the desired end, naval and air forces only ever act in support.

Move forward to 1956 and Suez. One of the high points was the use of helicopters to land 45 Commando from aircraft carriers stationed seven miles out at sea . . . actually, the first helicopter-born landing in history. The Suez Campaign might well have been a political mistake, or turned into one by politicians, but it was an unqualified military success. Which only serves to emphasize that all military activity is pointless without political objectives that are both sensible and sustainable.

None the less, as a result of Suez, amphibious operations achieved a new dimension . . . in fact, the doctrine of amphibiosity, an almost banal sounding word, was born. The laughter of those historians who also remembered Sir Francis Drake's exploits in the Americas now sounded a little hollow. The war that ultimately ensured that English would be the dominant language in the US and the Caribbean was fought by the Royal Navy as a series of amphibious, commando-style campaigns.

Power projection

Simply put, amphibiosity means the ability to influence near or far parts of the world without recourse to nuclear weapons. Remember how accessible the world's countries are by sea. Remember the striking range of an amphibious force. And remember that same force can strike at the point and time of its own choosing . . . but that it doesn't have to do so in order to make a point. The mere fact that it's somewhere out there provides much food for enemy thought. During the Gulf War, the presence of a comparatively small US amphibious force stooging around somewhere in the neighbourhood kept five Iraqi divisions fully occupied and thus unable to take part in the fixed land war. Critics argue that an amphibious force is vulnerable. Perhaps – but far less so than a massive airlift or parachute drop. As Sarajevo airport proved, a country doesn't have to have the latest in weapon systems and electronic gadgetry to blow aircraft out of the skies as they're landing or taking off. But both systems and gadgetry are needed to locate and cripple a modern amphibious force. Contrary to popular opinion, the world's oceans are not an open book. Aside from anything else, all the best satellites and underwater detection systems are owned by the US.

The self-sustaining aspect is worthy of comment, too. After it's disembarked, 3 Commando Brigade can operate without resupply for at least a month. This has an obvious bearing not only for acts of war, but also on mercy and peace-keeping missions, as witness the successful establishment of Kurdish safe havens in Northern Iraq after the Gulf War.

Presumably, a cavalry charge is out of the question?

Amphibiosity allows both political and military flexibility. As said, troops don't have to land in order to affect events. An amphibious force doesn't even have to be seen – just knowing it's there forces an enemy or potential enemy on to the defensive. But once the decision for military intervention has been taken, the commander has a large number of options open to him: a full-scale landing, or a series of commando raids; one beachhead or several; or even, for brief operations, no beachhead at all, but insertion by helicopter. In fact, modern military thinking tries to avoid the preoccupation with a beachhead that has characterized so much doctrine, especially naval, over the past few decades. Nothing is simple any more, if it ever was. The front line or FEBA (Forward Edge of the Battle Area) no longer exists in either space or time, for static troops concentrated in large numbers are horribly vulnerable. Instead there is one large politico-military mêlée existing on sea, land and air which probably also includes the UN Headquarters in New York, not to mention the BBC in London and CNN in Atlanta. The beach is just another landmark axis, en route to the real objective . . . but only if the spearhead troops know exactly what they're doing and have practised both long and hard. Of course it's not nearly that simple but the point about an amphibious force is that it represents total warfare. Politicians and the general public, not to mention the armed forces themselves, have become used to thinking in terms of the sea war, or the land war, or the air war. Nowadays no such creature exists, if it ever did. Sea, air and land are only three aspects of the whole; they do not exist in splendid isolation.

Whither excellence?

One of the great hallmarks of the Royal Marines Commandos is their capacity continually to improve their military skills and effectiveness, and then from within. Or as a senior officer commented: 'Why are we always innovating? Nowadays it's simply integral to the way we think. But I imagine it began as a matter of pure survival. We have to be the best. Ever since we were first formed, some bastard or another has been trying to close us down.'

At first sight, quite why the Royal Marines Commandos should have incurred such jealousy makes little or no sense. There is, of course, the very common, human reaction to any display of excellence: 'I could do that, just as well and probably better. Or if not me, I know a man who can.'

In defence circles there are always those weasely bean-counters who'll point out – with the utmost regret, naturally – that it might just be possible to have both the commando and amphibious roles undertaken by normal infantry . . . not quite as effectively as the Royal Marines, of course, but it would be so much cheaper. As E. L. Wisty (otherwise known as the late Peter Cook) said, he could have been a judge if it wasn't for the Latin. It's also true that most accountant-inspired cuts in military spending invariably cost more to put right than was initially saved, for world events have a nasty habit of ignoring the Treasury's best laid plans.

Not everyone can play

There are only four countries in the world with the necessary expertise and equipment to conduct successful out-of-theatre, high-intensity operations on their own, which invariably have to be amphibious if only for logistical reasons. These are the USA, Britain, France and the Netherlands, the latter probably relying in part on British expertise. And as said previously, an out-of-theatre operation can just as easily be Benign or Evacuation Operations (missions of mercy) as Peace Support or Constabulary Operations (force used in self-defence or as a last resort) as an act of war.

At times it's seemed as if the Royal Navy hasn't been quite sure what to do with the Royal Marines, especially since the Corps took on the commando role with such conspicuous success . . . with the Royal Navy but not necessarily of it, and if bootnecks fight their battles on land, then shouldn't the Army pay for them? Taking the argument further, without the Royal Marines the country could afford more capital ships, like aircraft carriers. To be fair, Britain's attempts to find its proper role in international affairs following the Second World War played havoc with all three Services, all of whom were reduced to believing that what was good for the Navy, Army or Air Force was automatically good for the country.

Who's for a little light conquest before lunch?

As an aside, any discussion of this general subject has to make the point that the British do tend to be natural soldiers. In his novel, *England, Their England*, written in 1933, with its wonderful description of a village cricket match, the humorist A.G. Macdonnell affectionately dubbed the English as being good-natured warrior-poets with a taste for good ale. Which was pretty good

14

coming from a Scot, even if he was born in India, and if anyone doubts that, read Macdonald Fraser's stories about life in a Highland Regiment. But overall the point – about all Britons – is well made. Whether it's to do with the fact that so many warrior peoples ended up concentrated in such a small country – Celts, Romans, Vikings, Jutes, Normans and so on – or whether it's to do with a tradition forced on the country by geography and history, is really beside the point The British are natural warriors. Just ask the rest of the world. Why else do you find so many foreign students at Dart-mouth and, especially, Sandhurst? Why else are British military training teams in so much demand worldwide? This might be a slightly unfashionable cause for pride, but it's also worth remembering that no other people since the Romans have ended up on such good terms with former enemies as have the British – with only a few notable exceptions, all of whose writers and politicians are invariably taken far too seriously. It was only war and conquest, and where's their sense of humour?

Even within each individual Service the battles rage – as Len Deighton pointed out, there was little love lost between the RAF's Fighter and Bomber Commands during the Second World War. A former head of Army Education once memorably described the British Army as being a federation of warring tribes (which could just as easily refer to the country as a whole). Yet the Services never just fight for a larger budget, but for honour, for their own Service's *amour propre*, one reason why the infighting can be quite so vicious. The fact that, post-Second World War, the two major political parties could never, would never, openly agree on defence matters only exacerbated the problems . . . especially with the ever-present civil service forever playing divide and rule. Or as it's known in the civil service, taking a long-term view in the light of current political considerations. All things considered, it's a wonder the Royal Marines have survived as long as they have done.

They're playing our tune

World events worked both for and against the Corps's survival. First, there was the Cold War which resulted in a static and extremely expensive military doctrine involving nuclear weaponry, blue-water fleets, vast tank battles and large air forces. It was also predicated on the assumption that both America and the Soviet Union would risk certain nuclear destruction in defending client or satellite countries. Or as was once explained to the author: 'Moscow never had to believe that it would happen, only that it might.' In other words, politicians on both sides had to believe that their counterparts were basically insane. There was also the slow disengagement of British forces East of Suez. What would 3 Commando Brigade do once it came home from Singapore, as one day it surely would? Come to that, what would most of the Army do once Empire had finally vanished?

But then little wars began breaking out, as they so often will. It has to be remembered that neither the war against the Mau-Mau in Kenya, or the Emergency in Malaya, were attempts to hang on to Empire. Well, some people might have seen them like that, not least the

Mau-Mau or Chin Peng, but in real terms they were wars fought to ensure that independence came peacefully and with a reasonable chance of success. Not wholly disinterested, perhaps, for Britain did have considerable economic reasons for wanting to ensure stability. The decades from 1950 onwards were a time when the pressure for conflict between the West and the Communist Bloc began to be relieved by proxy wars. In 1961, for example, Royal Marines Commandos prevented Iraq invading Kuwait. A few years later, 3 Commando Brigade was the main force used to prevent Indonesia taking over the newly independent Malaysia, during Sukarno's euphemistically-styled 'Confrontation' ('No, no, we're not at war with Malaysia, we're merely confronting it'). In fact, 'Confrontation' was made for the Royal Marines. In Borneo, where the main fighting took place, rivers provide the main lines of communication. The jungle imposes its own logic on text book military manoeuvring – a point that was to later escape both Secretary of State Macnamara and General Westmoreland in Vietnam. But if anyone deserves the title 'Reluctant and Probably Unwilling Friend of the Corps', Sukarno does. In Borneo there was ample opportunity for water-borne and fast helicopter commando incursions, in the case of the latter the Royal Navy establishing that it possessed the best helicopter pilots in Britain. Quite why naval pilots the world over, both helicopter and fixed wing, appear to be so much better than their air force comrades should really be the subject of another book. Confrontation was also the time when the SBS emerged as something considerably more than beach-reconnaissance and saboteur parties, just as the Malayan Emergency in the Fifties had seen the rebirth of the Special Air Service – although the SAS had to go and later help save Oman in order to hammer their point home.

Things will never be the same

In short, politicians and military planners began to realize there were still two distinct types of warfare: conventional and unconventional, often referred to as low-intensity, counter-insurgency, anti-terrorist or anti-guerrilla warfare. Nuclear weapons and vast conventional forces might be great for domestic industry, but were none the less an expensive, simplistic and slightly drastic way of solving certain problems. Nor could you send a gunboat, as in days of yore. At the risk of belabouring the point, the vast majority of human beings live permanently on the land. Control of sea and airspace is important, even vital, but true victory in war nearly always means the ability to take even temporary possession of the enemy's land-based assets, which in a major war will include political and economic structures and institutions. Otherwise the whole shooting-match breaks out again a few years later. The Royal Navy could, perhaps, simply have blockaded the Falkland Islands, and if so the United Nations would probably still be trying to broker a peace. Control of the air did not win the war in Vietnam. At the time of writing, Saddam Hussein is still causing problems. Short of full-scale nuclear, chemical or bacteriological destruction, a country can rarely impose its long-term will – even the will to kiss and make up – without troops on the ground at some time or another. This can even apply to peace-keeping and humanitarian operations. The Rwanda Hutu refugee camps in Zaire were allowed to become guerrilla bases, which in turn led to a Rwandan Tutsi invasion. One of the most successful humanitarian operations in the last fifty years, Operation Safe Haven in Northern Iraq, succeeded only because 40 Commando supplied the necessary military discipline within the refugee camps.

Horses for courses

During the 1970s it occurred to military planners that the Royal Marines Commandos could, in terms of a major NATO/Soviet Union war in Europe, be best deployed in a troubleshooting role on the flank. Between 1971 and 1978, 41 Commando Group was based in Malta – and deployed to Cyprus with 40 Commando in 1975 after the Turkish invasion. If only NATO hadn't decided that Turkey was a more valuable ally than Cyprus, or even Greece, 40 and 41 Commando might well have finished the job. Meanwhile, NATO's northern flank was also becoming cause for concern. Norway guards two sea-lanes considered vital to the then Soviet Union: north, from the Barents Sea and ports like Archangel and Murmansk, and into the North Atlantic; and south from the Baltic, and St Petersburg (Leningrad) into the North Sea. So do Denmark and Sweden, of course, but physical control of Norway would have given Moscow an incredible advantage. Nor would that

control have had to be achieved with nuclear weapons
. . . and even if Moscow had nuked Oslo, would America
or Britain have nuked Leningrad in turn? Or would
another, marginally less confrontational, target like
Leipzig have been chosen to make a point? Whatever,
45 Commando was given the specific role of defending
Northern Norway, which explains why 45 Cdo is
still a little larger than 40 or 42 Cdo. Like the now-
disbanded 41 Cdo, 45 is more of a Commando
Group. In time, NATO's northern flank became one of
3 Commando Brigade's main responsibilities and in the
process, the Royal Marines became the world experts
on cold-weather and mountain warfare . . . just as
the Confrontation had made them expert in jungle warfare.

1982, of course, saw Argentina invade the Falklands. The subject is covered elsewhere in the book, but
one lesson is worth repeating: any amphibious operation with a land-based, strategic objective must be
controlled by those directly responsible for achieving
that objective. The Royal Navy's decision to withhold
information from 3 Commando Brigade has been well
documented. Doubtless, too, Admiral Fieldhouse in
London had good reasons to make what amounted to
tactical decisions, if only for purely political considerations. But as Sun Tzu said: 'Those who know
when to fight and when not to fight are victorious.
Those who discern when to use many or few troops are
victorious. Those whose upper and lower ranks have
the same desire are victorious. Those whose generals
are able and are not constrained by their governments
are victorious.'

But then, how often does anyone get to play with a Task Force? Political and professional reputations have been made or salvaged by far less.

The other lesson worth repeating is that you cannot take normal troops without any form of specialized training and expect them to fulfil an amphibious or commando role. For by adapting to the capabilities of non-specialist troops, the operation loses the very qualities of flexibility, surprise and speed that makes an amphibious or commando operation so devastatingly effective.

Now you see them . . .

But now, with amphibiosity apparently firmly entrenched in Britain's military doctrine, it would seem that the Royal Marines Commandos' future is assured. Or is it?

Already the weaselly bean-counters are again whispering that perhaps, just perhaps, 'normal' troops could do the job nearly as well. Nor, must it be said, has the Royal Navy as a whole shown much sign of fully understanding what amphibiosity really means . . . other than having a few more ships . . . but even then, they're not exactly capital ships, are they? More like armoured ferries, really. Of course, amphibious shipping does have its uses when not being used operationally – acting as a floating exhibition centre for Britain's defence industry, training Royal Naval personnel, or even flying the flag in some far-off and hitherto forgotten corner of the Empire. In fact, if you added a rivet or two, and strengthened a few deck plates, specialized amphibious vessels might even be used as all-purpose fighting warships. Meanwhile, the Sea Scouts would dearly love a cruise.

It's not that the Navy isn't proud of its Royal Marines. Recently, RM Poole laid on a demonstration of amphibious warfare for an all-arms Staff College course. The expressions on the faces of the Royal Navy officers present, as the Royal Marines impressed the Army and RAF contingent, emphasized the pride and enthusiasm felt for their own Service's sea-soldiers. Yet there still seems to be a fear within certain Royal Naval circles that amphibious warfare could be a case of the tail wagging the dog. Heavens, it almost reduces the Senior Service to the role of mere taxi-driver.

Actually, it doesn't. Even if it did, it would be one hell of a good taxi. But again, amphibious operations with land-based strategic objectives can only be successfully controlled by those responsible for achieving them. It doesn't matter who's in charge as long as that person understands and appreciates all the ramifications . . . and that the land, air and sea battle inevitably merges into one large mêlée.

The USMC solved this problem years ago when they were given their own dedicated shipping and aircraft. But unlike the Royal Marines Commandos, the USMC is also considered a Service arm in its own right. Which is one reason why it's possible to see a Marine as one of the Pentagon Joint Chiefs of Staff, but never a Royal Marine in a similar British post. After all, amphibious warfare is only one of the Royal Navy's main responsibilities, and what would a Royal Marine know of, say,

Trident and how to deploy it? Or defending shipping lanes wherever they need to be defended? As long as the Royal Marines Commandos remain a Royal Navy asset, pure and simple, they will blush comparatively unseen in Whitehall's corridors of power.

And is that how the Corps should really be seen? Or as Royal Marines, but more importantly, also commandos? It's a question the Army has been quietly asking for some time, too.

On the other hand . . .

The idea of a Special Service Brigade – more probably, a small division – has been around for a long, long time. Actually, 103 RM Brigade had been renamed 3 Special Service Brigade in 1943, subsequently fighting in India and Burma, later changing its name to 3 Commando Brigade. The concept resurfaced in the late Eighties and for a while it looked as if the Royal Marines Commandos might be sailing – or abseiling – away from the Royal Navy, much as the Royal Flying Corps had once flown away from the Army. But not to form a separate arm, as had happened with the RAF. Rather, to be part of a separate unit that would cut across Navy, Army and Air Force fiefdoms – which more or less doomed the idea from the start.

Imagine, if you will, a permanent formation comprising Royal Marines Commandos, the Parachute Regiment, SAS and SBS, and with its own permanently dedicated armour, artillery, engineers, signals and logistics equipment and personnel. There would also be permanently dedicated shipping and aircraft, which could always be 'loaned' back to the Navy or RAF for brief periods.

The Navy, RAF and Army might also be called on to reinforce this formation, which can operate as a single entity, or detach smaller units as circumstances dictate. But any extra sailors, soldiers or airmen drafted in would come directly under the command of the formations' headquarters, as would their equipment, for the duration. It would obviously be trained to a far higher standard than the USMC, which would be the only other broadly comparable formation. It would be versatile, flexible and pack one hell of a punch. It would trial and develop new equipment and tactics. It would also act as an elite centre of excellence for the armed forces as a whole. It would, in effect, be a new, combined operations arm. Nor would it exist in splendid isolation – regular battalions, ships or squadrons could be attached for training so that in time, certain skills would filter throughout all the armed forces.

New jewel in the Army's crown?

Leaving aside all the arguments against this idea – and some were perfectly valid, concerned with matters of finance, recruiting and deployment – what was truly interesting about the concept was that it marked a decided shift in the attitudes of the Royal Marines and the Army towards each other.

There'd always been Army attached units with the Brigade – sappers, gunners, REME and even the occasional nervous-looking Intelligence Corps corporal wondering how soon before he'd actually have to kill someone – but since the Falklands Campaign the Army as a whole had taken a far closer interest in the Royal Marines Commandos.

First, there was no question but that the Corps was the acknowledged and worldwide expert in mountain and Arctic warfare.

Second, the Royal Marines appeared to have far more freedom to trial new equipment and develop new units, with the electronic warfare Y Troop and Commando Logistics Regiment being classic examples. In fact, as will later be explained, Y Troop could never have come into existence without the Army's enthusiastic support.

Third, those special forces skills developed by the SBS and the then Arctic and Mountain Warfare Cadre filtered down to the rest of the Corps in a way that SAS skills rarely, if ever, do to Army regiments.

Fourth, they regularly trained and exercised with foreign units, especially the USMC. In fact, the Corps had become the practical experts on American strategy and tactics. It knew a fair amount about the French Foreign Legion, too, not to mention the Royal Netherlands Marines, Danish Jaeger Korps, Italian Alpini, Swedish Coastal Defence and countless others . . . not the kind of information gleaned from attending courses together, but from actually operating together in the field. Doubtless the Army possessed similar knowledge and expertise, but it was spread throughout all the different regiments and corps. With the Royal Marines it was all under one roof and easily accessible.

And fifth, simply because the Royal Marines were extremely good soldiers.

Enter the JRDF. What?

For their part, the Royal Marines had lost some of that insularity which came from being part of the Navy. They'd worked with Army regiments in Northern Ireland since 1969, and while some had been less than professional, in bootneck terms, others had been pretty good. The traditional enmity between the Corps and the Parachute Regiment had been laid to rest during Operation Corporate. It seemed that the Army appreciated the Corps in a way that the Navy never really had.

For a while, a special forces formation was more than a mere gleam in the eye. But no one will ever know whether this latest love affair could have led to something more permanent. The Navy showed distinct signs of pique at what it possibly saw as betrayal. A more cautious counsel prevailed within the Royal Marine's senior levels and, in the words of a retired senior officer, 'people went cap in hand to the Navy and humbly apologized for ever having considered a divorce'.

Nowadays the Royal Marines Commandant General reports directly to the Commander in Chief Fleet (CINCFLEET) – an important man, but effectively the Corps has no direct and permanent access to the highest levels within the Ministry of Defence. And no matter how professional a man CINCFLEET is (contrary to popular wisdom and civil service gossip, senior military commanders are usually quite frighteningly skilled and intelligent), that means yet more layers of bureaucracy through which Royal Marines matters will be filtered, watered down or even ignored. Actually, given the importance that both Britain and the Royal Navy now attach to amphibiosity, one would have thought that the Commandant General Royal Marines should at least be equal in operational rank to CINCFLEET himself.

But isn't there this wonderful new formation called a Joint Rapid Deployment Force? True – and a very fine Headquarters it has, too. And both the Royal Marines and the Paras are integral components . . . when they're not doing something else. And in practice you still have three different sets of standard operating procedures: Royal Navy/Marines, Army and RAF. Nor does it have its own dedicated logistics. At the moment of writing, it's little more than a Joint Rapid Deployment Fudge.

Haven't we been here before?

While the Navy might still have been unsure how the Royal Marines can and should be used, aside from major amphibious operations, it did know one thing: if the Army liked them, the Corps had to be doing something right.

But what it means in practice is that the Corps will always run the risk of being misused by its parent Service unless and until some of the more senior admirals are true experts in amphibious operations and preferably, have also been 'green-hatted' and served for a time with 3 Commando Brigade . . . you simply cannot get the requisite experience at staff college. One would have thought that the Navy would see this as a sensible career path . . . perhaps the problem is that Royal Naval officers have become almost too highly specialized – electronics, engineers, weapons systems, etc. In terms of combat, the techniques involved in fighting a ship or even a fleet are very different from those required to command troops spread out in variously sized units over several hundred square miles of land.

Perhaps not surprisingly, Royal Navy/Marines amphibious operations seem to work at their best when conducted on a small scale. The retaking of South Georgia, for example, was a classic example of how well the two can work together when there is mutual trust and understanding. But then, what marked that operation was independence of command: no interference – or none that couldn't be safely ignored – from more senior commanders many miles away. It's also arguable that the Falklands Campaign owed a considerable part of its success to the presence of Commander Clapp, the then Commodore of Amphibious Warfare. Too bad that some of his own superior officers seem to have considered that he'd gone native and became a little too fixated on the needs of 3 Commando Brigade.

But in the final analysis, it's rarely individuals who are truly at fault, but the system that creates them. In terms of Britain's armed forces, the system appears to have learned nothing and forgotten everything. Perhaps it's time that defence itself was taken out of party politics, just as the Bank of England has been. Certainly the Ministry can do without being second-guessed by a Treasury which often appears to be more loyal to the electoral needs of the government of the day than to the nation of the future.

The reason why

The Corps does not lack volunteers. Over the past ten years alone more than fifty thousand men have applied to join the Royal Marines. Of these, less than half have been accepted for a Potential Officers' Course (POC) or Potential Recruits' Course (PRC). Of these, less than a quarter have been accepted for training. And of these, less than sixty per cent have managed to win a Green Beret – the headgear that marks a man as a commando, rather than a Royal Marine.

While a family military background can play a part in a man wanting to be a Royal Marine, it's by no means the only reason. After all, since the demise of National Service, there are far fewer parents and relatives who have any direct military experience.

One officer told how he'd 'sort of drifted' into the Corps while still at university. Something of a radical to begin with, he'd become disenchanted with student politics ('too much time and money spent writing letters of solidarity and attending conferences that never achieved anything; too little thought for student welfare – like proper accommodation or the price of beer in the Union bar'). He'd met a few Royal Marine Reservists through playing rugby ('very unradical that – playing rugby') and had visited them on their training nights – as much out of idle curiosity, or even morbid interest. But he found himself drawn more and more to the life, particularly its outdoor aspects, joined the Reserve and, when he discovered that the Corps would pay for the rest of his time at university, joined up. Somehow, he said, he'd felt that he had come home.

Another Marine, a recruit, remembered how he'd been running a successful transport business with his brother when he suddenly woke up one morning with the fixed determination to join the Marines – much to his family's (and his own) surprise. The only reasons he could think of at the time were that he loved playing about in boats, that he felt there was more to life, that he wasn't being stretched or challenged enough – and that the Marines represented some sort of elite. 'I knew knack-all [nothing] about the Corps, can't really tell you why I joined. Anyway, that's not important – it's why you stay [in training] that counts.'

If there is a common factor, other than a sense of service, running through the motivations of those who want to be Royal Marines, it is possibly a feeling of wanting to be the best, of wanting to prove themselves: not so much for the opinions of others, not to impress family or friends, but simply to prove something to themselves. And it's sad but true that the majority of men who do join for the uniform, or out of bravado, will painfully discover in the first few weeks of training that there are easier ways of achieving the same objectives. There are also those who, having decided to join the armed forces, look around to see which Service offers them the most. But again, this often comes back down to a basic desire to try for the one they see as being the toughest, with the accent on self-discovery. For many would-be Marines, it's also something they've always wanted to do, ever since boyhood. Quite how such a desire lasts throughout puberty and adolescence remains something of a mystery – unless the desire to be a Marine is as much a vocation as anything else. Certainly the training (and operational) demands on a Marine are tough enough to exclude all but the most determined.

Every now and then the odd psychopath attempts to join the Corps – as they do with the Paras, USMC or French Foreign Legion – attracted by what they see as a licence and opportunity to hurt people – by the power inherent in a gun. Men like these are not welcome and if by chance they get through the recruiting screens, the first month or so at Lympstone will find them out, and they will quietly be told to leave. Moral considerations aside, psychopaths do not make good soldiers, and definitely not good special forces. They don't respond well to discipline (and would be an extreme liability, say, on the streets of Belfast), tend to be egocentric to the point of unpleasant (and dangerous) selfishness, and contrary to the myth of *The Dirty Dozen,* psychopaths are not usually very courageous.

Of course the Corps teaches aggression; but it also teaches how to channel and control that aggression – how to use it only when it's absolutely necessary. Remoulding a warped character is not on the Lympstone curriculum.

Degrees of ability

At first sight the educational standards required of a potential Royal Marine are not exactly stringent. Five GCSE's, including Maths and English, plus two A levels are required for officers (the equivalent of a good high school diploma in North America). Recruits need to be able to read and write and to be numerate to a reasonable standard. All of this adds to the myth of the, well, slightly 'thick' Marine, who shouldn't be trusted with anything requiring too much brainpower.

In fact, the majority of potential officers possess degrees while the general academic standard among recruits is one of the highest in the Armed Forces. But the Corps has never fallen into the trap of believing that a good honours degree or A levels are necessary to command in battle.

They might, perhaps, point out that a junior officer – or a senior NCO – is trained to make the type of split-second analysis and decision that currency and commodity dealers have to make on the financial exchanges in London, New York, Chicago or Tokyo. A more senior officer is under the same stress as a director of a large company would be if he had to produce, day after day, the optimum business plan – and be able to change it at a moment's notice. There is the added pressure in both cases that if the soldier gets it wrong, he and his men will probably die, whereas the businessman will merely dust off his CV and go in search of a new job.

What this means in practice is that the Corps looks for intellectual potential and refuses to accept that an academic qualification always indicates that a man possesses it; nor that his intellect will hold up in times of stress. Yet, given that, the Marines do go to great lengths to recruit from the universities, for two reasons. First, in an attempt to get graduates possessing more practical degrees – a language, science or possibly engineering. Second, the Marines are well aware that the corridors of power are stalked by men and women who enjoy a similar academic background. It would be useful, the

Corps possibly feels, that it should have senior officers who can reminisce about dreaming spires and May Balls with the best of them. Also, despite its reservations about purely academic abilities being relevant to a soldier's life, the Corps recognizes that some aspects of military planning do require extreme intellectual ability. At the same time, many officers say privately that any man who shows the potential can be trained and taught within the system; including being sent to university at a later date.

Classless society

If there is one quality the Royal Marines look for, it is the mental ability to become a commando. It's not enough to want to be 'green-hatted', or believe that you deserve it. You have to be capable of developing the necessary psychological strengths – and that ability cuts right across society. For all ranks it begins with a basic integrity, for no one can pass commando training without the ability to recognize their own personal weaknesses – and then do something about them, without always waiting to be told. It later includes the ability to function under extreme pressure . . . the ability to endure . . . the stubborn determination to succeed in any way possible, but without falling apart if ever defeated . . . overall, the triumph of mind over body. And, as the author's own observation, it also includes a marked degree of imagination and common sense.

Objectives like these require a meritocracy based purely on personal ability. The days of the majority of would-be officers (Young Officers, or YOs) coming from the public school system are long gone. As long as the candidate can demonstrate an early-developed sense of responsibility and integrity, ambition and intellectual ability, it doesn't matter where he comes from. Although thanks to England's confused educational system – something else the two major political parties have never managed to agree on – many YOs will be from either public or grammar/grant maintained schools.

Similarly, other ranks are no longer recruited exclusively from the working classes, if such a group still exists and if they ever were. In fact, as a retired Royal Marines general pointed out recently, there is absolutely no difference between the parents attending a Young Officers or recruit passing-out parade. There is the same mix of accents, backgrounds and professions. Increasingly, recruits and to a lesser extent YOs are those young men who want to join the Corps, but no longer for life. They are looking for a challenge and to be part of something they consider meritorious, but either have other plans for the rest of their lives or merely want to keep their options open. So it is that many a recruit is someone who has the ability but no interest in being commissioned. Although, that said, there are also those recruits who failed the Potential Officers' Course, but decided to join the Corps anyway. For first and foremost one is a Royal Marines Commando, secondly one is an officer or other rank. This is reflected in the responsibility given to an individual in specific circumstances. For example, the coxswain of a landing craft is the man in charge, no matter what his rank. He could, possibly, be over-ruled by a senior NCO or officer – but whoever tried to do so would have to have a very strong case. Mere rank would not be enough. Similar with a Mountain Leader, the specialist in Arctic warfare and climbing, a sniper or an assault engineer. The specialist is the man responsible, and, therefore, the man in charge. Underlying this is the deep trust Royal Marines Commandos have in each other. A senior officer can safely take the advice of a comparatively junior NCO because he knows the man has been exceptionally well trained and won't let him down. It goes beyond a commitment to the Corps itself . . . it is a personal covenant that each man makes with his fellow Royal Marines and is one of the, perhaps the most, important aspects of commando training.

A special flair

Royal Marines officers are trained to be well mannered, hard and extremely professional. They should also possess one other quality, which has to be apparent from the beginning: a quality that is difficult to define, but is variously called flair or personality – the ability, often bloody-minded ability, to dominate a situation. And although it's been said that officers who show too much flair find it difficult to make it to the higher echelons of command, since the job then becomes as much political as military and one should not cut too much of a dash, it is true that officers with flair will command the greatest respect and affection from their men – assuming that it's allied with both professionalism and integrity.

There's a story that's passed into Corps folklore that,

perhaps, exemplifies the type of officer whom the men will respect, whatever his superiors may think of him. A Royal Marines officer had been sent on a particular course, which meant living in an Army mess. Coming down to breakfast one day, he found the dining room deserted save for a Guards officer, sitting at the table and wearing his cap peak over his eyes in true Guards manner. Grunting a greeting, the Royal Marine sat down, and looked around him for a moment before asking the Guardee to pass the sugar. Absolutely no response. Not even an indication that the Marine was in the room. Again, the Marine asked for the sugar. Again, no response. He asked for a third time, and finally the Guardee condescended to speak:

'When a Guards officer wears his hat to breakfast, it is an indication that he does not wish to speak to, or be spoken to by, anyone. It is a tradition of the regiment.'

The Marine thought about it for a few moments, then climbed on to the table, walked over to the Guardee and stood in his cereal.

'When a Royal Marines officer puts his boots in your cornflakes, it means pass the bloody sugar!'

Now that probably wasn't very polite. It may even have been a tad disrespectful. But it does indicate the bloody-mindedness with flair that marks a good young officer – not to mention the aggression.

CHAPTER TWO

Lympstone

The best form of welfare for the troops is first-class training, for this prevents unnecessary casualties.

Erwin Rommel

Untutored knowledge is useless in the face of educated bullets.

George S. Patton

It all begins at Lympstone.

If the soul of the Royal Marines resides anywhere, it is in that two square miles of accommodation blocks, classrooms, offices, assault courses, and, of course, the parade ground standing full square in front of the Officers' Mess.

Commando Training Centre Royal Marines (CTCRM) is on land once part of Sir Francis Drake's estate. Royal Marines have been training there since 1939 – one of the original wooden huts has been deliberately preserved. At present, CTCRM forecasts and manages its own budgets. To quote from official literature: 'The role of the Commando Training Centre Royal Marines is to train regular and reserve new-entry personnel for service within units of 3 Commando Brigade and other operational units within the Royal Marines Command, as well as support the structure of the Corps by providing an extensive package of continuation courses which enhance infantry and Commando skills.'

All Young Officers and recruits are trained at Lympstone by the Commando Training Wing (CTW), occasionally taking part in field exercises together, always aware of each other, thus helping forge a unique bond of comradeship of which the Corps is justifiably proud. CTCRM is the only military training centre in the world where men are trained to 'Operational Performance Standards', that is, capable of taking their place in an operational (commando) unit the moment they leave. For example, in 1982, Royal Marines went directly from their pass-out parade to join 3 Commando Brigade in its deployment to the Falklands. In 1991, Marines and officers who'd just passed out were sent directly to join Operation Safe Haven in Northern Iraq – including one entire troop who passed out on the Friday and were in Iraq by Saturday night. The point to remember is that these men were trained to commando Operational Performance Standards.

CTCRM also trains Non-Commissioned Officers (see Annexes B and C), Signallers and Clerks, and within the Infantry Support Wing (ISW) trains Snipers, Assault engineers (AEs – see Annex E), Platoon Weapons Instructors (PWs – see Annex D), Heavy Weapons (HWs – mortars, anti-tank, air defence), Drill Instructors (DIs), and Physical Training Instructors (PTIs). Again, both Officers and Marines receive specialized training in the same location and occasionally, on the same course. Like all other training wings, the ISW acts as a resource for the whole Corps. It will trial new weapons and equipment, and always provides advice and assistance throughout the Royal Marines as and when needed. Nor is this limited to the Corps – the Signals and Clerks Training Wing trialled the new, £2 billion BOWMAN project that will replace the Central Net Radio system used throughout the British Armed Forces. In a less dramatic, but equally vital manner, the specialist rehabilitation and remedial sub-unit called Hunter Troop now shares its knowledge and experience throughout the Armed Forces.

In fact, Hunter Troop is a perfect example of the Corps's ability to turn a problem into an opportunity. Most if not all YOs and recruits will receive some sort of injury during their training. If it's serious, they'll be transferred to Hunter Troop, run by the PTIs and the CTCRM's medical staff, for rehabilitation. Alternatively, a recruit may be sent to Hunter Troop for remedial therapy, say to strengthen specific muscle groups or while recuperating from illness or an operation. Realistic recovery targets are set, so that the YO or recruit will return to full training with the optimum chance of success. Over the past few years, Hunter Troop and the CTCRM medical staff have even become the military experts in handling stress fractures. As a result, traditional gym-shoes have been replaced by proper trainers, worn when exercising on a properly sprung gym floor. Nor are YOs or recruits allowed to run wearing boots until feet have hardened and boots been broken in. Time was when the mere thought of Hunter Troop brought a YO or recruit out in a cold sweat. Nowadays it has to possess one of the highest *esprits de corps* of any sub-unit within CTCRM, a source of considerable and justifiable pride to the PTI Branch . . . especially when Hunter Troop actually beats its PT Instructors at sports like basketball.

But this book is actually more concerned with the Commando Training Wing. No matter how professional the other wings are, all Royal Marines primarily associate Lympstone with the day they were awarded the coveted Green Beret.

It's at Lympstone that a young Marine first makes his covenant with the Corps and his comrades. At Lympstone that he first realizes the trial is as much psychological as physical. That personal integrity is as important as the ability to do fifty sit-ups in as many seconds.

Young men arrive there for all manner of stated reasons. Perhaps there's a relative in the Corps. Perhaps they once saw a Royal Marines Commando demonstration when they were kids. Or simply want to join what they perceive is the best. But the ones who stay the course are nearly always those who are as attracted by the Corps ethos and dedication as by the purely military side of things. The true call to arms was never, is never, solely about excitement. It's about dedication and humility. Testing oneself. Achieving more than you ever dreamed possible. And as so many discover when they leave the Corps, it's a hard act to follow for civilian life rarely offers the same levels of responsibility and courtesy . . . the same sense of being part of something that's really quite exceptional. So if anyone reading this has a former Royal Marine Commando for a civilian colleague, please ignore the occasional look of total disbelief and frustration that sweeps across those manly features whenever Marketing, Accounts or Human Resources does something particularly asinine. Listen kindly to his stories, even for the second or third time: it means he thinks quite highly of you. Just remember that he brings with him a world more intense than anything you have ever imagined.

Potential Recruits' Course

Potential recruits are not allowed to mix with recruits in training. Aside from the fact that the recruits in training are too busy to talk to them, they are already in another world. The three days of the PRC are going to be strange enough as it is without adding to it. Besides, recruits in training invariably spend a good deal of their time talking about leaving as soon as they can. Mostly it's a way of letting off steam, but the effect on would-be Marines could be upsetting, and they (the Corps) lose enough as it is.

When potential recruits first arrive at Lympstone – say, on a Sunday afternoon – they draw the kit they'll be using, are given a short brief about the programme, are taught elementary marching (they will not be allowed to shamble around the camp), and are taken to the induction block where they'll be staying. The lights are turned out just after 2200 hours.

The following morning begins with a room inspection. Then comes a visit to the gym, where each man has to do as many squat jumps, sit-ups and straddle jumps as he can in one minute respectively. This tests them for physical ability, potential and mental approach – commonly known as guts.

Then comes a series of lectures about the various Technical Qualifications and Specialist Qualifications open to a Royal Marine (TQs and SQs) and how much they'll be paid. This is followed by a visit from the one recruit they do get to meet – the King's Squad Diamond. The King's Squad is the senior recruit troop in training, and the Diamond (or Diamonds, there can be more than one) is the recruit (or recruits) most likely to win the King's Badge, even though it's not always presented. Probably, the Diamond is more of an unofficial recruit NCO. It's unlikely a Diamond will tell them how perfectly bloody the whole thing is and that they should leave for home immediately. A Diamond is a very motivated man – his job is really to say yes, the training is tough, but there is light at the end of the tunnel. And if he hasn't just come back from a ten-day exercise on Dartmoor, he'll probably look as if he means it.

The following day begins with another room inspection, followed by a 1.5-mile run, to be completed in less than 11.5 minutes, followed by breakfast, and a series of character and ability interviews. Then comes a visit to the weapons museum, with a brief description of the weapons the Royal Marines use, and why, followed by a visit to the assault course. Here they're tested for vertigo, given a 200-metre fireman's carry to do in less than ninety seconds, interviewed individually by the instructors and briefed on the following day's log race.

On the final day, after room inspection, they're taken to the assault course, and split into teams, and each team is presented with the inevitable telegraph pole which has to be taken around the assault course as quickly as possible. Unlike the POC, there's no set time – deliberately, because the instructors want to see how much pressure the recruits can apply to themselves. The point is that Royal Marines Commandos learn how to motivate themselves without relying on orders. Log race over, stores are cleaned and returned and the potential recruits assemble to hear their fate.

For those who've failed, it can be a deeply traumatic experience. It's not unknown for a potential recruit to break down in tears when he's told by the Warrant Officer in charge that he's not been accepted, such as the young man who'd even been a member of the Royal Marines Reserve. When he'd left home to go on his PRC, so sure was he of passing that he'd told all his family and friends that the next time they saw him – some six months later – he'd be wearing the Green Beret of the fully fledged Royal Marine Commando. All he'd ever wanted to do was to join the Royal Marines. And here the door was being slammed firmly in his face, without even the comfort of being asked to try again in six months. He was merely told that it was his right to try again in a year's time – but really, wouldn't he be happier in one of the other services? For the rules are very strict. The instructors will not pass a man unless they are positive that he's capable of staying the course. Not that he's guaranteed to pass the course, merely that he's got the potential. Otherwise, it's not fair to the man, his fellow recruits, his instructors and even the Corps itself.

It's not enough that you want to do a thing so badly you've been unable to think of anything else, of any other career. This is the first harsh lesson taught by the

Royal Marines – wanting is not enough, wanting does not entitle you to try. Only your own ability and real commitment will do that . . . plus the pragmatic consideration that even if you do manage to pass that course, will you be of any use to the Corps?

A question of commitment

Officers train at Lympstone for a total of forty-seven weeks, recruits for thirty. Including holidays, that makes a year for officers and six months for recruits. The difference between the two courses is that a YO does have to learn far more – when he leaves Lympstone, although he's still on probation for another year, he's expected to be able to begin to command a troop (equivalent to an army platoon, theoretically numbering thirty or so men), whereas a young Marine leaving Lympstone is only expected to be able to take his *place* in a troop. Both will still be faced with a deal of learning, but the responsibilities of a 'sprog' officer in the Corps are that much greater – he's trained to take command from the beginning, whereas in the army he may often spend the first year or so as another officer's second in command. But of the two, the army system is probably preferable since it gives the officer more time to grow into the job – and possibly more practical experience.

But it should also be remembered that the Young Officer will have been trained to a far higher infantry standard than his Sandhurst contemporary. Similarly, the recruit training is the longest and most intensive within NATO, arguably throughout the world.

The sheer intensity and professionalism of the training at Lympstone comes as a total shock to YO and recruit alike. Tough as the POC, AIB and PRC were, they were no indication of what training will really be like. The method of instruction appears to have changed, too. Before, at the POC or PRC, candidates were encouraged to pass. Now, they are being challenged to prove they really want to be Royal Marines Commandos – and that they're good enough. This type of approach has come under attack recently, for some modern thinking holds that recruits should be led by the hand through flower-bedecked meadows to where a wonderful rainbow marks success. Well, there is a crock to be found in this approach, but it's not gold. Young men join the Royal Marines specifically for the challenge. Take it away, and you'll lose them. Then, too, successive defence cuts have reduced the time available for basic training, which only adds to the overall pressure. Ministry planners and cost analysts now demand a fast through-put, with optimum success rates, whatever the hell that means in relation to training men for war. If you reduce the intensity of training, you will not be producing commandos capable of taking their place within a fighting troop as soon as they leave Lympstone. For as has been said before, one of the lessons learned at Lympstone is that the mind can triumph over the body. There is no point in reducing the cumulative, physical and mental effects of the training and final commando tests. Because if you do, no matter how good the final product, it won't be a commando. This is one reason why the Corps demands such a high standard of physical fitness from the very beginning. Essentially, every person who passes the POC or PRC should be physically capable of completing training. The rest is all in the mind. Incidentally, the reason why the Army has now been forced to consider longer basic training is not really because today's young men are so horribly unfit. It's because the original training time was cut back by the Treasury several years ago. Naturally, the cost of putting right the original mistake will be more than was originally saved. But don't tell the bean-counters because they know the numbers are never wrong.

Most YOs and recruits start out by making up a calendar to chart their progress week by week, month by month. The calendar is soon ignored. It is as much as they can do to get by on a day-to-day basis – sometimes, from morning to afternoon – without even thinking what next week or next month will bring. Reasons for joining are soon forgotten, appear trivial when men are living for days on end in a narrow trench – a narrow, flooded trench with the temperature below freezing. Or when they're speed marching nine miles with equipment weighing up to thirty pounds on their backs (just a foretaste of what life will be like in a unit). It is not why they joined that's important. It's why they stay. And that depends on how truly committed they were (for a sense of commitment often outlasts more logical reasons) and how determined they are not to be beaten. It becomes a very personal battle: the man (or rather the YO batch or recruit troop, because no man can succeed on his own) against the course itself. Certainly loyalty to one's fellow YOs or recruits will become one of the biggest reasons for not quitting.

This is as it should be, for as author James Jones

noted in *The Thin Red Line,* men do not, in battle, normally commit acts of bravery and endurance out of loyalty to an abstract ideal. They do so out of loyalty to each other, which makes far more sense, because they're less likely to get each other killed, or to expect someone else to die for their own beliefs.

The instructors demand that YOs and recruits grow up very quickly. All the instructors have served with one or other of the commandos. All make it very plain that playtime is over and this is for real. For although it is extremely difficult to simulate battlefield conditions during training – far too expensive and resulting in an unacceptable casualty rate (and God knows it's high enough to begin with) – you *can* simulate the mental and physical pressures of the battlefield. This is exactly what the instructors try to do, while teaching YOs and recruits their trade. Learn how to fire and clean your rifle. Learn how to do it when you're dog tired, at night, living in two feet of mud and already late for the next rendezvous. Learn how to keep yourself and your clothes clean. Learn how to do it when there are only minutes between lectures, no matter what the programme claims. Learn how to go around the endurance course in a three- or four-man syndicate, each helping the other. Learn how to do it when one man's injured and if you don't achieve the correct time, you'll all have to go round again. Learn how to lead or take part in a troop attack. Learn how to do it when you haven't slept for three days and you're suffering from mild exposure. Learn how to live out in the wilds for a week or so. Learn how to do it when you've fallen into a river (not a deliberate part of the curriculum) and you, plus all your spare clothes, are soaking wet with little prospect of drying out. Above all, perhaps, learn how to take responsibility for your mates. Learn how to do this when there are at least three or four of them you can't stand – and who can't stand you. A yo-yo's (YO) or nod's (recruit) life is not an easy one.

Potential recruit training

If those who've passed the PRC and arrived back at Lympstone to begin their training proper think that they can immediately become part of recruit training proper, they're sadly mistaken. First, they have two weeks in an induction block – time intended to bring them to the point of *beginning* to be recruits. Time for the Corps to take a much closer look at them and decide if it really does want them. Time, come to that, for the recruits to take a closer look at the Corps and decide if they still want to become Marines.

The two weeks are spent learning the more basic aspects of soldiering: how to wash and iron one's own clothes and how to keep the living accommodation clean and tidy. Let it be said that these two aspects of recruit training are not a reflection on the standard of recruits applying to join the Royal Marines (despite the basic academic standard required, many boast two or more A levels, and may have joined from a successful job in civvy street). It is more a comment on the fact that today's young men appear to be far more spoilt than those of a decade or so ago. Spoilt not just by their parents, but by fashions and fabrics, for example, that appear to require very little ironing – or by the ready availability of dry cleaners and washing machines. By the fact that trainers (sneakers) don't need polishing – whereas military boots do, because if they're not polished, the leather will crack and no longer be waterproof. The shine is just an added bonus.

Feet brought up exclusively in trainers are also soft, which among other things means a greater risk of blisters. Perhaps would-be Royal Marines should spend a few months walking around in leather boots before even trying for the POC or PRC.

This is a time when the recruits begin to think like recruits, when they realize how ill-equipped they are to last the training, when they begin to understand that military discipline in the Royal Marines is largely a matter of self-discipline. No instructor will continually badger a recruit to do a certain job. He'll tell him once, and that's it. Often, he won't tell him at all, expecting that the recruit will see the necessity of doing such-and-such before he gets shouted out – it's called developing one's initiative.

This is a time, too, when the recruits first make their acquaintance with the drill square. Much to their surprise, they discover that Royal Marine drill instructors do not scream in high falsettos – do not go in for the eyeball-to-eyeball confrontation that one finds at Quantico (USMC) or Catterick (Brigade of Guards). Commands are audible, but shouted only if the troop is some distance away. And a rebuke – the recruits soon discover – is all the more effective if it's delivered in a coldly contemptuous tone, almost conversationally, rather than screamed into one's ear from a distance of two inches.

At the end of the two weeks the recruits can decide if they want to stay or not. The Corps can decide if it wants to keep them or not – although the Corps can decide to dispense with a man's services whenever it wants to. Between twenty and forty per cent will leave at this point. Some leave because they've become intensely homesick, others because they've realized that there are easier ways of impressing a girlfriend.

The recruit who had to be 'let go' when it was discovered he didn't know how to wash himself properly has passed into Corps folklore. It turned out that although he was eighteen, his mother still supervised bath-time. Some people wondered why she hadn't tried to join up herself. In fact, the Drill Instructors who act as surrogate parents to the recruits will go to considerable length to help the lads adapt to the rigours and confines of training. All the same, bathing a recruit by hand would be taking this a little too far. Aside from anything else, all the recruits would probably want their backs scrubbed, as well . . . and then so would the YOs and eventually the Corps would develop a special Personal Washer Branch, and you'd find them lurking throughout NATO armed with large scrubbing brushes and Badedas.

But back in reality, the first two weeks are up and the recruits move out of the induction block into proper recruit accommodation. It's not all that different, really, but the point is that they're now considered fit to mix with more senior recruits.

And now the pressure really begins. Why, sometimes their instructors actually appear to want them to leave – which they can do, but not until the twelfth week. 'Go on, make my day and wrap (quit),' is an oft-heard refrain, which surprisingly has the opposite – and desired – effect of making the recruit determined to stay and tough it out, if only to prove the instructor wrong. But if the instructors were kind and understanding at this stage of training, they would lose far more recruits later on when the going really gets tough. This initial approach also encourages the recruit troop to unite together against the common enemy, their instructors. Later on they'll discover that the real enemy is the course itself, or rather those personal weaknesses that might prevent them from succeeding. But for now, the troop is beginning to work together . . . and learning that other invaluable lesson taught at Lympstone: one fails, we all fail. The recruits are learning to look after each other.

By the same token, the recruits are not broken down and then reassembled in the Corps image – as tends to happen in the USMC or the French Foreign Legion. Brainwashing is out, if for no other reason than that brainwashing creates men with little initiative – and is ineffectual anyway at moments of stress, leading to a breakdown in battlefield discipline. Rather, the Corps encourages the recruits (and YOs) to grow in those directions that will help them to become Marines, to grow both physically and psychologically, to become elite soldiers in body and mind.

But recruits are never that much aware of the mental changes they're going through. Only when they look back at the end of it all and compare their characters then with the type of men they are now, do they realize that they have undergone a sea change from boy to Marine.

A good deal has been reported about 'beasting' at

Lympstone – the unmerciful bullying of recruits by savage and sadistic instructors. Undoubtedly, it does happen occasionally. In a Corps numbering some seven thousand men, there'll always be at least one bad apple. And Sod's Law (the Corps version of Murphy's Law) states that not only *will* something always go wrong, but that it'll go wrong in a manner calculated to produce the worst publicity for the Royal Marines. None the less, true cases of beasting are mercifully rare and are dealt with severely. What does often happen is that neither recruit nor parent (nor the parent's local Member of Parliament who inevitably becomes involved) realizes that recruits are not being trained to look good in their Green Berets; not to look good on guard outside Buckingham Palace; not even to exercise interminably with 42 and 45 Commando in Norway. A recruit is trained to fight and survive on the battlefield, as a commando, as a Royal Marine. Again, it's a question of simulating the mental and physical pressures that occur in war. But at the same time, the instructors are not only being cruel to be kind. They are attempting to turn out Marines who can do their job – and if being able to do that job means the ability to eat a dead rat and fire a rifle before the other guy, that's what they'll teach.

Not, one hastens to add, that recruits at Lympstone are ever taught to eat dead rats. But they are taught to develop the ability to do whatever they must to get the job done. Again, not in terms of savagery in war, but in terms of being able to drive themselves to the very limit and beyond. And it is an inescapable fact that no one ever knows what they're truly capable of until they're forced to find out.

The longest days

Let's take a look at a 'day-in-the-life-of' a recruit in, say, the tenth week of training, nearly half-way through the course. One thing's for sure, this recruit wouldn't stand out in a crowd of other recruits for they all tend to look alike. It's not their comparative youth. Nor their short hair. Nor the fact that they all wear identical clothes. It's the fact that all recruits have the same deadpan expressions. In the early stages of training the only emotions they appear to show are dismay (when something's gone wrong, and it always does) or relief (when something's gone wrong but the instructors haven't noticed. Yet). A deadpan face is the natural camouflage of the recruits, reflecting a desire to go unnoticed from one embuggerance to another.

Even asleep, recruits all look alike – which is how we first meet this particular man, lying in his bed at 03.30. But not for long, as the door is flung open and he plus the rest of the troop are told by an instructor to get dressed (in PT kit) and get outside.

By now the recruit has learnt not to ask too many questions, but to accept as cheerfully as possible everything that comes his way. There is a reason, he's sure, for shaking him and his mates out of bed at an ungodly hour – and that reason is bound to be Something They've Done (or Not Done). Sometimes, it's better not to ask.

It's cold outside and the troop stand shivering for a while before being marched off towards the water tank. This is an open-air tank measuring some forty feet across. Its metal sides are about eight feet tall, the water inside is five feet deep. Ropes are strung some eight feet above the surface – single ropes, reasonably taut but not so taut that they won't swing and sway when someone is crawling across them. Here the recruit troop is told to practise regains for the next half hour. A regain is the method by which having crawled half-way across the tank on top of the rope, you stop, let yourself down so you're hanging by your hands, and then try to swing back on top of the rope again to carry on crawling. It is very difficult at the best of times; it requires strength, and agility and timing. At nearly four in the morning, it's well nigh impossible. Within a few minutes all the recruits are wet.

At that point one of the instructors gently reminds them that the previous day's weapon inspection had been bad in the extreme. Dirty barrels, dirty moving parts, mud-encrusted magazines – over half the troop had had something wrong with their rifles – and this after being warned that an inspection was due. In itself that had been a mark of favour, since recruits are not normally warned but are expected to keep their rifles spotless at all times. As the instructor points out, it's unlikely that so many of them will fail an inspection ever again. Somehow the recruits feel that he's telling the truth.

That lesson over, it's back to the barracks for as much sleep as they can get before reveille at 06.00.

Our recruit gets up, grabs a quick shower, shaves, makes his bed and does his share of the barrackroom chores. He tries to be as quick as he can, because breakfast is at 06.30 and he has to draw his rifle from the armoury before 07.00. If he's lucky he'll have about twenty-five minutes to check his rifle for cleanliness –

very important after the earlier event – help to give the room a once-over, get his kit ready for the day and get dressed for first parade at 08.00. This lasts for the best part of an hour and is followed by three-quarters of an hour's drill.

Between 08.45 and 09.40 he has a map-reading lecture. The instructor continually questions the class to make sure that they understand and are not simply pretending to do so. Map reading over, the recruit has ten minutes to get ready for the next lecture, on platoon or troop tactics, to be held on the Lower Field. Platoon or troop tactics are over by 10.35. According to the timetable he then has a ten-minute stand easy (tea break). But the next lecture is PT in the gymnasium, for which he has to get changed. Together with his troop he doubles back to the accommodation block, gets changed, and doubles over to the gym. No stand easy – some recruits claim that they never had a stand easy throughout their training, were convinced it was a figment of someone's imagination.

PT finishes at 11.40 and he has ten minutes to get showered, get changed again and be with his rifle at the next venue for weapon training. Lunch is between 12.35 and 13.35. He spends most of this time making sure he's ready for the afternoon. At 13.35 – on the dot – he's on the 25-metre range for live firing, which ends at 14.40. He then has the inevitable ten minutes to get back to his barrackroom, stow his rifle in his locker, make sure the locker's locked and muster outside where a three-ton truck is waiting to take the troop to Woodbury Common for a map-reading exercise, when he'll be tested on the morning's lecture. Woodbury Common is the most relaxed part of the day so far. He even has time to notice another recruit troop, two months senior to his own, who are on exercise up there. He notices, somewhat enviously, that those recruits appear to be far more in command of the situation – and that their instructors appear to treat them as being at least semi-human. Map reading finishes at 16.30 and, since the truck has vanished, the troop must run the four miles back to the camp. His rifle and any other stores must be cleaned and returned by 17.30. Supper is at 17.45. He wolfs down his food, in a hurry to get some time to himself before official lights out at 22.30. In reality, he's still up and the lights are still blazing at 22.30 since he has to help a mate with the other man's ironing – a favour which will be returned the next day.

And as he does finally fall asleep, he wonders – not for the first time – why on earth he wanted to join the Royal Marines. And shouldn't he opt out in week twelve as is his right? For if he doesn't do so then, short of a medical discharge – or being simply declared unsuitable by the Corps – he's theirs for the next four years. And then he may remember the other recruits he saw on Woodbury Common, and how they appeared to be coping so well, and he'll probably promise himself to give it one last go before calling home with the news that he couldn't hack it after all.

Every recruit wants to leave at some time or other during training. The course wouldn't be hard enough if he didn't. And if the above 'day-in-the-life-of' appears to be lacking in commando skills, and mainly concentrates on the type of training one could expect in any military unit, there's a reason. You cannot teach a man all those arcane disciplines that help to make him an elite soldier unless you get the basics right. Before he's a commando he must be a very good soldier indeed. He must also grow from adolescent to mature man in a far shorter time than nature or society usually allows.

One of our sheep is missing

In fact, recruits are introduced to those commando skills quite early on in their training – but on exercise, in the field where it counts. Their first taste of being a commando comes in week twelve, on an exercise called either Omega Man or Hunter's Moon – both rather emotive names which conjure up much skulduggery and creeping about at night. But while they appear, at face value, to be the stuff of *Boy's Own* books and war comics, the reality is – as always – very different.

In principle the exercise is a simple one. The recruits are taken to a fairly deserted part of the moors (usually Exmoor), given an area to live in and told to get on with it as best they can.

It begins with drawing stores. Each recruit can take a set of denims, a pair of overalls (ovies), a waterproof jacket (made of nylon so that sweat vapour condenses inside and makes one's clothes damp), two pairs of socks, a shirt, underwear, a pullover if it's really cold (woolly pully); a pair of boots and a sleeping bag. (The sleeping bag is a comparatively recent innovation. Not so very long ago, the recruits were allowed to take only a single blanket.)

The recruits are also issued with a survival kit – fish

hooks, nylon line, waterproof matches etc. – mainly useful for the psychological comfort it brings. Additionally the troop will take radios, maps, compasses, protractors – and also load on to the three-ton truck all the stores that the instructors will take with them – a somewhat poignant moment as they lift up stoves and camp beds and tents and food. For the meal they have before leaving will be the last real meal for at least two days.

The troop is then trucked to Exmoor, disembarked in a lonely spot and searched for any contraband items like chocolate bars, cigarettes or even money – particularly money, since one troop managed to smuggle out quite a considerable sum and used it to pay a local farmer's wife to cook for them.

'Great initiative, lads,' one of the instructors is reputed to have said. 'Now let's see you yomp (trek) back to camp.'

The search over, two instructors lead them across the moor for some twelve miles, at night, to the area where they're to set up camp. This tends to be in a well-wooded valley that runs quite precipitously down to a river or stream. Here the recruits will make their brushwood 'bivvies', using whatever materials they can find in that one area. But there's never any time – or enough light – to make a bivvie on the first night. Instead, the recruits grab whatever branches they can find, make some sort of rudimentary shelter, and huddle together inside. If nothing else, this does wonders in dispelling any inhibitions they may have about cuddling up to each other for warmth.

The next day, and depending on the weather conditions, they may be given one tarpaulin (a small tarpaulin) between four of them. Or if they've been allowed to take ponchos (and this decision is left up to each individual training team) they can tie them together to make a single sheet. With that as a basic floor covering – and sometimes as any sort of covering, if it's too warm for sleeping bags – they begin to make their bivvies. The training team will offer some advice, but mostly they watch to see which recruit is coping well, which recruit has remembered the lecture on the subject or is showing some initiative – and which recruits are either content to follow someone else's lead, or are beginning to sink into damp apathy (damp because it's nearly always raining). Most importantly, the instructors are watching for the recruits who appear to be determined to enjoy the experience, who can still keep their sense of humour even as it dawns on them that this is not going to be the fun time that they'd imagined. For it's one thing to be told that you're going to have to live off the land, another to be faced with the difficulty of doing so – and subsequently, of not eating at all. (It's doubly hard when the smell of cooking from the instructors' tent often wafts across in your direction . . .)

On one survival exercise the weather conditions were so bad that two recruits went down with exposure on the first night and the training team had quickly to pitch a marquee to shelter the rest of the troops from freezing rain and gale-force winds. Both recruits were taken to hospital that same night – and taken back out to the exercise the following morning.

'It was really rather pitiful,' remembered an instructor who'd fetched them from hospital, 'the way one of them lay there, staring up at me, his little eyes pleading not to be taken from his nice warm bed. But the doc had passed him fit (a civilian doctor) and so back out he had to go. Nurses thought I was some sort of monster. The Nod knew I was. But the main thing wrong with him was simply lack of guts. If you think you can't make it, if you don't want to dig out and try and make it, you won't – you'll go down, no question.'

Recruits in the field on a survival exercise are meant to be tactical most of the time, meaning that they must assume that an enemy may attack at any moment. They are not, to be truthful, as tactical as they will be in some other exercises – when they'll spend many hours, even days, wearing NBC suits (anti-nuclear, bacteriological and chemical warfare protection clothing), but they can expect the occasional thunderflash thrown in their direction, invariably when they're just getting *off* to sleep. Nor are they necessarily told what the exercise programme is going to be. Again, the training staff are looking for those recruits who either react well or badly when one surprise after another is thrown at them.

The same troop who suffered so badly on their first night experienced just such a surprise two nights later. They were still living in the marquee. Conditions were simply too bad to allow them out on the moor, even in the comparative safety of a wooded one-in-four slope. But as the marquee was a mere few yards away from the instructors' own tent complex, meaning that the recruits were continuously aware how warm and dry – not to mention well fed – the instructors were, any scant extra comfort was offset by a certain mental torment. The recruits had been allowed to settle down for the night, when they were suddenly woken up. They were told that a night navigation exercise (night navex) had been planned; that they were to get up, get into their wet clothes (leaving their dry ones for when they returned) and muster outside as soon as possible. There they were issued with radios, maps and one emergency bergen (rucksack) per four-man team. The route was explained to them – eight miles, passing through four checkpoints across the highest part of Exmoor – and they were marched to the starting line and sent off at staggered intervals. But not before one of the teams had reported to the training sergeant that one of their number – the recruit who'd gone down with exposure and hadn't wanted to leave his hospital bed – had become totally withdrawn, wouldn't say a word except to complain about the cold, and they really didn't want the responsibility of taking him up on to the moor. The sergeant sent for the recruit and asked him if he was fit enough to take part in the night navex. The recruit hummed and hawed for some time before allowing that he didn't really think so – but that he wanted to do it in case he was back-trooped.

In reality, this particular recruit had guessed that failure to complete the exercise would probably mean being discharged from the Corps – as turned out to be the case. The training team had had their eye on him for some time, feeling that probably he should never have been accepted as a recruit in the first place.

And so, minus one recently hospitalized recruit, thankful to be now out of it and already looking forward to the day when he would leave Lympstone altogether, the team set off.

For all that it's supposed to be so beautiful, Exmoor

is a wicked place. Somehow its hills seem steeper than those on Dartmoor. Being so close to the Bristol Channel and thus the Atlantic, Exmoor catches the full force of those gales that sweep in from the sea. The fact that more of it is cultivated than Dartmoor works against the night walker too: more barbed-wire fences – often just a single strand, invisible in the darkness – to rip and tear. The temperature was close to freezing – cold enough to make the recruits want to run all the way. As it was, they managed to trot a good deal of it. They also discovered, by good map reading, that if they missed out the one checkpoint that was unmanned, so saving about two miles, it would still be possible to approach the next checkpoint from the correct direction. As against that, they *had* been told to go to each checkpoint, and if they were caught they knew they'd have to go round again. In the end, the two miles that could be saved won the day and the team managed to complete the night navex without being found out.

And if to the weary writer allowed along for the ride it seemed that they spent so much time in the new route they had to follow – so much time and energy in making sure they approached the manned checkpoint from the right direction, that they might just as well have done the thing properly – that wasn't the point. It was that, by using the skills the instructors had taught them, they had managed to outsmart the instructors themselves. Any time a recruit can get one over on his instructors, he's a happy man.

This attitude came to a head a few years ago. It all started when the recruit training wing received a phone call from a local Exmoor farmer. He was missing two sheep, couldn't even find the bodies, and since a recruit troop had been in his area a month or so before he wondered if they'd seen or heard anything suspicious – like a wild dog, or even strangers with a van.

The message was passed to the training team who'd taken the troop into the area. No, there'd been nothing suspicious, though the troop in question had looked far happier and well fed than they should have done. The instructors had remarked on it at the time, and merely concluded that for once they had a bunch of exceptionally well-switched-on men, and left it at that. But then the instructors remembered that amongst the troop was a man who had been a butcher in civilian life . . . surely he, *they* couldn't have? But they had. Two sheep had been captured, stunned, expertly slaughtered, butchered, cooked and devoured. The troop admitted their guilt by the fact that when they were told they would have to pay for the animals, they did so without question. Smugly, and without question. 'You know,' an officer said, 'you could almost be proud of them – to do that under the very noses of the training team and not get caught. Except, of course, that one is so terribly shocked by the whole thing . . .'

Since that day, recruits have been kept well away from sheep. Now, the only meat they have to eat on their survival exercise is the rabbits which are given to them at some stage – given to them live, and which they then have to kill, skin, and clean before eating. It is the first time that most recruits have ever killed anything in their lives.

'Killing itself isn't the point of the exercise,' explained an instructor, 'or it better not be. God help any recruit who we think actually enjoys it. See, it's not that we're starting them off on killing rabbits and graduating them on to killing enemy soldiers, maybe by way of a few politicians. What it is, it's a hard lesson in self-sufficiency. And they learn that no matter how squeamish you may think you are, there comes a time when you're so cold, tired and hungry that your scruples vanish. Not that we'll make a guy kill a rabbit if he honestly can't bring himself to do so – but that's not for his sake, it's for the rabbit's. A nervous guy will botch it, and that'll make the animal suffer.'

The recruits are told that if they don't manage to kill their rabbit quickly and cleanly, an instructor *will* make them suffer for it. This produces a slight nervousness – often manifesting itself in a certain black humour. It is not uncommon to see a line of recruits, each holding a rabbit and waiting their turn at the killing block, suddenly launch into a chorus of 'Bright Eyes' from *Watership Down*. Not quite what Art Garfunkel had in mind, but it seems to calm the rabbits.

Lessons learned

What do they learn from exercises like these? For many of them, city born and bred, it's learning to get closer, almost to merge with nature in the wild. For all, it's a time when they discover that they can manage to survive even though the only hot drink they've had in three days is nettle tea. That in itself brings a tremendous sense of accomplishment. But then, all of recruit training is designed to do just that – to build up their self-esteem by giving them a succession of harder and harder tasks. In the process they graduate from being boys to becoming a certain kind of man – not necessarily the kind of man today's society feels totally at home with, but the kind of man society needs to defend it.

The cost of effectiveness

Long and hard as recruit training is, it's not nearly long enough. Over the past five years, at least a month has been lost – and most instructors are adamant that not only do they want that month back, but probably another two months added on. But these demands have fallen on deaf Treasury and MoD ears: it costs somewhere in the region of £35,000 to train a recruit as it is and a man in training is hardly cost effective in terms of defending his country. At the same time the Royal Marines do suffer certain manning problems, in common with the rest of the Armed Forces. Officialdom's inspired response to this is not to deal with the root cause, but to insist on as many men getting through Lympstone in as short a time as possible in order to make up the shortfall.

Sometimes, one has the unworthy thought that despite the Cold War being over, Whitehall is still full of Soviet moles, all rather sadly wondering when they'll meet that nice KGB handler again . . . but all still loyally beavering away to ruin the country. The only other explanation is sheer stupidity and a preoccupation with short term gain.

Manning problems within the Royal Marines are due

to two main causes. The first, that pay and conditions – especially for junior ranks – have not kept up with the equivalent civilian sector. It isn't just that Royal Marines are expected, if necessary, to put their lives on the line for their country. They're also expected to spend long months away from their families . . . while married accompanied postings are only allowed if the posting is for a year or longer. It was estimated that in 1986 between a tour in Northern Ireland, winter deployment in Norway and standard training exercises, the men of 45 Commando spent less than six weeks at home. And while it can be argued that men who join up are aware of all this beforehand . . . and that purely commercial considerations shouldn't come into it (but they always do when the Treasury begins to sharpen its knife) the fact is that a long history of insensitivity and trying-to-do-things-on-the-cheap has resulted in a far higher leaving rate – particularly at the corporal level – than is truly necessary or desirable.

It's an argument that's slated to go on for a long, long time. After all, it's been around for well over a thousand years. And just as it probably escaped a new recruit to a Roman Legion, so too it escapes Royal Marine recruits as they sweat, strain and stumble towards that magical moment when they're presented with their Green Berets as newly fledged Royal Marine Commandos.

Pongos and matelots can be green, too

Lympstone is also home to the All-Arms Commando Course. (See Annex F.) As we have seen there are certain

Army units attached permanently to 3 Commando
Brigade. 29 Commando Regiment Royal Artillery,
equipped with 105mm light guns, 20 Commando Air
Defence Battery Royal Artillery, equipped with Rapier
FSB2, and 59 Independent Commando Squadron Royal
Engineers, equipped with all manner of sexy kit, are all
highly valued by the Royal Marines Commandos – not
least because all these Army personnel are entitled to wear
a Green Beret. As are various REME, Royal Signals and
Royal Logistics Corps personnel who will also be found
scattered throughout the Brigade and Commando
Logistics Regiment. Green-hatted Royal Navy personnel
will include photographers (among the best in Britain, let
alone the Armed Forces, as witness the awards they keep
on winning) and possibly medical staff: doctors, dentists
and sick-berth attendants, the latter trained to civilian
paramedic standards. The general rule is, if you want to
serve with the commandos, you get yourself commando-
trained. There are some exceptions: you just can't do without a doctor, dentist or even a cook – but all the same, no
unfit and overweight Army cooks need apply. Yet it's surprising how many people who could possibly claim
exemption from the rule are determined to win a Green
Beret. Which includes a currently serving chaplain who'll
proudly – and a little ruefully – point to the steel shepherd's crook the CTW made for him, a crook weighing
exactly the same as the old SLR 7.62 semi-automatic rifle
and which he carried throughout his commando course
. . . because, of course, chaplains never carry weapons.

Why? Why do all attached personnel have to be commando-trained? Why do they want to be commando-
trained?

First, the obvious reasons.

Passing the All-Arms Commando Course helps you understand what makes the Royal Marines tick and how they operate. It establishes that you've gained a necessary level of fitness and developed commando skills. The average Royal Marine will be inclined to respect the fact that you, too, have suffered but ultimately prevailed. Whether Pongo or Matelot, you're now part of the Royal Marines family.

But it's also to do with the commando spirit.

Pause for the usual cracks about 'make mine a large Scotch'. Or 'I thought the Navy had stopped the rum-issue.' OK? Once again, then: the commando spirit.

One fails, we all fail. Integrity. Trust. Loyalty to each other. Determination. The ability to endure. Selflessness. Responsibility. Humour in the face of adversity. Mutual respect and courtesy. Rudyard Kipling's poem 'If', but taken to the nth degree.

As green-hatted Navy and Army personnel discover – if they didn't already know – the Green Beret is not a symbol of physical prowess. It's a symbol of shared ideals and mental strengths. Being awarded a Green Beret doesn't actually turn men into supermen, although it may feel like that at the time.

The All-Arms Commando Course, which runs for six weeks, is also mandatory for any attached training personnel. There'll always be at least one member of the USMC attached to CTT, and possibly someone from the Royal Netherlands Marines, plus an increasing number of British Army officers and NCOs, all of whom have to be 'green-hatted'. It's an excellent way of sharing different skills, even if there is a slight suspicion that anyone who spends too long with the Corps inevitably goes native. As witness the attached USMC captain who once marched his company into the jungle in Brunei because he thought the CO was picking on them unfairly . . . and refused to come back until promised fairer treatment.

CHAPTER THREE

Officer Training

A military decision is not merely a mathematical computation. Decision-making requires both the intuitive skill to recognize and analyze the essence of a given problem and the creative ability to devise a practical solution. This ability is the product of experience, education, intelligence, boldness, perception and character.

General A. M. Gray, United States Marine Corps

Potential Officers' Course

Each year, some four hundred bright, young, hopeful and nervous faces will grace the breakfast table at Lympstone Officers' Mess. These young men, aged between seventeen and twenty-three are attending the three-day Royal Marines Commandos Potential Officers' Course. They already know that if Sandhurst requires at least one hundred per cent commitment, Lympstone will require one hundred and twenty per cent: the course is that much more intensive and considerably tougher. Safe to assume that they are all totally committed to becoming Royal Marines officers.

Quite *why* is never satisfactorily answered by Young Officers in training, nor by recruits nor even by trained

Royal Marines themselves. True, all the standard reasons are given: 'a family connection'; 'want to join the best, most professional body of men in the British Armed Forces' – that compliment always accepted gracefully by, the Corps itself, albeit with a certain wry amusement . . . for how could any young man be in a position to judge in the first instance? The truth is that for most, the reasons are as much emotional as logical and often barely understood by the potential Royal Marine himself. No matter: he'll discover during training that the reasons for successfully completing the course can and do change.

On a recent POC, fifteen candidates arrived at Lympstone at midday. Walking in through the main gates can be the first shock, for the palpable air of professionalism is as much combat as regimental. Even the civilian staff seem to be more purposeful . . . but then, CTCRM is a high security base, by the very nature of some of the more arcane and secret courses it also offers.

In parenthesis, all Royal Marines are NVd, or Negatively Vetted, which gives them automatic access – if necessary – to information graded 'Secret'. Negative Vetting simply establishes that there's nothing in a person's background to suggest he might be a security risk, whereas Positive Vetting is more concerned with building up an individual's personality profile. Neither is as cut and dried as it sounds and different Government organizations might well adapt the rules to suit themselves or specific circumstances. Royal Marines standards, however, remain fairly exacting especially in terms of officer selection.

Back to our fifteen hopefuls. After meeting the officer

and senior NCO who'll be looking after them, they were given a light lunch, necessary kit and posed for the obligatory course photograph. Then came the presentation about the Corps' history and what it actually does today. By now the fifteen were feeling suitably excited – just as well, for they're going to need all the enthusiasm they can muster. At 15.50 hours (three p.m.), the fifteen moved to the gymnasium for the Royal Marines Fitness Assessment. They'd already been given a booklet which suggest the fitness levels to be obtained before arriving. At least three of the fifteen were now looking distinctly nervous. But first there was a comprehensive warm-up, followed by vaulting. The Corps isn't looking for trained gymnasts – but it is looking for co-ordination and determination. One of the fifteen proved to have little of either.

Incidentally, all the candidates were free to leave whenever they wanted. Staying for the full POC is not compulsory.

Now came the RMFA itself. As many sit-ups as possible in two minutes – the optimum score is eighty-five. As many press-ups as possible – no time limit, as long as only toes and hands touch the floor – with an optimum score of sixty. As many burpees as possible in one minute, forty-five being the magic goal. As many pull-ups as possible, to a maximum of eighteen, until the candidate drops off the beam. And finally, a continuous 300-metre grid-sprint in 30-metre legs, to be completed in under forty-four seconds.

An hour and a quarter later, eleven showered and changed candidates sat down to write a current affairs essay. Two of them were still feeling sick from the

RMFA. Points are awarded for reasonable – i.e. good – grammar and spelling plus written communication skills. Plus proof that the candidates read more than the sports pages. Each candidate now had an individual interview with the Course Officer, whose task it is to find out why they really want to join the Royal Marines Commandos and if they understand what it actually entails.

At 18.30 hours (six-thirty p.m.), ten candidates met YOs in training for drinks in the Officers' Mess. This is not purely social. Aside from the fact that most of the YOs were drinking orange juice – they've learned to leave alcohol until the weekend – it gave our hopefuls a chance to learn what officer training is really like. Not deliberate horror stories, but just the plain, unvarnished facts. Then dinner and after that the rest of the time was the candidate's own. By now two of them had discovered they shared similar doubts and misgivings and discussed these in greater depth. The rest got an early night.

The next day, ten candidates sat down to breakfast but only eight arrived at the assault course. After a warm-up, a PTI showed them how to tackle each obstacle. Then they were split into teams and given the ubiquitous log – which had to be taken round the assault course without touching the ground. Each candidate was given the chance to be team leader on at least one obstacle, when they had to produce a plan, brief the other team members and make sure they followed orders. The ten, increasingly shattered, hopefuls were also judged by how well they cooperated as simple team members. But on some of the obstacles no team leader was designated . . .

And after a short interlude for rope climbing and a fireman's lift, the eight went round the assault course again. But this time they were being timed.

Then came the visit to the Tarzan course. They weren't allowed to do the entire thing, only the end jump into a vertically-hung scramble net, about fifteen feet above the ground. It's intended to measure natural aggression and commitment. It does.

At 11.00 hours, nine cleaned-up candidates mustered in a classroom to give three-minute lecturettes on any subject of their choice. One of them realized he should have prepared his lecturette in advance, as the pre-course information had suggested.

Eight candidates sat down to an early lunch.

At 12.30 hours, they were taken to Woodbury Common, some three miles east of the CTCRM and introduced to the endurance course. This is a collection of tunnels, pools and swamps. Going around it can be a deeply depressing experience. Especially if you know that afterwards you're faced with a four-mile run back to camp. But for the POC, it's new and possibly a little exciting. It lacks the panache of the Tarzan course – but then there's always the water tunnel, which is just that: a fully flooded, eight-foot tunnel, and never mind that a man is both pushed and hauled through, it still indicates any tendency towards claustrophobia. As do many of the other tunnels, particularly those which seem to get smaller and smaller as you crawl along them. Perhaps a few of the brighter, potential YOs realize that the Course doesn't so much test one's physical as mental endurance. But either way, it hurts like hell.

At 15.00 hours (three p.m. remember?), eight weary

candidates went into a discussion group, when the Course Officer gave them topical and always controversial subjects to debate. Points awarded for articulation, logical and courteous argument plus listening skills.

The evening was free.

At 08.00 hours the next morning, seven candidates went for the Battle Swimming Test. Wearing full battle kit they had to jump into the pool from the three-metre board and swim sixty metres without drowning. It's not marked as part of the POC, nor does it matter if the candidates are poor or non-swimmers – buoyancy aids are provided and swimming is taught in training. What it does do is emphasize that Royal Marines Commandos do have a lot to do with water, in one way or another. Any hydrophobes who manage to survive the endurance course may find the deep end a little hard to take.

At 09.30 hours there was another presentation about Royal Marines officer training, careers and specializations.

At 11.00 hours, the eight individually learned their fate. Three had been recommended to attend the next stage, the Admiralty Interview Board (AIB). Three were told that they'd failed the POC this time, but they might like to try again when, say, they'd achieved the necessary fitness standards . . . or even matured a little more. Two were simply told that they'd failed . . . nothing to stop them applying again, of course, but it was felt that they didn't have the right motivation to complete officer training successfully. Or the necessary personal skills to be a Royal Marines officer, given that the job involves commanding Royal Marines Commandos. One of these two subsequently joined the Corps as a recruit.

Of the three who'd been told to try again later, one did and passed; one went to Sandhurst; and the other eventually ended up in the Royal Marines Reserve.

As for the three who'd passed? Too soon for rejoicing. Next, there'd be the hurdle of the AIB. If that was successful, a full year of the toughest officers' training in the world.

Passing the POC isn't necessarily the beginning.

'You think the POC was tough?'

All potential officers in the Royal Navy have to undergo the AIB. Since the Royal Navy is the parent service of the Royal Marines, all potential YOs also have to attend the AIB as well. While future Royal Marines officers are not tested in quite the same way as are Royal Navy officer candidates – the difference resulting from basic job function – the AIB for potential YOs is just as searching. It takes place at HMS *Sultan* in Gosport, Hampshire, is controlled by a Royal Marines colonel or half-colonel; a Royal Marines major; a civilian headmaster (not necessarily from an independent school), one of whose functions is to interpret the candidates' academic background; and a Royal Navy careers officer – often a WRNS officer. Lurking somewhere in the background is a psychologist. While he doesn't sit on the Board as such, he – or she – will be asked to comment on certain, often borderline, cases.

The AIB lasts for three days. It is based around three 'pillars': the gymnasium; a discussion exercise; and an interview. All the while the candidates' characters and motivations are probed to see if they have the ability and the will to give that one hundred and twenty per cent commitment.

Candidates will also have to show a detailed knowledge of Royal Navy history (slightly unfair, but the Senior Service will have its pound of Royal Marines flesh); Royal Marines history, organization and tactics. Candidates will also be asked why they want to be officers in the Royal Marines . . . with the standard reply that 'I-want-to-be-a-leader-of-men-and-serve-my-country, Sir (or Ma'am)' only ever eliciting the answer 'why?' No one likes pat answers.

Should the candidates ever breathe more easily on discovering that they're also to be tested – during a discussion exercise, say – by a charming and doubtless sympathetic Wren, it's wishful thinking based on naivety. 'Who would have thought', moaned a young man who'd failed, 'that such a good-looking, nice woman could be so bloody hard!' Sexual equality begins for many candidates at the AIB. The Wren officer in question had given the failed hopeful plus three others a scenario: a shipwrecked party on a bleak, inhospitable island and how could they survive – and eventually be saved? And as the candidates had stammered their way from one disaster to another, the Wren had pointed out exactly where they'd gone wrong – forcibly and with an apparently mounting impatience. Never had the candidates felt so pressured – and from such an unlikely source, too. When the Wren finally informed them that they'd managed to kill off the last survivor, any sense of failure was lightened by an overwhelming relief that their ordeal was over. The point being, of course, that no one expected any of the candidates to be survival experts. The idea was simply to see how they coped under increasing pressure. For it's pressure like that that helps reveal young men in their true colours.

This possibly explains why one young man, suddenly asked how he'd spent the last year in preparing himself for a career in the Royal Marines, answered that he'd been working in an abbatoir to get used to the sight of blood. While another candidate seemed to be a little excited about what form the medical examination would take. Would he have to strip or not? Told it would be a comparatively simple affair, requiring no more than unbuttoning his shirt (the Wren privately amused at his modesty, knowing it wouldn't survive Lympstone), the hopeful breathed a sigh of relief and revealed his true fear. He'd been worried in case he had to wear clean underpants, but as it wasn't going to be a bare-buff examination, there wasn't any need and he could keep on the ones he was already wearing. A subtle question or two established that he'd been wearing them for quite some time . . . for whatever reason, he preferred it that way. Needless to say, neither candidate passed – other than into Corps folklore of the Ones Who Got Away.

Generally speaking, out of every ten would-be officers in the Royal Marines, only one will successfully complete the POC and the AIB and the final Royal Marines Selection Board (at which point the results of the POC and the AIB are brought together for the first time).

Perhaps it's the very difficulty of becoming a Royal Marines officer that makes it so appealing. Although the Corps would also argue that since it costs approximately

£100,000 to train an officer (as near as these things can be computed for the edification of Ministry of Defence and Treasury pundits), failures are expensive and the Corps must be sure that every man accepted as a YO has the potential to complete the course.

But who are they?

Lympstone trains – or gives places to – fifty-eight Young Officers each year, plus four to foreign or Commonwealth candidates. (Whose governments pay dearly for the privilege, raising the possibility that certain branches of the Royal Marines could almost become profit centres in their own right.)

Not all the fifty-eight will pass: the average failure rate, for whatever cause, is 28.7 per cent (the .7 conjuring up the image of a, well, *damaged* young man being returned home, in fact simply a statistical aberration). The fact is that even given the extensive, not to say exhaustive, pre-testing, up to a third of all YOs will fail. While not happy with that, short of making the course easier, the Corps feels that it simply has to live with that figure. (It's probably small consolation, but the failure rate amongst potential life insurance salesmen and women is even higher. As it is amongst would-be journalists, doctors and prospective parliamentary candidates. So perhaps the Royal Marines pre-selection courses and Boards are a little more effective, even professional, than many would have you believe.)

The average age of a Young Officer is twenty-three. At first sight, it might be thought that the Corps breeds two types of officer: the 'character', perhaps something of a rough diamond; and the academic. However, many a YO who may have indeed begun service life as something of a 'character' will in time discover an unsuspected academic flair. While many of the academics have discovered a basic, near consuming, love for soldiering itself. Any preconceptions about Royal Marines officers are quickly dispelled in discovering that Captain So-and-So, now on leave of absence to do an MBA, originally scraped into the Corps with border-line 'O' Levels. Or that Major Such-and-Such, as close to Central Casting's ideal of a square-jawed commando as it is possible to get (and probably SBS or ML trained) originally joined with a good degree in French Literature, intending only to stay a few years before becoming a university don. Well, a slight exaggeration, perhaps – although in one instance, not too far off the mark – yet the overall points that a) it's difficult to type Royal Marines officers and b) the Corps is less interested in what a man's done before joining than in what he'll do afterwards, so long as it's beneficial for the Corps, do hold good.

Nor should it be thought that the majority of graduates are Oxbridge. It's just that at the time of re-writing this revision, there were two, both with Firsts, going through Lympstone. As one member of the Officer Training Wing said, 'This underlines the fact that nowadays we can attract people who have plenty of other options . . . it's good that we continue to be able to pick and choose from a complete cross-section of society.' And the point here is that the Corps does try to mirror a changing society in its officer selection. An all-graduate, or all-public-school background might appear to have certain advantages – academic/used to all-male environments – and it would certainly be far more Services traditional, yet so much variety would be lost in the process. The Corps would become, like certain Army regiments, far too inward looking and identified with a certain narrow, perhaps anachronistic section of society. Nor would the NCOs and Marines themselves, necessarily of a very high standard, respond well to an officer class that appeared to be as much rooted in traditional class distinction as in ability. As with the Paras, Royal Marines' NCOs and men tend to discover that the presence of a high percentage of 'good' officers makes soldiering that much more worth while.

Officer training

The Royal Marine YO is being trained to lead a troop of thirty commandos. In practice, detachments, courses, leave and undermanning may result in a slightly smaller troop. If nothing else, this teaches him to re-evaluate his tactics.

As a troop commander, the YO will be totally responsible for the welfare and administration of his men. Naturally, he'll have alongside him an experienced troop sergeant – but however much the officer may lean on the sergeant in the beginning, there must come a day when he's fully capable of taking over. Otherwise he runs the possibility of failing the year's probationary period that follows the year already spent at Lympstone, and being asked to resign his commission.

That Royal Marine officers are expected to take on

such early responsibility is reflected in their pay – a Royal Marines captain, for example, is paid the same as an Army major. Nor is it uncommon to find a Royal Marines captain or lieutenant doing a job that would be done by an Army major or captain. Against that, promotion tends to be slower in the Corps than in the Army, if only because there are fewer jobs available. In terms of YO training at Lympstone, this means that the course is designed to produce young officers (sprog officers in Marine-speak) who are trained to a higher military standard at troop or platoon commander level than their equivalents from Sandhurst. And while the course of thirty-four weeks is the longest of its type in the world – and arguably the toughest, since the physical pressure is applied from Day One – it is not generally felt to be long enough. A tremendous amount of work is crammed into a relatively short space of time.

If there is a comparison with civilian life, it would probably be like studying for an honours degree while also training to compete in the pentathlon at international standard, while semi-permanently wet and cold.

The pressure on YOs to 'grow up and grow into the job' is far greater than on recruits. Whereas recruits maybe, often are, told in some detail about their mental or psychological shortcomings and suggestions made as to how they can overcome them, YOs are generally expected to sort out those problems for themselves.

A YO asking one of his instructors how he could best improve in a certain direction is liable to be given short shrift. At the most he can expect the question: 'Well, Mr So-and-So, how do *you* think you can best improve?' In this way YOs are far more aware of the maturing process they're going through – and far more aware of the penalties of failure.

The physical horrors of YO training are worse than those facing recruits. For while the demands are very much the same, the average YO is expected to perform better than the average recruit. In fact, the most incompetent YO is expected to perform better than the average recruit. The Royal Marines do not believe that leadership is a function of class or education, but that it is a function of a man's ability to win the respect and trust of those whom he would lead – and in the very physical sense, of being able to keep up with them – in the field, in battle.

YOs are trained mainly by Royal Marine sergeants with Royal Marine officers overseeing the course and taking some of the lectures. It has been suggested in the press that the sergeants take this opportunity to impress their charges with a 'Sergeants Rule, OK' philosophy. Nothing could be further from the truth. YOs leaving Lympstone will probably go to a troop whose sergeant is a personal friend of the men who've been training him. And since all senior NCOs are well aware of the importance of having officers, and the vital role a troop officer plays in war, they are unlikely to turn out meek and cringing men who will do whatever the troop sergeant tells them. To do so would be to court disaster.

Perhaps it's best at this point to try to explain what the function of an officer in the Royal Marines is (not so very different from an officer's function in the Army) and how he interacts with his senior NCOs and men, particularly at troop level.

However the distinction between officers and men

first came about, it is today based on several unassailable facts. First, men do need a 'figurehead', someone to inspire them, someone they can trust, particularly in times of stress.

Second, it's far easier for a man to make life-and-death decisions about other men if he's one step removed from them, if his rank carries with it the implied right to make such decisions.

Third, a man cannot be expected to make decisions continually about men under his command unless there is someone who can help him to implement them, that is, his senior and junior NCOs (colour sergeants, sergeants and corporals).

Fourth, as a system it works extremely well. And until another one can be proved equally effective, no one is going to change it.

This means that senior NCOs act as a type of middle management. They are the link between officers and men. And while, at troop level, it would be a foolhardy officer who always made decisions without asking his sergeant for his opinion, at the end of the day the sole responsibility is the officer's alone. Rule by committee does not work on the battlefield.

All military rank structures are designed to work in times of war, not peace. Where the Royal Marines differ perhaps from some other units is that they expect a good officer to command by virtue of his ability and personality and not by virtue of a piece of paper saying that he's been awarded a commission by the Queen. And that his men had better obey him, or else. It is for this function that YOs are trained at Lympstone. That is why it's in their instructors' own best interests that they produce the type of officer whom they would, one day, be happy to serve with. Indeed, given the relatively small size of the Corps, it's quite possible that a YO training sergeant will at some time serve with an officer he once trained.

The situation is affected by the fact that Royal Marine senior NCOs are generally regarded (by the USMC in particular) as being the best in the world. This in itself puts an enormous pressure on YOs in training; they have a far higher standard to follow and live up to – a standard set by men who are nominally inferior in rank and status.

Sometimes this situation results in a YO effectively hero worshipping his instructors – a situation the instructors themselves try hard to discourage since the man must learn to stand on his own feet, must finish training convinced in his own mind that he's capable, in the not so distant future, of leading the very men who have been teaching him. In a similar way, a student at university may well be extremely grateful for the advice, the teaching his tutor gives him. He may respect his tutor enormously, but a certain type of student will want to better his tutor one day – out of the realization that if he's to be successful in his chosen career, that is the standard to aim for. Ambition does play a major part in a YO successfully completing training.

A senior Royal Marines commanding officer was asked what moral qualities he looked for in his officers. 'You know the expression "lovable rogue"? Well, I could never accept an officer who was one. There is no place for that type of moral ambivalence.'

A slightly harsh judgement? Not when you consider an officer's responsibilities. Or that he has to win the respect of senior and junior NCOs. The qualities of dash, flair, even a certain eccentricity are all welcome in the Corps. But lovable rogues need not apply – aside from anything else, they'd never last the training.

YOs United

Probably one of the biggest contrasts between YO and recruit training was pinpointed by the man who'd gained a Corps commission. (There are a limited number of Corps commissions open to trained Marines under the age of twenty-seven.)

This particular YO said that the difference was that he could ask as many questions as he liked as a YO – was encouraged to do so – whereas recruits were not given quite the same leeway. Describing himself as 'a bit of a gobby [talkative] bastard, really', he also pointed out that while recruits could often relax at night, YOs had to study: less free time, less opportunity for sleep.

In order to get through training, YOs must – like recruits – work together. Like recruits, a YO batch will turn a united front to the rest of the world. Like recruits, YOs will not suffer a man to stay if he neither fits in nor pulls his weight.

'I remember one guy in my batch,' reminisced a serving officer, 'who was got rid of by the rest of us. It just seemed obvious that he wasn't cut out for the life, never tried to mix with the other guys, kit was always shambolic, so we simply asked him again and again if he *really* wanted to be a Marine. After a month or so he wrapped [quit] and having experienced life in a troop since then, I think we were right to behave like that. No way could he have survived.'

Welcome to Salisbury Plain

It's true. Battlefields, even simulated battlefields, do possess a certain beauty at night. But the eerie green of the flares, the flash and delayed crump! of the explosive charges, felt before being heard, and the crack of their own weapons, were aesthetically wasted on the section of YOs practising live firing at night on a very wet and cold Salisbury Plain.

They had been in position for well over an hour, lying full length in the mud, the rain trickling down their backs and oozing through to their skin – not for the first time prompting the question 'What the hell am I doing here, anyway?'

What they had been doing was waiting for a sergeant instructor to appear with the remote-control radio transmitter that would activate the targets they were to shoot at – that they were to shoot at and hit. No matter how bad the weather, no matter how tired and cold they were (barely five hours' sleep in the past four days), they were expected to be at their best.

Their sergeant had finally arrived together with the assault engineer who'd spent the previous afternoon laying charges that would simulate grenade, artillery and mortar fire. The control box was produced, the button pressed and suddenly the area was illuminated by flares, followed immediately by explosion after explosion as the charges disintegrated in a shower of mud and stones.

Simultaneously, targets popped up in front of the section. The section leader for the night remained calm and gave the correct fire orders – an overexcited, ragged volley would not have been permissible. And the first few rounds were disciplined, the right men shooting at the specified targets, before the order 'Fire At Will' came, allowing the YOs to pepper the targets as they liked – targets that were falling down and springing up again like so many demented jack in the boxes – and all the time the bright green of the flares, the noise of explosions and a shower of earth as a charge exploded nearby.

That phase of the exercise had been designed to accustom the YO to fire weapons, not in the comparative peace and tranquillity of the range, but in highly unpleasant surroundings. To fire and hit the target without forgetting safety drills. (To learn to be as professional as possible – for if he's not, when he's posted to a unit, both brother officers and senior NCOs – not to mention his men – will soon let him know exactly what they think of him.)

That night, the YOs had done well. Good, accurate fire. Good weapon drills. The only slight mistake occurred after the firing had stopped and the section leader had begun to lead the other YOs out of the valley. The pass he'd chosen would have taken them directly into the path of live rounds being fired by a machine-gun some thirty feet further up the hillside.

'Dear me,' said the training sergeant, 'we are feeling a little confused tonight. . . . Not that way, Mr—, think of all the paperwork I'd have to do. Follow the contour line we're on until the GPMG [general purpose machine-gun] is well behind us.'

It is an interesting experience to walk along the side of a valley with a machine-gun firing away over your head – firing live tracer rounds that streak away into the darkness before impacting with an audible thump on the target area. Rounds that sound as if they're at least the size of chickens' eggs, even though you know they're only a few centimetres long. Even though you know that the machine-gun is on a fixed mounting – and that's secured to a concrete block buried deep into the earth – you can't help but wonder what would happen if the mounting suddenly broke and the gun barrel depressed to fire directly at your own little group.

Safely away from the SF (SF = Sustained Fire = machine-gun), the section had made their way out of the valley to where they could be inspected.

It is a crime, punishable by Court Martial, for any soldier of any rank to have any unauthorized ammunition in his possession, particularly during an exercise, when live rounds can easily become mixed up with blank rounds. The YOs had given all their live ammo to the training team before lining up to be searched.

'I have no live rounds in my possession, Sergeant': a time-honoured legal statement followed by a thorough search of each YO's webbing pouches and his combat suit pockets. But one YO was discovered to have three live rounds still in his possession, and the dressing down he received was shattering.

'You were told. You were warned. You know the dangers. You're supposed to be a man, a leader. So for God's sake behave like one – get over there, put the live rounds with the rest of the spares. There's no excuse. If you can't learn to look after yourself and obey orders, how the hell do you think you'll be able to lead a troop and look after the men under your command?'

The rebuke was doubly devastating because it was delivered by a man the YO both liked and respected. But that YO will never forget his range safety again, nor will any of the other YOs in the section.

Finally, the section made its way back to the trenches they had been living in for the past week – a week in which they'd been bombarded by thunderflashes, subjected to simulated gas attacks and overrun by tanks.

Tank trap

Admittedly, there had been a slight mistake during the tank attack.

The entire YO batch had joined up with young army officers who were on a command course at nearby Warminster. The difference was, as one of the Marine YOs ruefully commented, the army officers were allowed to go back to a nice, warm officers' mess at night whereas the Marines had naught for comfort but a three-foot by fifteen-foot trench – admittedly roofed over in parts, but still narrow, wet and uncomfortable.

On the afternoon before the live firing, the Marine YOs had borne the brunt of a simulated armour (tank) attack – simulated in so far as the tanks hadn't actually fired live rounds. But then, they hardly needed to since the Engineers had laid explosive charges that, when detonated, mimicked perfectly the effect of tank and artillery gunfire 'walking' toward their target – that is, coming ever closer and closer. Following the artillery bombardment had come the tanks, straight through the YOs' position. Unfortunately, one of the tanks had come a shade too close to a trench – ran over part of it, in fact. The fact that trenches are designed to withstand a tank running over them, and that this trench had behaved perfectly, had been totally lost on the four YOs who'd dived into the far end, away from the tank's tracks, cursing every single tank driver who ever lived.

A trench designed and built to withstand a tank running over it is one of the more curious concepts of the military mind. For in battle, tanks do not quickly and politely pass over a trench. They reverse back and forth over it, swinging from one track to another, so collapsing the trench and burying its inhabitants. But a static infantry defence against an armoured attack is one of the more cherished concepts within certain defence circles.

A hard night

The final part of the night's activities, a few hours after the live firing was over, had begun for the YOs with an eight-mile yomp, carrying all their gear, across Salisbury Plain to a rendezvous at a deserted farmhouse. Needless to say, during the last hour of their yomp the weather had turned particularly nasty. Winds gusted to forty miles an hour, bringing with them abnormally large hailstones. Hard enough at the best of times – but when you're exhausted and carrying close to a hundred pounds on your back. . .

When they had reached the farmhouse the YOs had done what all good YOs and recruits do – found a sheltered spot and gone to sleep. Typically, one YO had been so tired that when spoken to by an instructor who wanted to know if the batch understood their instructions for the rest of the night, he had managed to answer all the questions while still asleep.

Shortly before 03.00 the YOs had been woken, got their kit together and joined the army officers for a four-mile yomp to the start line for a series of troop attacks against a fortified position. That attack had been a bit of a disaster. Enemy supposedly killed had suddenly resurrected as the YOs advanced, and attacked the Marines from behind. One YO section had disintegrated in a welter of accusation and counter-accusation, the men deciding that their commander for the night had made one mistake too many, telling him so in no uncertain terms. And all the while the instructors were following and watching, only becoming involved when things had got too much out of hand.

'Yeah, it was a bit of a shambles,' one of the instructors admitted afterwards, 'but that's what war is like. You can't figure out who's going to make a good officer until things do go badly wrong. But I was badly surprised by Mr —. He let us all down tonight.'

To be told that he's let everyone down is the worst rebuke a YO can receive. It implies that he's betrayed the trust placed in him, that he's unfit to be given command, and that he thinks more of himself than he does of his fellow Marines. A YO who continually lets his instructors, his batch-mates and himself down will not stay long at Lympstone.

Tricks of the trade

While YOs and recruits are naturally aware of each other's existence, they usually train together only on exercise. The YOs in particular welcome this because that's when they learn all the little tricks of keeping comfortable in the field that the instructors never seem to teach. Like, for example, taking babywipes (impregnated tissues used for cleaning babies) – so much easier to keep oneself clean.

Also, the recruits have a well-deserved reputation for knowing where and how to get the best deals on civilian manufactured equipment, bought to supplement official issue. It might be a petrol cooker, a Gortex bivvie bag (a sleeping bag cover that's waterproof, yet still allows sweat vapour to escape) or even a particular brand of bergen – before the Crusader model became standard issue, recruits used to buy their own. Whatever the piece of kit, the recruit will know if it really works and how cheaply it can be bought.

By and large, however, neither YOs nor recruits are encouraged to buy their own kit until they've been at Lympstone for some time. They're not officially encouraged in the first instance, since the standard-issue equipment is, in theory, perfectly adequate for all their needs . . .

The fact that YOs and recruits train in the same establishment begins to foster the family atmosphere that the Marines are so proud of. For Lympstone is a time of shared experiences, the time when YO and recruit alike begin to appreciate the ugly side of war . . . that it's not all *Boy's Own* fun or gung-ho heroics, but a deadly serious business. Very deadly, since soldiers are not so much taught to die for their country as to kill for it.

YO and recruit alike have it hammered home to them that, for example, the bullet from a modern rifle hits with such an impact that it will disable, even kill from shock alone. That if you *have* to move through a mine-field in a hurry, the best way is simply to run as fast as you can in a straight line – apparently this gives a reasonably good chance of survival, if the mines have been sown in a standard pattern. That if an officer is saluted on the battlefield, or his rank indicated in any way, then a sniper may well shoot him seconds later. YOs and recruits are taught that the only way to make sure that these – and all the other nasty things that can happen to a man in war – don't happen to them is by being extremely professional – and by getting their retaliation in first.

It is perfectly true: it all begins at Lympstone and if the heart of the Corps resides anywhere, it resides there. It is a superb centre of professional excellence, with an air of quiet dignity and even humility in remembrance of all sacrifices made in the past . . . and all those that will be made in the future. It's an atmosphere often mistaken for unbending discipline by the newly arrived or the civilian. Discipline undoubtedly does exist at Lympstone. It is far more regimental than any other Royal Marines establishment. Yet it also gives young men the ability to develop those qualities of self-discipline and self-motivation which are the hallmark of any elite soldier. Most members of the Special Air Service, for example, can point to a similar, strongly 'regimental' background in their own early military training. They may not have liked it at the time – whoever really does? – and may have found it pointless and irksome when carried over into active soldiering. But before a soldier can begin to develop those special, elite qualities he must first develop the necessary dedication, character and determination on which to build . . . and that always begins with basic training. Ask any world-class athlete: it's exactly the same for them. As it is for any profession: there are no short cuts to excellence. This is one reason why the British Armed Forces have earned a worldwide reputation: get it right in the beginning, and far more becomes possible. It is a lesson that Britain's educational establishment is only now, belatedly, beginning to accept. Lympstone is particularly special because its Young Officers and Marines leave with that core already well established.

Some years ago the Officer Commanding Recruit Training was chatting to a Platoon Weapons corporal. The conversation turned to how they both approached the job of changing recruits into Marines. For the twenty-four-year-old corporal it was exactly the same every day: rolling out of bed at some ungodly hour, doing fifty press-ups . . . and continually reminding himself that once again he'd be spending the day teaching children. Within the context of the Royal Marines, Lympstone marks the transition of child to adult, of soldier to commando. The Green Beret doesn't only represent physical prowess or military skills. Arguably, they both take second place to character development.

Nor can one overemphasize the value of officers and men training in the same establishment or being faced with identical challenges. It can happen to a limited extent elsewhere in the Armed Forces, but usually in relation to advanced and specialized training, when both officers and NCOs have already served for several years. At Lympstone the kids start out together and so begin to form that bond of shared values . . . shared qualities . . . and, probably, shared painful memories . . . that so impresses other soldiers. Assuming they can understand it in the first instance.

'Oh, I know all about you Marines,' an Army infantry major once commented, only part humorously. 'The sergeants really care about the men and the officers really care about both. Can't make life and death decisions easy, can it?'

Aside from the obvious comment that life and death decisions should never be easy, the major did have a point. Royal Marines do care about each other, both as individuals and as members of the same Corps. It's one of the reasons why they hate letting each other down. Not only is that a civilized attitude, it also helps enormously in war. For the vast majority of truly elite troops have always been imbued by a mutual respect and affection . . . and this is what begins at Lympstone.

And yet . . . at the moment of writing, the idea is being mooted that perhaps Lympstone should be closed down, or irrevocably changed. Do Royal Marines officers really have to train alongside the men? Shouldn't they be with other officers at HMS *Dartmouth*? Just think of the costs savings. Come to that, why can't Lympstone also help train naval officers? I mean, are we really maximizing our investment?

One of the biggest threats to any civilization, anywhere, has always been the inexorable rise to power of the unelected, unaccountable bureaucrat . . . which also results in the drive for a 'common currency' by which all human activity can be measured. Being essentially non-productive, the bureaucrats' own currency is control.

But the currency of, say, the health profession is saving lives. That of teaching and science, ideas. The currency of the military is both these plus victory. When all are replaced by money, nowadays often referred to as efficiency savings – note the implied assumption that all cost cutting is automatically efficient – the culture changes and becomes both narrow and short term. Instead of being the enabler, money becomes the goal.

Japan did not become a world industrial power simply because everyone wanted to get rich. As has often been pointed out, Japan was driven by other, greater considerations. Of course there have to be financial controls . . . but how can you ever put a monetary value on the commando spirit? How much does it cost to enable a man to drive himself beyond the limits of endurance, or willingly sacrifice his own life for others?

Close down Lympstone, begin monkeying around with a tried and tested system, and we may soon find out.

Commando tests

The commando tests also take place immediately following a week-long exercise which will have entailed living rough in the field; very little sleep; a sea-borne raid; abseiling; and a full-scale assault. After the nine-mile speed march, the men must take part in a troop attack. After the endurance course and four-mile run back, the men must be able to fire their rifles on the range and score four out of six hits on the target. All tests are taken wearing full-order battle kit which weighs 14 kg (30 lb) when dry, plus carrying a rifle weighing just under 4.5 kg. When wet – and it nearly always is – the equipment weight increases by at least another 4.5 kg, giving a total of 23 kg (50 lb). Overall, the passing grades for Young Officers are higher than those for recruits. This is not mere embuggerance, but emphasizes that the job of an officer is to lead by example. There are a few, a very few recruits and YOs who pass all the tests with comparative ease. Some people, however, find that there's always one particularly harder, or easier, than the rest. Other people find them all equally hellish. The thirty-mile load carry used to be the main obstacle, coming as it does at the very end of training and all the other tests, by which time most recruits and YOs are feeling just a little weary. Nowadays the thirty-miler is broken down into three sections of ten miles, with a high-energy carbohydrate break between each section: hot, sweet tea and/or a fruit pie. There were those who scoffed slightly when this was first introduced, remembering that when they did the thirty-miler there were no breaks and you carried your own chocolate – until it was pointed out that the pass-times themselves hadn't changed, so that any time lost had to be made up by moving even faster on each section.

Tarzan and assault courses combined

Recruits thirteen minutes, officers, twelve and a half. If thirty seconds doesn't seem very long, remember that many people only pass by a scant five or ten.

Endurance Course
Recruits seventy-two minutes, officers seventy.

Nine-Mile Speed March
Recruits and officers both ninety minutes.

Thirty-Mile Load Carry (across Dartmoor)
Recruits eight hours, officers seven hours. Taking into account break-times, this represents an average speed of four m.p.h. for recruits, and just under four and a half m.p.h. for officers. The route is not flat, but takes in every steep valley, every hill, every long, aching, uphill grind and the worst underfoot conditions that a sadistic directing staff could possibly find. At least, that's how it feels half-way through.

CHAPTER FOUR

The Specialists

Part of the uniqueness of the Royal Marines lies in the Corps's ability to handle a wide variety of military jobs – an ability born of its determination to be as self-contained as possible. To illustrate that facet of the Corps, here is a brief look at a few of its specializations

The very nature of their role demands that Royal Marines Commandos be as self-sufficient as possible. So it is that all Royal Marines are encouraged to obtain either Specialist Qualifications (SQs) or Technical Qualifications (TQs) which relate to a specific branch. An NCO cannot progress beyond sergeant without either an SQ or TQ. Most officers will also gain specific qualifications, although some are impractical by virtue of the length of time required to qualify. There are a few officers who manage to remain GD (General Duties) throughout their careers, often regarded with a certain envy by their comrades. However, just because a man 'belongs' to a specific branch, e.g. Landing Craft, Platoon Weapons, Heavy Weapons or Drill Leaders (NCOs only) doesn't mean he spends all his time there. First and foremost, he is meant to be a combat-ready commando, capable of taking his place in or leading a troop, company or brigade, whatever his specialization.

It isn't possible to cover all the branches, SQs and TQs in detail – that would require a book in itself – but the ones chosen will hopefully represent the way the Corps goes about its business. You should also remember that each branch becomes its own centre of excellence, responsible for teaching, innovation and maintaining professional standards throughout the entire Corps. The value of this system can't be over-estimated, especially when it comes to formulating new doctrine at staff level. One phone call gets directly through to a fellow Royal Marines Commando who is the expert on a specific subject. It also works in the opposite direction: a branch that comes up with a good idea is assured of a speedy hearing at the highest Corps levels. The fact that so many specialists are scattered around the Corps encourages officers and NCOs to look beyond their own specialization. While the young Marine, newly out of Lympstone, might well find that one of the troop corporals is a qualified Assault Engineer, and another one is a qualified Landing Craft Coxswain. Or that the Troop Sergeant is a PTI or Mountain Leader – although that would be more common in Recce Troop. The overall effect is that Royal Marines Commandos tend to be far more rounded as soldiers, and far more aware of all the different aspects of warfare. Which, as an officer once almost ruefully remarked, makes it that much more of a challenge to command them.

There are so many SQs and TQS because the Royal Marines insist on being as self-sufficient as possible.

Marines themselves fulfil many of the functions that in the Army are undertaken by specialist corps. Two that they can't do account for the presence within 3 Commando Brigade of 29 Commando Regiment Royal Artillery and 59 Commando Regiment Royal Engineers. But everything else must be done by the Royal Marines.

Drill Leaders (DLs – NCOs only)

The Royal Marines would probably be the first to agree that drill for drill's sake has little or no relevance to modern warfare. Ceremonial parades may look grand, but unless they have some relevance to the job in hand, they're largely a waste of time and money. Worse, they may even detract from a soldier's ability to fight and survive on the battlefield, since a man trained only to respond to and operate within a rigid chain of command will suffer if a link in that chain is killed.

So for the Royal Marines, drill and ceremonial are merely the outward signs of self-discipline and high personal standards. To be more specific, to the Corps drill is the 'cold face of discipline' – initially, the discipline instilled in a man before he can begin to learn the self-discipline that the Corps values so highly. Responsible for instilling that initial discipline are the Drill Leaders – the men who 'mother' recruit and YO alike through the first difficult weeks of training.

As well as teaching their charges how to march and salute, the Corps traditions and history, the DLs also teach recruit and YO how to look after themselves. How to wash and iron their clothes. How to keep themselves clean in the worst conditions; to take pride in their personal appearance not only because it looks good on parade, but because it's a boost to morale, particularly in the field.

DLs are born, not made. It takes a special kind of person, one who wants to communicate his own enthusiasm for the Corps in such a way that he can fire the imaginations of the men he's responsible for. Most if not all DLs are 'Corps pissed', as the Marines say, meaning a man who is totally in love with the Corps and his job within it. As witness the fact that progress through his branch is left very much up to the man himself. While there are courses he takes before promotion to corporal or sergeant, he is expected to do much of the work beforehand, in his own time.

For most men who've been in the Army, their memories of drill instructors distil down to a loud, well-creased voice that squawked, screamed and squeaked its way into their dreams. Royal Marine DLs, however, do not believe in shouting on parade. They'll spend many hours practising voice projection so that they can make themselves heard without frightening everyone within earshot.

And as to whether it's all worth it? During the Korean War, elements of a USMC division were in retreat from Choisin Reservoir, and 41 (Independent) Commando was sent to help them get back to the safety of the UN lines. The US Marines were openly impressed at the way the men of 41 Commando marched and generally deported themselves; with how they managed to remain neat and clean in the worst conditions; and how their self-discipline helped to turn what could have been a rout into a successful retreat – or tactical withdrawal, in correct military parlance. Those attributes of self-discipline and pride in oneself and one's corps are initially taught to Marines by the DL Branch – who also see themselves as continually responsible for overall standards within the Corps.

Platoon Weapons (PWs – NCOs only)

Corps folklore has it that most PWs took so long to decide on an SQ or TQ that their minds were made up for them by higher authority and they ended up in the PW Branch. This slightly unkind attitude is probably due to the fact that PWs are responsible for most of the YO and recruit training at Lympstone – and few Royal Marines enjoy their time at Lympstone. PWs also supervise the Junior and Senior Command Courses that have to be passed before promotion to corporal or sergeant. Overall they are responsible for the standard of infantry skills within the Corps. As such, they spend a good deal of their time telling others what they've done wrong. But the PW Branch also organizes sniper training (of which more later) and is the authority on all individual weapons within the Corps. PWs teach men how to shoot and how to read a map. They are, as one said, one of the few branches that actually sees an end product from their work (at Lympstone) – the recruit or YO who's successfully completed his training – a claim that can also be made by both the DLs and the PTI Branch. PWs are also responsible for organizing live firing, on a closed or open range. Although in theory officers are also taught range work, in practice the job is invariably given to the nearest PW. In an age of more and more esoteric specialization (clerks are now expected to master computer programming, for example), some PWs feel that they're not quite so appreciated as they would like. The problem is that the total professionalism of the branch has come to be expected to such a degree that PWs are taken for granted. Also, because PWs are responsible for so much that is basic to the making of a Royal Marine, the smallest mistake that a PW makes (even, for example, confusing northings and eastings on a map reference) is gleefully seized upon by other Marines with less than happy memories of life as a recruit.

Without taking anything away from senior NCOs, PW corporals are probably the most important members of the branch. Corporals in the Corps as a whole have tremendous responsibility and the PW corporals at Lympstone are responsible for most of the day-to-day training of the recruits, working closely with them under the direction of the team leader (a PW sergeant) and troop officer.

Snipers (Additional Qualification, or Adqual – officers and other ranks)

In theory, the sniper's course is the basic PW course – the one a man must first pass in order to gain further promotion within the PW Branch. In practice, because the sniper's course is to such a high standard (Royal Marine snipers are the best in the Atlantic Alliance, among the best in the world) it has the highest failure rate of any course in the Corps. For that reason, sniping is not regarded as being an SQ or TQ, but as an Adqual (additional qualification) in the same way as is completing a parachute course.

How and why the Royal Marines developed sniping as a tour-de-force explains a good deal about how the Corps thinks and operates. Although sniping had proved its value down through the centuries – in the Civil War many officers brought their gamekeepers from their own estates into battle to fulfil the sniper's role – at the end of the Second World War sniping fell into disrepute. The new scenario called for a massive Warsaw Pact armoured advance to be met by a massive NATO armoured counter-attack. Plainly there was no room for a sniper on that juggernaut-dominated battleground, and the British Army more or less forgot about them. At that point Britain became involved in a series of 'low-intensity operations', as Sir Frank Kitson dubbed them, in places like Kenya, Aden, Korea (more of a full-scale war, that one), Malaysia, Borneo and, latterly, Northern Ireland. These were basically infantry wars – as was the Falklands – demanding exceptional infantry skills. Among those skills is sniping. In a conventional war a sniper is trained to dominate the ground between opposing troops. His targets are any men engaged on a specialist task (an officer, signaller, heavy-weapons crew etc.) whose loss will cause even more disruption and dismay than is normal on a battlefield. A sniper is also trained to lay down harassing fire at distances of up to 1,000 metres. This means that all the opposition keep their heads down, greatly adding to the confusion. Snipers are also trained to infiltrate behind enemy lines, or 'stay-behind' if the enemy advances, to try to shoot senior enemy commanders.

In unconventional war, say in Northern Ireland, snipers are extremely effective at hiding up, sometimes for days on end, and killing known terrorists; or in covering demonstrations or riots when it can be reasonably expected that a terrorist sniper will also be present.

So snipers do have an extremely important part to play, notwithstanding the dreams of the technocrats, planners and cavalry. As luck – and good foresight – had it, the Royal Marines had insisted on keeping their own sniping skills alive and well after the Second World War, since they saw them as integral to commando-style operations – yet another example of the Corps going its own way and ultimately being proved right. (A similar situation arose with the creation of the Mountain Leaders Branch.)

As it was, the Royal Marines were in a position to pass on their skills, not only to the British Army but also to the USMC who modelled their sniper's course on Lympstone's. The irony of it all is that the Argentinian snipers who posed some problems during the Falklands War may well have been trained by the USMC. Certainly they were probably the recipients of training methods that originated with the Royal Marines.

Where the sniper's course at Lympstone (lasting some six weeks) differs from the British Army's sniper training is that the Royal Marines centralize all training at Lympstone, whereas the Army trains sniper instructors, who then go back to their own units and train their own regimental snipers. Obviously this type of approach can only result, over a period, in a dilution of standards. But with centralized control the Corps can ensure that standards remain as high as ever. So all Royal Marine snipers are trained at Lympstone, together with a few selected police officers and some Army personnel. Less than forty-five per cent of all men taking the course pass completely – a figure that does not include police attendances, since policemen are less concerned with the military aspects of sniping. None the less, the sniper's course is one of the very few that will make a man a better soldier even if he fails. Often, a man who does fail the course will become a sniper's number two – the man often responsible for providing protection for the sniper himself.

The Corps claims that there is no reason why any trained Marine should not be able to pass the sniper's course. But then, it claims exactly the same for the SC3 course (SBS) and the ML2 course (Mountain Leaders). What they really mean is that the course starts at the standard of the trained Marine and goes on from there – no special preparation is needed in the first instance. A sniper does not even have to be a natural shot – shooting can be learnt. But he does have to be a natural soldier to whom fieldcraft comes easily. He must have a natural awareness of his surroundings and the ability to merge into the background, which probably explains why most snipers, even those who operate well in an urban environment, were born and raised in the country. Finally, contrary to popular opinion, snipers do not have a favourite rifle. That is to say, they are not encouraged to have their own personal weapons, for the very good reason that a man who places too much faith in a particular weapon will not be effective if anything happens to it. He will have forgotten that a rifle by itself possesses no special skills – those belong to the man who uses it. Similarly, when Marines first go on the course and are issued with their gilly suits – combat gear covered with strips of cloth – they tend to add all manner of leaves and grass in the field. Later, as their confidence in their own ability increases, they tend to discard most of the foliage since a gilly suit by itself will hide a man who knows how to take full advantage of any cover that's available.

Assault Engineers (AEs – NCOs only)

The Assault Engineers are unique to the Royal Marines. While there is a permanent unit of commando-trained Royal Engineers (men who've completed a five-week All-Arms Commando Course, run independently of recruit training), and while the Marines are positive that the men of 59 Squadron RE are the best in the business (Marines are inordinately proud of both the Royal Engineers and the Royal Artillery units who choose to serve with them), the Corps has found it necessary to maintain its own military engineering capability, operating at troop or company level. Whereas 59 Squadron deal mainly with heavy plant equipment, most of the Assault Engineer's kit is either man-portable or can be carried on a Land-Rover or three-tonner – or, occasionally, lifted into place by a Sea King helicopter.

Assault Engineers are expected to undertake a variety of tasks, ranging from establishing fresh-water supplies to sowing a minefield, or clearing one; from building or blowing up a bridge, to overseeing the building of trenches strong enough to withstand an artillery bombardment, with one shell landing every five square metres (one shell in every area measuring seven and a half by six feet); from setting up booby traps, to training others how to disarm them. Assault Engineers are also trained coxswains, since theirs is the branch responsible for river crossings. There are never any more than fifty or sixty Assault Engineers scattered throughout the Corps, possibly because promotion within the branch tends to be slow. Some AEs have had to wait for up to six years for the course they must take in order to be promoted to sergeant.

Possibly their versatility is best illustrated by the AE colour sergeant who was pressed into service by the Royal Engineers in the Falklands to help defuse a mass of unexploded Argentinian shells. He'd never done the job before, but after a quick on-the-spot training programme (and how many men get to train on live shells?) he started work, winning the British Empire Medal in the process.

Once, the Corps contained all manner of little, but vital, branches. But now there are no more grooms or helicopter air gunners. The Carpenters and Tinsmiths Branches, however, have found a good home with the Assault Engineers. However, that little known and unofficial branch of ocean-going yachtsmen – the Corps maintains several yachts – is happily as strong and as professional as ever. As witness Pete Goss who in 1997 was awarded the MBE and the Legion d'Honneur for one of the most remarkable sea rescues in history.

Clerks

One does not, it must be said, associate Royal Marines Commandos with pen-pushers. Pause for everyone to think again. Earlier on, this book emphasized that while amphibiosity is one of the most effective methods of power-protection, it is a little more complex than bog-standard warfare. Actually, that's not altogether accurate: there is no such thing as bog-standard warfare, and all warfare is becoming more complex – especially for those at the cutting edge, like Royal Marines Commandos. The point being that someone has to administer the Corps overall and 3 Commando Brigade in particular . . . and that means clerks who are far more than mere pen-pushers and who've all been commando-trained and, probably, spent time in a fighting troop before taking up this particular specialization. The NCOs, by the way, will do exactly the same Command Courses – run by the NCOs Training Wing at CTCRM – for promotion to corporal and sergeant as do men from the Landing Craft, Weapons and other branches, as well as the promotional courses relevant to their own branch. No matter what your specialization, promotion is only for those who can prove their ability to lead men in battle.

The Clerks and Signals Training Wing is at CTCRM Lympstone. . . two main branches under one roof, for both are concerned with the fast, accurate processing of information. All clerks are computer literate, to the minimum level of Information Systems Operators. Advanced level training includes data protection and computer security . . . and courtesy of the Computer

Awareness and Applications Training School (CAATS), the understanding of what type of computer technology and programming will be available in a few years' time, always relating it back to the needs of the Corps: reconnaissance is not only used in battle. Naturally, the Corps being what it is, clerks can also specialize in areas like stores accountancy, men who store and distribute equipment obtained from both military and civilian sources, or service funding which deals with the management of non-public funds and includes double-entry bookkeeping, VAT property management, investments and banking. There is no truth, however, to the rumour that a foreign exchange dealing room is hidden away somewhere in the Training Wing. Given the number of former Royal Marines working in the City, there's no real need.

The Wing also trains illustrators, a comparatively recent innovation since the branch was only formed in 1968. Illustrators provide many skills that used to be exclusively supplied by attached Royal Engineers and Intelligence Corps personnel, since one of their skills lies in producing detailed maps and three-dimensional terrain models working from air photographs. The branch works closely with the SBS, for should an oil rig or ship be hijacked by terrorists, an illustrator would produce an accurate scale model so the rescue operation could be planned in meticulous detail. However accurate, maps never tell the complete story and the details provided by a model are far easier to remember. Recently, Royal Marine Illustrators built a terrain model of the former Yugoslavia as used by British and NATO troops operating in Bosnia. Illustrators are also trained to first-year art college standard in graphic design and design most of the printed material the Corps produces internally . . . always refreshing to hear a man talk about different typefaces with the same enthusiasm as he'll discuss the relative merits of the M16 and the SA 80 rifles.

CHAPTER FIVE

RM Poole

The truth is, not many Royal Marines like Lympstone. With its major responsibilities for YO and recruit training, for Senior and Junior NCO Command Courses and for the All-Arms Commando Course, it is possibly a little too regimental – it has to be. It also carries certain memories for all Marines – ones that they're proud to hold, but don't like to be reminded of to any great extent: to the Marine, Lympstone is indelibly associated with being either a yo-yo or a nod.

But Royal Marines Poole – now that's different. For although it's the Corps's other major training establishment, it's altogether far more relaxed. Since it's responsible for specialist training, it receives only fully trained Marines – other than YOs or recruits on short landing craft or SBS briefings. The atmosphere is totally different. As a Royal Australian Navy officer said, one of the more noticeable facts about Poole is that when you're saluted by someone junior to yourself, it's always with a cheerful 'good morning' or 'afternoon'. Plenty of eye contact, as often as not a smile and as much a way of saying hello as anything else. Whereas saluting at Lympstone tends to be far more strictly regimental.

Royal Marines Poole trains Landing Craft personnel; the SBS (but not exclusively); ships' detachments, that is, those Royal Marines who will be part of a ship's company; Royal Marines divers; Reconnaissance Troops; and the Corps's drivers. For Trivial Pursuit freaks and pub quiz enthusiasts, Poole has the second-largest natural harbour in the world, the biggest being Sydney, Australia. Overall, RM Poole acts as the amphibious training centre for the Corps and, indeed, for the rest of Britain's Armed Forces, especially the Army's 17 Port and Maritime Squadron, Royal Logistics Corps which possesses its own Landing Ships Logistic (LSLs); 33-metre-long Ramped Craft Logistic (RCLs); and Mexeflotes, large pontoons used for landing heavy equipment or constructing a floating quay. RM Poole also conducts training courses for NATO troops.

Royal Marines Commandos Landing Craft Branch

For most people the Royal Marines are synonymous with landing craft – with men leaping into the sea and battling their way through waves and bullets to the beach. The official term for that type of operation is an opposed landing – and while the Corps does train for opposed landings, it doesn't like them one little bit.

For whereas the amphibious armoured personnel carriers used by the USMC can – in theory – provide a high degree of protection, at least against small-arms fire, only the very largest of the landing craft used by the

Royal Marines can do the same – and even then, a .50-calibre machine-gun bullet has the unhappy ability to go through quite thick armour plate. It's not that the Royal Marines can't or won't undertake opposed landings, but they point out that such landings have always had the least chance of success, and obviously result in great and sometimes unacceptable casualties to one's own side. The object of war is, after all, to win and not simply to look good on the newsreels or provide the inspiration for a thousand books, plays, poems and films. But an unopposed landing demands speed, mobility and surprise (commando attributes all) and this is one reason why Royal Marine landing craft, while offering less physical protection than their US counterparts, are quicker; why the Royal Marines are trained to land in spots previously regarded as being inaccessible; and why they're also trained to land and fight in small units, only linking up later in larger formations if necessary.

The other reason is that the US equipment is extremely expensive. As a colonel in the US Army once remarked, if Britain had had the same amount of money to spend on arms as the Americans had, her troops would not be as well trained as they are today. In British forces, training and tactics have had to make up for budgetary shortfalls – which is no very bad thing, since it produces soldiers less dependent on high-tech equipment that invariably breaks down just when it's most needed. As can be imagined, this amphibious ability of the Royal Marines demands very high standards of landing craft officers and NCOs, and Poole is where they're trained.

The Royal Marines use six types of craft for landing commandos on shore:

Landing Craft Utility (LCUs). 27 metres long, with a cruising speed of 9 knots and a range of 200 nautical miles. These can carry a fully equipped rifle company of 120 Royal Marines Commandos; or four lorries, or four All Terrain Vehicles (ATVs)/Land Rovers plus trailers. The six-man crew have their own extremely basic accommodation, which includes a small galley. It will usually be commanded by a senior NCO or officer. A new roll-on, roll-off LCU is due to replace the current Mk OR in the year 2000.

Landing Craft Vehicle and Personnel (LCVPs). 13 metres long, with a cruising speed of 14 knots and a range of 150 nautical miles. Can carry a troop of twenty-eight Royal Marines, or a single ATV/Land-Rover plus trailer. LCVPs have a crew of three and can be weatherproofed for Arctic operations.

Landing Craft Air Cushion (Light), (LCACs (L)). 12-metre-long hovercraft, capable of 30 knots with a 12-hour range. Can carry sixteen Royal Marines or two tonnes of stores.

Rigid Inflatable Boats (RIBS). Similar in size and design to the fast inshore boats used by the Royal National Lifeboat Service. A RIB can carry up to ten men with their kit and will reach a speed of at least 50 knots.

Rigid Raiding Craft (RRC). The new Mk III is a wonderful piece of kit (yes, the author got to drive one),

some 8 metres long, that can carry a section of eight
Royal Marines plus all their kit for an optimum range of
80 nautical miles. It can be carried while underslung by
a Sea King or Chinook helicopter. The Mk III has a
diesel engine, and can achieve speeds in excess of 35
knots. Yes!

Inflatable Raiding Craft (IRC). 5-metre-long Zodiac-
style craft, which can carry four Royal Marines plus kit
at a speed of 8 knots for two hours. These tend to be
used in a special forces role, that is, delivering the SBS or
elements of the Brigade Patrol Group, Y Troop, Royal
Artillery or Royal Engineers Reconnaissance Troops, or
a Recce Troop from 40, 42 or 45 Commandos. IRCs can
also be launched from a surfaced or submerged submarine, or dropped from Sea King or Chinook helicopter.

Not so very long ago, a senior admiral in the Royal
Navy was heard to comment that he couldn't understand why the SAS bothered having their own Boat
Troop, since the Royal Marines Landing Craft Branch
produced the best military small-boat handlers in the
world. More about this later, but the point was well
made. True, techniques like driving an RRC full-tilt at
the beach, so that when the craft hits it flies snarling
towards the enemy for some thirty or so metres, are
usually reserved for displays. But what isn't always
apparent is the sheer level of seamanship fostered by the
branch, underlying the Corps's ability to provide a secondary vocation for its men. As said, first and foremost
one is a Royal Marines Commando . . . and then one
belongs to a branch not just because there's a vacancy,

but because that branch has a specific and personal appeal. All Landing Craft personnel have an inbuilt love of the sea and boats, and most of them give the impression of being more at home on water than on dry land. It also carries enormous responsibility, for the coxswain of an IRC, RRC, RIB or the skipper of an LCAC (L), LCVP or LCU is the man totally in charge, no matter what his rank. But in war, it's also a dangerous job: Landing Craft coxswains and crew are always those first targeted by enemy sniper fire.

Because of their greater size, LCUs can and do become 'mother' ships for an amphibious operation, allowing the infinitely larger LPDs (Landing Platform Dock, e.g. HMS *Fearless* or *Intrepid*) to slope off into the wide blue sea where they'll run less risk of being attacked by enemy aircraft or submarines. LCVPs may also be used as temporary HQs, as well as mounting diversionary or surprise attacks in areas other than the main landing beach. And, if radio silence is being rigorously enforced, Raiders can and do act as high-speed couriers between the various elements of the amphibious landing force. During the Falklands, LCVPs were also used as inshore minesweepers. Much to their own and everyone else's relief, it transpired that no mines were actually in the area around San Carlos, but it did demonstrate the versatility of these craft, and indeed of the Landing Craft Branch as a whole.

Not only is the Landing Craft Company at Poole responsible for training men in the branch, it also trains all Royal Marines how to function in landing craft. It is possibly here that a Royal Marine begins to develop, for the first time, that sense of caution that is very much the

Corps's own trademark. It is impossible to spend any time in or around the sea without learning to expect the worst as a matter of course. (The worst, in the case of a recruit practising landing drills for the first time, is discovering that the coxswain of an LCVP has not dropped the ramp on to a gently shelving beach. He's dropped it on a sand bar some distance offshore and the recruit has to wade ashore, rifle held high, in water that comes just under his chin.)

539 Assault Squadron

Based in Plymouth, 539 Assault Squadron is yet another example of the Corps's ability to develop specialized units on the spot, as it were, and to train its personnel to fight for the next war as opposed to the last. 539 was first formed during the Falklands War, but officially disbanded soon thereafter, although it never seemed quite to go away. It was then officially re-formed in 1984, thus carrying on the Corps tradition of forming, disbanding, renaming and re-forming units until the powers-that-be give up the unequal struggle – or simply become totally confused – and allow the Corps to do what it wanted in the first place.

539 is equipped with LCUs, LCACs (L), LCVPs, RIBs, RRCs and IRCs. Plus other bits and pieces that have probably been loaned by various manufacturers desirous of the best trialling available. The Squadron can and will take part in a main amphibious landing, but its other roles include inserting special forces and reconnaissance troops and providing the capability for fast

flank or diversionary attacks. This comes back to the concept of amphibiosity discussed at the beginning of this book. There is a tendency for amphibious force commanders to become fixated on a specific beachhead, and restrict all operations to a comparatively small area – in effect, a funnel between sea and land. But in fact the wider the front, the more difficult it is to defend and while large amounts of men and material do have to come ashore somewhere, restricting operations to that 'choke-point' can be playing right into the defenders' hands. As it is, 539 Squadron allows diversionary or specific-target operations to be conducted up to two hundred miles either side of the main landing area. It can also conduct riverine warfare and decoy operations, that is, confusing enemy signal intelligence to suggest that an LCU or smaller just might be an aircraft-carrier. If it gets the new armoured hovercraft that the Americans have recently developed, 539's strike range will extend many more miles inland . . . as said earlier, the object of an amphibious assault is never the beachhead per se, but what lies beyond it.

Marine Drivers

The other major training responsibility at Poole is for Royal Marine drivers. Driving is never seen as being one of the more glamorous tasks in any armed force. The general impression is usually of a surly, dirty driver managing to hide both himself and his vehicle with practised ease. That may have been good forty years ago but military drivers nowadays must be more skilled and responsible, particularly Marine drivers. Think about it for a moment. Before a truck or Land-Rover can be driven off a landing craft, its engine must be waterproofed, since it may well be under water for some considerable period of time. It must be waterproofed in such a way that the vehicle doesn't have to be stripped down immediately, as in the old days, as soon as it reaches dry land, in order to remove all the waterproofing. Nowadays, a Land-Rover or three-tonner, when waterproofed by the Marines, can be driven for the next six months or so. It doesn't do the vehicle a power of good, but it does save time. That waterproofing is the responsibility of the drivers themselves, who have to know how to keep their vehicles moving when they're one hundred per cent submerged for well over a minute, being guided by a man standing behind them with his head just above the surface. Having a good lung capacity helps.

They also have to know how to make the BVs (bandwagons, tracked vehicles used on snow and ice) perform to a level that the manufacturers never intended. Sometimes it feels as if a good driver can make a BV walk on tiptoe through an icefield. Of course he can't, but the skill with which he moves the BV across the most dangerous terrain is something to experience – to experience with a certain amount of alarm, actually, until one discovers how far a BV can lean to one side without overbalancing.

There's one aspect of the Marine Drivers Branch that, again, epitomizes the Corps's penchant for perfecting a particular military skill to the point where they become the experts. Poole teaches the VIP staff drivers, who learn anti-terrorist techniques, taught to a standard considerably higher, say, than that of the civilian police. The Marines teach not only how to use the car as a weapon in case of ambush, but also how to execute particularly snappy U- or J-turns, and how to do so without becoming disoriented, so that the driver can immediately and accurately fire his weapon after the car has come to a shuddering halt or crash. In other words, weapon training is as much a part of the VIP staff driver's course as driving itself.

Yet with all that, the Drivers Branch never has enough volunteers. Traditionally, a Marine driver used to be a man in his mid to late thirties whose knees had grown tired of all that yomping . . . and who, wanting to gain a skill for civilian life, became a driver in the knowledge that he'd end up with a Heavy Goods Licence. Problem is, there aren't as many 'Three-Badge' Marines around as there used to be. Today's Generation X as often as not will join the Corps for a fixed term, say five years only and have no intention of driving for a living when they leave. So any 'suggestion' that becoming a driver is exactly what a young Marine fresh from training has always really wanted to do, is likely to be greeted with a polite 'thanks, but no thanks'.

CHAPTER SIX

Royal Marines Special Forces

Wars are won by the average quality of the standard unit . . . any action in which more than a handful of men are engaged should be regarded as a normal operation.

Field Marshal Slim

Special Forces are . . . ordinary men doing extraordinary things.

Major-General Julian Thompson OBE, RM

Special Boat Service

One of the great strengths of the British military lies in its willingness to experiment with new ideas, especially in wartime – often with a degree of desperation, or over the dead bodies of its more hidebound commanders. This attitude of 'what if we tried that?' has never gone away . . . possibly derived from a combination of natural inventiveness, pragmatism, a sense of adventure, and a low boredom threshold. All probably influenced at times by the basic desire common to so many British servicemen, namely to control their own little armies. It's an attitude that during the Second World War resulted in the SAS, SBS, the Long Range Desert Group, Popski's Private Army, the Chindits, Force 137, Phantom and one of the most efficient 'black' propaganda and signal deception operations ever known. (See Annex G.) In fact the tradition goes back much further than that, as witness licensed buccaneers in Elizabethan times, the Guides of the North-West Frontier, and even Wellington's use of 'intelligencers', many of whom worked closely with the Spanish guerrillas during the Peninsular War. The other inescapable fact is that special forces are usually regarded with deep suspicion by their own side . . . a suspicion as often as not based on the understandable jealousy about men excused parades, guard duty and even regulation boots. They seem to have much more fun, too. One of the other hallmarks of special forces units is that they tend to be formed either by civilians who've been called up during a war, or by annoyingly eccentric officers who've been driving their comrades insane with their wild ideas. Even more galling when either prophet is proved correct.

Well, it was this way . . .

The Special Boat Service first came into being during the Second World War . . . often claimed by the Army as an off-shoot from the Special Air Service, but in reality a child of many and varied parentage. One of these antecedents, the Sea Reconnaissance Unit (SRU), mounted the first-ever military paddle-board invasion of California during a successful exercise against the US Rangers. The SRU was the brainchild of Lt Commander Bruce Knight, Royal Canadian Navy, who in peacetime was responsible for vast tracts of Canadian forest – yet another bloody eccentric who was ultimately proved correct. (Not with the paddle-boards, although some still swear they ultimately became surf boards, and without them the world would never have known the Beach Boys.) But it was Lt Commander Knight who later established the SCUBA (Self-Contained Underwater Breathing Apparatus) Sections that in 1945 would recce the Irrawaddy river in Burma before the Fourteenth Army crossed. The overall point is that nearly all these units – except perhaps for Raiding Forces Middle East – tended to specialize in particular aspects of amphibious, special forces warfare: beach reconnaissance; anti-shipping raids; sabotage against land-based targets; transporting agents; decoy operations; liaison with Resistance groups; strategic intelligence operations and so on. By 1946 all but the Royal Marine units had been disbanded; in 1947 these became the Small Raids Wing and in 1975 eventually became the Special Boat Squadron, to be much later renamed the Special Boat Service because the word 'Squadron' was no longer accurate, if it ever had been.

. . . or was it?

But just as the Special Air Service ended up combining the roles of the Long Range Desert Group, Popski's Private Army and a few others it discovered for itself, so too did the Special Boat Service eventually end up combining many of the amphibious, special forces roles developed during the Second World War.

But not immediately. During the Malayan Emergency

in the early Fifties, the SBS was mostly used in a sea-borne-raiding role against specific terrorist targets, although some personnel were involved in surveillance operations, working with the Malayan Special Branch. In fact, the Emergency was successfully fought by Field Marshal Gerald Templar as the century's first counter-terrorist 'intelligence' war, proving how blurred the demarcation lines between civilian and military operations can become . . . a lesson repeated a decade later in Borneo, and a decade after that in Northern Ireland.

During the Korean War, the Royal Marines were represented by 41 (Independent) Commando and an ad hoc unit of swimmer-canoeists called Pounds' Force, named after its leader Lt E. G. D. Pounds RM – who actually went on to become a Major-General, proving that those bloody eccentrics do occasionally receive due recognition. Pounds' Force successfully mounted a decoy beach reconnaissance at Kongsoon, twenty-two kilometres south-west of the planned beachhead at Inchon. Later, reinforced by Marines from 41 (Independent) Commando, and working closely with US Underwater Demolition Teams, Pounds' Force mounted a series of successful sabotage operations against land targets – mostly railways – as well as carrying out reconnaissance duties for the USMC and US Navy. They also began taking – volunteer – artillery officers ashore in order to direct naval gunfire, a technique that today is carried out by 148 Commando Battery, based in Poole, who work closely with the SBS and the Brigade Patrol Group. There's no doubt that the existing close operational relationship between the Royal Marines Commandos and the USMC dates from the Korean

War. Certainly the US Navy's Seals (Sea, Air and Land forces) that replaced the UDTs were prompted in part by the way the SBS was busily evolving.

No, we're purely defensive troops. Honest.

In 1961, a triumphant 3 Commando Brigade returned to Singapore. In 1962 President Sukarno of Indonesia declared Confrontation with the newly independent Malaysia, on the spurious grounds that it really belonged to his country. Malaysia called on Britain and the rest of the Commonwealth for help and the subsequent fighting took place mainly in and around Borneo, lasting until 1965. It was a messy campaign, not least because cross-border operations by the British forces were officially banned: the Malaysian Prime Minister, Tunku Abdul Rahman, had appealed to the UN for help, as had the Indonesians, and as far as the UN was concerned the British and Commonwealth forces were there in a purely defensive role. This resulted in Operation Claret, those unofficial cross-border operations which the Malays didn't – officially – know about, although the Indonesians certainly did.

As a passing comment, it appears to be a truism that whenever the UN is directly responsible or even heavily involved with military operations, the result is always total fiasco. Perhaps the problem lies with the UN being an equal opportunity employer par excellence which wants to be nice to absolutely everyone . . . which so often results in totally inadequate troops and commanders being given an impossible job. South Korea was doomed until MacArthur and the Americans effectively took over. There are those who still remember certain Swedish UN troops in Cyprus during the Sixties who turned out to be university students picking up a bit of extra cash. And Bosnia had no chance until NATO moved in under the guise of I-FOR. Jaw-jaw might be preferable to war-war, but only when all parties are actually jaw-jawing.

In fact, Sukarno pretty soon gave up his plans for military conquest and the campaign settled down to one of counter-insurgency and counter-terrorism in which the SBS was heavily involved, along the way proving the value of military hovercraft.

It was the other guy

Meanwhile, back at the ranch as it were, the SBS had also become increasingly active in Europe. They were heavily involved with the planned defence of the Rhine if, as and when the Warsaw Pact arrived uninvited. They were also responsible for beach reconnaissance throughout the eastern Mediterranean, since much of the information dating from the Second World War had been destroyed in 1945–6 – or more probably, misfiled beyond human ken. And gradually, the civilian agencies like MI5 and MI6 realized that here, like the Special Air Service, was an asset simply too valuable to be left to the military. And the wonderful thing was that outside the military, few people knew very much about them. Even when most people in the forces did think about the SBS, they thought beach reconnaissance or small raiding operations and left it at that. So it was that a Minister could rise to his feet in the House of Commons and deny with complete honesty that the Special Air Service had been responsible for a specific operation or incident. No one ever thought to ask if the SBS had been involved. Even in the late Eighties, when newspapers on the Continent carried stories about submarine-delivered SBS spying on the then Soviet Union, plus delivering or collecting agents from Soviet territory, the press in Britain ignored it. There might well have been pressure from the Government, of course, in the time-honoured tradition that the British public should always be the last to know – Moscow certainly did. But more likely the stories simply weren't believed. Everyone knew the SBS didn't do stuff like that. That was SAS business.

SB who?

That said, the SBS themselves were always far more security conscious than their SAS cousins, and deter-mined to avoid the type of publicity that the SAS always attracted. One of the obvious operational reasons for this concerned one of the SBS's prime roles, the defence against counter-terrorism at sea. It is extremely difficult to retake an oil rig or civilian ship that's been captured by Greenpeace, let alone terrorists, and the less any potential terrorist hijackers knew about the people and techniques likely to be used, the better.

Another reason is cultural, since Royal Marines Commandos tend to be a fairly close-mouthed bunch. The need for security awareness is built into their basic training at Lympstone to a far greater extent than in the Navy, Army or RAF, because it isn't only the SBS who find themselves doing interesting but highly classified work. Generally, the Corps's attitude was that as long as the powers-that-be knew what the SBS had done and could do, then there was no need to seek more open publicity – especially as the Royal Navy didn't approve. A somewhat short-sighted attitude, perhaps, since all too often military decisions are made by politicians and civil servants with half an eye on what the public thinks. Change is often less important than the image of change. Everything is a brand.

The SBS was always far smaller than the SAS – say around fifty serving in the branch at any one time. Nor was it a separate regiment, which helped the SBS to remain comparatively hidden and protected by the Corps. Because it was such a secretive and little-known organization – except by the GRU and KGB, and they never shared information with anyone, not even each other – the SBS became even more of an asset for MI5, MI6, the Joint Intelligence Committee, the Defence Intelligence Agency and even GCHQ. This didn't always go down well with the Corps hierarchy, who felt that they should at least be told when the SBS were off doing something terribly secret, instead of hearing a recorded message that so-and-so can't come to the phone right now, but please speak after the beep. OK, that's a slight exaggeration (OK, a big one), but intelligence services always operate on the need-to-know principle. If there is no operational need for the Commandant General of the Royal Marines to know where certain SBS troops were operating, then don't tell him. He can always complain to the First Sea Lord. Or the Home Secretary, Foreign Secretary or Prime Minister. Throughout the Sixties and Seventies, the SBS increasingly came to be seen as a strategic intelligence asset, which in a sense brought them into direct competition with the SAS. While this hardly worried the guys on the ground, it did concern many of the senior NCOs who formed the SAS permanent cadre, and a few officers who believed that their own careers depended on the SAS having overall supremacy in the field of clandestine warfare.

Someone had a cunning plan

This would ultimately lead to the current joint Special Forces Headquarters and combined training . . . which however much it might please the planners, isn't working particularly well. You would have thought that the government had learned its lesson when it tried to develop a joint MI5/MI6 headquarters in the Eighties, as recommended by a firm of management consultants. Although just to prove that not all management consultants are totally insane, another later report recommended that the joint HQ should be closed down, largely on the basis that neither MI5 nor MI6 were paying too much attention to it. But to understand why the forced marriage between the SAS and SBS hasn't worked, it's necessary to take a closer look at the SAS itself.

Pause for the author to take a deep breath. Nowadays, any criticism of the SAS is likely to result in screams of anger from all those fierce armchair warriors, or shouts of jubilation from those who combine sensitivity and smugness in equal proportions . . . actually, opposite sides of the same moral and intellectual coin, and probably only really happy when wearing hairy sandals and doing something meaningful with free-range goats. Not to mention Defence Ministry officials, modish spectacles glinting with fury, because criticism amounts to treason and worse, total ingratitude for the way said officials have always manfully struggled to do their best for the Defence of the Realm. Interestingly enough, this hatred of criticism or even mild dissent is a comparatively new phenomenon. Up until the Second World War it was considered perfectly normal for even serving officers publicly to criticize aspects of defence strategy and tactics. Not always a wise career move, perhaps, but never assumed to be treasonable. After all, Basil Liddell Hart was a serving officer when he began formulating those doctrines that so upset the then War Office, if only because they so often proved to be right. (And no, the author is not claiming to be in the same league.) A combination of Cold War secrecy and a Whitehall establishment desperately seeking Britain's new place in the world – without too much early success – changed everything, the situation heightened by the intense secrecy verging on genuine paranoia that marked Margaret Thatcher's last years in office . . . for Thatcher had managed to politicize Whitehall and the defence establishment in a manner that Churchill and certainly Wilson could only have dreamed about.

While it can be said that the SAS are spectacularly good they may also be spectacularly awful. In either event they're still streets ahead of most if not all other countries, but this is primarily a discussion about Britain's special forces. Let it also be said that the Ministry of Defence and the Army allowed the situation to develop where one could find such a wide disparity of performance within a single unit . . . if there is blame, it belongs at the very highest levels.

Are you sitting comfortably?

SAS operations in Malaysia (Fifties), the Radfan (Yemen, Sixties), Northern Ireland (mostly) and the Iranian Embassy were extremely good, some spectacularly so. Plus countless other operations that no one has ever heard about. But there is a tendency for the SAS to believe their own publicity, and give the impression of being all-knowing and invincible. During Operation Corporate (Falklands War), the decision to land men from SAS D Company's Mountain Troop on the Fortuna glacier, South Georgia, was pig-headed stupidity backed up by the sort of arrogance so often the hallmark of a closed, inward-looking organization. Nor did their Boat Troop, also acting against advice, fare much better. And while Andy McNab is undoubtedly a brave man, his Bravo Two Zero patrol during the Gulf War made the type of mistakes you wouldn't expect from a highly trained special forces unit. Or even a well-trained infantry unit. Two examples: first, anyone with any experience of that part of the world knows that no matter how deserted even a patch of desert might be, let alone somewhere reasonably green, if you stop for a moment either a goatherd or someone wanting to sell you something suddenly appears. Secondly, when crossing a road used by the enemy, you use a certain procedure. First you send one person across to secure the left- or right-hand flank, then another to secure the opposite one. Then a third man to move a little further out between them, forming the apex of a triangle. Then the rest of the patrol crosses one by one, either taking up the first three positions, or moving through them to a previously arranged rendezvous. You don't all rush across as soon as the coast looks as if it might be clear.

And overall, it's really best not to use Chinook helicopters to insert special forces, even if this would mean taking away one of the RAF's playthings, their special forces unit. Chinooks are fairly chunky pieces of kit and not always easy to disguise. Nor is it easy to fly them at several hundred miles an hour only a scant few feet above the surface, which is the Royal Navy and Royal Marines tried and trusted method, using much smaller aircraft. Besides, Chinooks are far too valuable in terms of moving regular troops and equipment around the battlefield. If this seems carping criticism, former SAS soldiers themselves have made the same points, and more. Which raises the question: how can the SAS simultaneously appear to possess some of the best soldiers in the world – and some of the biggest cowboys? And to those with any military background the other question: where, oh where are their officers?

For it is one of an officer's prime roles in any military unit to ensure that 'cowboys' – or bullies – or general idiots never get to a position to do any real harm. The first assumption one makes, for example, when hearing about a particularly unpleasant, long-term case of sexual harassment in the armed forces, is that an officer has been derelict in his or her duty . . . and it's no good pleading that they didn't know what was going on, because it's their job to know. *Quis custodiet ipsos custodes?* Officers are also supposed to monitor each other, with a little help from the RSM. Within a normal battalion, say, the overall maintenance of both moral and professional standards is the responsibility of a triumvirate composed of the Commanding Officer, Adjutant and RSM. But this relies on a degree of continuity of all ranks . . . without it, the system breaks down.

Time for a little compare and contrast

Any serving (male) member of the Armed Forces can apply to join the Special Air Service. Women can apply to join 14 Intelligence Company, which may or may not be an SAS operation but is certainly trained by them. And while Hereford might be a little choosy about who's permitted to attend the pre-selection course, there'll always be those who are as hopeless as they are hopeful. Hereford will, with considerable justification, point to the fact that good special forces soldiers have come from the most unlikely military backgrounds . . . and that a wide trawl brings in all manner of different attitudes and skills, will even prevent the type of inward-looking attitude that people have critized in the past. But the suspicion remains that Hereford is equally looking for people who will accept the SAS ethos as promulgated by the Regiment's permanent staff – who are all NCOs. There are no permanent officers within the Regiment, and most officers will only do only a single, three-year tour. Which means that when they're being selected, effectively by the permanent cadre, it's on the basis of how well they're going to fit in . . . and won't try to tell a sergeant who's on his third tour how to do his job. Which is not to say that good officers can't be found in the SAS . . . just that sometimes, remembering how egalitarian the Regiment actually is, respect and acceptance by your new 'mates' becomes more important than your true role. And while it's normal to hear men carping about their officers, at times the SAS does seem to take this to extremes. Raising the question: if those 'Ruperts' are quite so incompetent, how on earth did they manage to pass the training in the first instance? Or wouldn't it perhaps be better if all men joining the SAS did so at the rank of trooper, so that the Regiment's officers were commissioned from within? And why aren't there any permanent officers in the SAS, to help provide the continuity that any regiment, any corps always needs? There are a number of reasons, some more sensible than others. First, that's the way it's always been. The SAS was a special unit raised at a special time (Second World War) and never intended to be permanent. Second, membership of the SAS requires that every man is fully capable of operating in the field. What do you do with an officer who's no longer able, by virtue of injury or age, of acting as a troop or company commander – have him put down? Third, this is, actually, one way of spreading SAS skills throughout the Army. Fourth, there are many officers who want to spend time with the SAS but obviously, only a few places are available. A high officer turnover ensures that as many people get the chance as possible – and once again, helps spread SAS skills and so on. Perhaps there are a few other reasons, too, as in fifth: all in all, the Army would rather not see the SAS develop into a full-fledged regiment, in every sense of the word regiment – for then it might become even more influential. Or sixth: perhaps a lack of permanent officers makes the SAS more MI5 and MI6 friendly: with the Army but not always of it.

Royal did it this way

Nor were there any officers permanently attached to the SBS. But then, there are never any officers permanently attached to any branch in the Royal Marines – even if the occasional one has managed to do a couple of terms back to back. As he progresses higher up the chain of command, a Royal Marines officer is supposed to understand how all the different Corps components and branches operate. And that's all the SBS ever was – just another branch.

In the old days, a serving Royal Marine of any rank had to be recommended for the SBS, and only then after he'd been in the Corps for a couple of years. More likely than not the branch would already have become aware of him . . . a badged swimmer/canoeist could have casually suggested one day that he might like to think about 'going SB'. All candidates would have one thing in common: all would be commando-trained, that is, had already reached a standard of infantry skills far in advance of the average candidate for Hereford. There was no particular branch 'ethos', either, no tremendous sense of exclusivity. Loyalty to their branch, definitely, but many of their closest friends would be in other branches. Above everything else there was their loyalty to the Corps. Swimmer/canoeists were also well aware that their lives could depend on skills other Royal Marines possessed. A serving SBS sergeant once told the author that he couldn't understand how anyone would even want to pilot a helicopter travelling at full speed only a few feet above the ground. But luckily there were Royal Navy pilots who did and could. Another serving SBS corporal made the point that his life could depend on the ability of a Landing Craft coxswain, or a Royal Marine driving an ATV in the Arctic. In effect, the Royal Marines Commandos was seen as an elite Corps to begin with, and the SBS only another speciality among many. Which didn't always explain why so many swimmer/canoeists had to be dragged kicking and screaming back to regular duties, but the original comment was none the less valid. Which leads to another point of difference between Poole and Hereford.

Spreading the skills around. Or not.

'You've no idea', a serving Royal Marines major said recently, 'of the value guys who've been SBS or Mountain Leader trained can be when drafted into a fighting commando. When I was OC Recce Troop, I had an SBS sergeant and an ML corporal – and we all learned from them. The Corps's ability to spread knowledge around has always been one of its greatest strengths. We can do it because we're obviously smaller and more tightly organized than the Army. All the same, I can't help thinking it's a pity that the SAS often seem to be so far removed from the rest of the Army – except maybe the Paras, but then they can be pretty exclusive, too.'

In fact, for a long time the Paras looked upon the SAS as their own private reserve. Even today cliques can occasionally be seen – former Paras at this table, Engineers or Gunners at another – explained by the fact that while it might officially be a regiment, not everyone stays with the SAS for any great length of time. As often as not when they do leave, they'll become civilians because the SAS is a very hard act to follow. And nor, must it be said, are men who've served with the SAS always welcomed back to their parent regiments or corps with open arms. Some are even viewed with outright suspicion. Overall, SAS skills are not spread around the rest of the Army as SBS or ML expertise is spread throughout the Corps. Which in this cost-conscious age is rather a shame.

The SBS existed, and to an extent still does, within the larger family of the Royal Marines. No such luxury, even necessity, exists for the SAS which in itself leads to a defensive, inward-looking attitude, heightened by the Regiment's transitory nature. Men come and go, either back to the Army or to new lives as authors or security consultants. The system breeds a strong individual, but one who often ends up extremely isolated. But all SBS personnel belong to the larger Corps family. Many would have known each other since recruit or officer training at Lympstone. A greater sense of security led to a branch far more at ease with itself, never falling into the trap of believing it always had some point or another to prove. Which again leads to an area that has to be discussed, the traditional rivalry between the Paras and the Royal Marines. Although this was mostly laid to rest by the Falklands War, it had long affected relations between the SAS and SBS.

Whither the Paras?

Suez was the last campaign that saw a full-scale parachute drop, but the Paras had been feeling under threat ever since the battle of Arnhem. This had highlighted the major problems of resupply and using comparatively lightly equipped troops against a professional army. The value of diversionary attacks, or *coup de main* attacks against particular targets like an airfield, was never in doubt. But if these were only most likely to succeed against a relatively disorganized, badly trained and even worse led enemy, was there any point in possessing such a specialist unit? Both parachutists and their aircraft are extremely vulnerable before and during the actual drop. It was true that the German use of parachutists on Crete during the Second World War had been highly successful. But later analysis suggested that the British commanders had been the true architects of their own defeat. In any event, time and weapons systems had moved on . . . and although Warsaw Pact military doctrine called for massive para-drops to capture key points ahead of an advance, or outflank the NATO defenders, there were many who wondered how effective it would be in real life (see *The Third World War* by General Sir John Hackett). Of course, in a very real sense Warsaw Pact/Soviet military doctrine dominated NATO military thinking during the Cold War, for NATO only ever saw itself as the defender. So it was a question of what do we do if, as and when they do that? Naturally Moscow saw it differently, especially when the defence against the possible attack included surrounding the Soviet Union with nuclear missiles . . . but the general – NATO – feeling was if the Soviets set so much store by parachute troops, then so should we. Besides, every country likes to have an elite military regiment or two. Britain had several. Aside from known crack infantry regiments, there were the Gurkhas, the Paras and, of course, the Royal Marines. Then dawned the era of a new defence policy. Before, it had been a question of what the country needed to do, and how to do it with limited resources. Gradually, beginning in the Sixties, this began to change to 'Here's how much money we have, so cut your cloth accordingly. And by the way, it'll probably be even less next year.' It's not generally appreciated, by the way, that this approach was instrumental in Britain becoming one of the world's major arms suppliers – which means that other countries end up paying for much of Britain's own military research and development.

This greater cost-consciousness resulted in regiments being amalgamated. But with whom could the Paras amalgamate? The Royal Marines, as we've seen, survived because of world events that worked in their favour . . . the growing acceptance of amphibiosity . . . and because their very structure allowed them to adapt and develop in all manner of interesting directions. The Royal Marines were old hands at the business of survival. The Paras were in nothing like such a favourable position. To begin with, they were one of the youngest of all Army regiments. Secondly, they appeared to be trained for only one thing, dropping out of the sky. But other units could also be para-trained. And wasn't it a little risky to stake the survival of a regiment on a technique that might never be used? But in fact there was more to the Paras than that. Aside from their infantry skills, Paras were trained to be extremely aggressive, very fast moving troops on the ground. Fast moving in terms of physically running, that is. Armoured Personnel Carriers are not normally included in a parachute drop. There could be no question about it: the Paras were extremely aggressive. Para junior and senior NCOs often seemed to keep the men wound up in a permanent state of aggression, the idea being that the dislike felt by the men for their NCOs would, in action, be channelled against the enemy. But while all types of war need blind aggression at certain times, at others a cooler and more rational approach is required. Northern Ireland's Bloody Sunday pointed that one out. Much later, Goose Green was to emphasize the point further.

So it was that the Paras assumed the role of the Army's own, airborne commandos. Except other regiments weren't altogether happy with the idea; except Britain already had commandos; except as technology improved, there were few parts of the world outside the striking range of helicopters operating from a carrier at sea. Small wonder that the Paras came to see the Royal Marines as one of the biggest threats to their existence.

For without the commando role, the Paras were essentially nothing more than a superbly fit and well-trained body of men capable of operating at speed and independently of a main force under conditions of extreme hardship. Which is extremely impressive, but not necessarily enough to save them from the chop.

In search of identity

The Paras also saw the Special Air Service as the logical extension of their own skills, almost a branch of the Parachute Regiment in the same way that the SBS was a branch of the Royal Marines. SAS pre-selection training was a harsher version of P Company, and the two-week beat-up that proceeds para-training itself. It's not totally true that you only need to be able to run fast while carrying a heavy weight in order to pass either – guts and determination play a pretty important part – but there's no question about the two regiments' extremely close bonds, especially in terms of the SAS's permanent training cadre. And one of the weaknesses of the SAS is that parent regiment loyalties – and rivalries – tend to be carried over, certainly during training and the early years, for no one knows if he'll be invited to stay on.

The Special Air Service is also a very young regiment. Unlike most other Army regiments, it recruits from no special part of the country. It is as much defined by what it does, as who it is, similar to the Intelligence Corps. In time, all regiments develop their own particular character – but it's hard to say what the SAS character in the regimental context actually is . . . special forces operations and clandestine warfare in general are only an extension of essential soldiering skills. Of course, the SAS can point to numerous medals and an ethos that demands a continuing drive for professional excellence. But so can many other regiments. There are also those lines taken from James Elroy Flecker's poem, *The Golden Road to Samarkand*, engraved above the clock tower at Hereford, that begin: 'We are the Pilgrims, master, we shall go, Always a little further . . .' The same poem ends with a night-watchman consoling the wives left behind: 'What would ye, ladies? It was ever thus. Men are unwise and curiously planned.' And the wives agreeing: 'They have their dreams and do not think of us.' This almost mystical approach to warfare is nothing new, but tends to be regarded with a degree of suspicion throughout the British Armed Forces . . . who none the less also feel a little aggrieved if any one unit appears to claim that it's 'more committed than thou'. No one has a monopoly on duty or commitment. Perhaps the best way of describing the SAS's regimental character is to say that it's composed of individuals who all share certain professional and personal ideals. What military unit isn't? In the end, the SAS is only as unique and as valuable as its last operation. This alone tends to result in a certain inward-looking attitude, heightened by the fact that only a few people may ever know what that last operation actually was. It is perceived by many within the Army as being run by its senior NCOs, and too exclusive for the rest of the Army's good. The fact that the SAS also produces some of the very best soldiers in the world often passes people by . . . as does the fact that different types of war require different techniques.

So there you had it. On the one hand a young regiment that wasn't one at all, in the strictest sense of the word, and which was also viewed with considerable suspicion by many people throughout the Armed Forces. It had survived various attempts to close it down – and an attempted take-over by the Guards in the late Fifties. Continuity was represented only by a small band of senior NCOs. Its closest ties were with a 'proper' regiment, albeit one that was far more under threat. On the other hand you had the SBS which belonged to the Royal Marines.

One small happy family?

As mentioned, the SAS and SBS had worked together over the years. There were cross-training and joint exercises. Two SAS NCOs who'd passed diver training accompanied the SBS during the first recce of the Falklands War, which meant parachuting into the Atlantic to rendezvous with a waiting submarine. That had been at the SBS's own request, for they'd been short-handed at the time. Later the same two SAS NCOs were allowed, as honoured guests, to activate the charges that would send an Argentinian spy-trawler to the bottom of the sea, after the first fast-rope descent in warfare. (A fast-rope descent means putting on a special glove and controlling your descent by squeezing the rope – assuming you managed to catch hold of the rope when you leaped out of the helicopter.)

'They could hardly believe their luck,' remembered a man who was there. 'I mean, how often does an Army guy get to blow up a ship?'

The point is made to emphasize that relations between the two Services could be extremely good, at least on an operational level. At senior levels it was a different matter – for a confused defence policy over the decades had pitted regiment against regiment, service against service, with the Treasury moving from expediter to prime mover. Actually, there was never any question that the Royal Marines wanted to see either the SAS or the Paras disbanded – unless it was the only way of saving the Corps. But it was against this background, with all the historical baggage, that the SAS and SBS were effectively combined and the problems really began.

In one way it made a great degree of sense. Why have two separate headquarters for men who were engaged on similar, if not identical tasks? Why not combine pre-selection training, too – just think of the costs savings. Nor was everyone within the SBS totally against the idea – and the reason for that also had its roots during the Falklands War.

The SAS/SBS recce teams that preceded the Task Force reported directly back to the overall Campaign HQ at Northwood. This in turn passed any relevant information on to the Task Force. Much to his surprise – read anger – Major-General, then Brigadier, Julian Thompson OBE, RM discovered that a great deal of information simply wasn't being passed on by the Task Force naval intelligence cell. Perhaps it was something to do with the SAS/SBS being regarded as very highly classified, strategic intelligence assets. Or the old need-to-know principle: since the Task Force was still at Ascension, there was little need for 3 Commando Brigade to know. Or the problem associated with a mixed command. The SBS themselves were horrified when they discovered what had happened, as were the SAS soldiers accompanying them. Whatever, General Thompson 'remonstrated' with Admiral Woodward and that particular problem was solved. But in General Thompson's own words, the episode had only strengthened his determination 'to get a grip on the SBS'. (Naturally, the SBS later drew him a cartoon commemorating this resolve.) Like many others in the Corps, he was concerned that the SBS was becoming just a little too semi-detached. Aside from the Falklands episode, which actually was more to do with personalities and a botched chain of command, there was little point in the Corps training men at great cost who could be taken away for other, unnamed duties at a moment's notice. And how could a land commander be expected to operate efficiently when friendly special forces were conducting missions in his area of which he knew nothing? It's a point that many an Army commander has made in the past, too. But there were those swimmer/canoeists who enjoyed dealing directly with the civilian intelligence agencies and resented any attempt to bring the branch back under the Corps umbrella. Men who envied the greater freedom apparently enjoyed by the SAS and perhaps saw the SBS not as a branch, but as a whole different service.

Maybe it made sense at the time

In 1983, Major-General Julian Thompson, now responsible for RM Special Forces, began getting a grip. First of all he moved the SBS contingent attached to Commaccio Group in Scotland back to Poole. Commaccio at the time was a near battalion-sized unit with three main functions: providing security for the Royal Navy's nuclear weapons; operational sea and riverine duties in Northern Ireland; and providing anti-terrorist protection for Britain's oil rigs and merchant shipping. It takes a force of between sixty and seventy men to retake an oil rig, of which approximately ten will be the SBS spearhead, the remainder specially trained Marines. And when the SBS returned to Poole, the specially trained Marines came with them. Poole was anyway a far better location, especially given that the ship rescue remit covered any British-flagged ship taken over by terrorists or pirates anywhere in the world. This was the time that SBS finally came to stand for Special Boat Service, with the branch divided into three squadrons: Headquarters, M (maritime) and C (conventional, i.e. all the other stuff). Each squadron contains two or more sixteen-man troops, which may actually be serving anywhere in the world.

Meanwhile the amalgamation theory was being pushed extremely hard, initially by Admiral Woodward who later, and to his credit, changed his mind. But the MOD bean-counters held sway. Aside from the reasons already given, it would allow joint operations to be more easily planned and executed, and provide a single tasking point. Military planners like single tasking points, probably because it makes for a neat organizational chart. The trouble is that you can lose a certain amount of flexibility, and often end up concentrating many problems in one place. Interestingly enough, there were many in the SAS who were also worried about the possible results of any amalgamation, seeing it as an attempt by the Royal Marines to take over the SAS itself. But in the end the Navy agreed that the Director of Special Forces would always be a member of the SAS, although a Royal Marine would probably be his second in command. Et tu, matelot.

Of course it made sense. At the time.

The next, logical stage was to combine pre-selection training. So was the next decision that non-Royal Marines could join the SBS. Funnily enough quite a few Royal Marines who went to Hereford thinking they had every chance of passing pre-selection were failed. Even those who were selected for full training were often failed, and in the case of one SBS officer on the very last day of the course. It was almost as if someone, somewhere was trying to make a point. Or didn't want officers around who weren't prepared to be good little boys and do whatever they were told. Paradoxically, it later transpired that the highest percentage of Army passes come from those soldiers who'd been 'green-hatted', that is, passed the All-Arms Commando Course and subsequently served with 3 Commando Brigade. Given that the Commando course is considerably more arduous – and longer – than the SAS pre-selection course, and given that a large part of it is concerned with developing commando, battlefield skills, which applicants for the SAS won't always possess to the same extent as someone from, say, the Paras or Light Infantry, it would seem logical that all SAS candidates should first spend six weeks on the All-Arms Commando Course, followed by P Company at Aldershot with the Paras.

It walks like a duck. Quacks like a duck. But even so . . .

Meanwhile, what to do with all those special forces personnel who weren't Royal Marines and had never been 'green-hatted', but who opted for the SBS? Especially if and when it was discovered that some of them had no aptitude for diving? Because the type of diving the SBS are required to do demands men without even the slightest hint of claustrophobia. Not men who can control it, because there always comes a time and place when no amount of self-control will slow the beating of your heart.

It was a Canadian scientist who first pioneered the technique of diving under the ice, using specially designed suits, in this case warmed by hot water pumped down from the surface. The SBS watched the news report with interest as the then very young Prince Charles was lowered through a hole in the Arctic ice. Nowadays the ability to approach land or a specific target by swimming under the ice is one of the SBS diver's more impressive accomplishments – especially at night, when you can't see a hand in front of your face and are only too well aware of the cold, hard ceiling just above your head. Imagine, too, the sensations going through a man's mind as he's attempting to attach a limpet mine to the bottom of an enemy ship in harbour

– and the tide's going out. OK, so he knows that there should be at least five feet between the ship's hull and the sea floor at low water. But suppose this is a freak tide? All that weight above, pressing down on him . . .

'It's when a trainee reaches out and clutches your hand,' said a former SC sergeant, 'that you know he might be having problems.'

And why use this technique in the first instance? It's simple. Imagine that an SBS sabotage team has been seen or captured after they've set their charges. The enemy will send down its own divers – assuming it can find any prepared to go – to check for mines. If the ship's bottom is only a scant few feet above the sea floor, the job will be that much more difficult, verging on the impossible.

How, also, will non-Royal Marines SBS fit into the overall practice of spreading SBS skills throughout the Corps, with each branch specialist also trained as an instructor? And do Army personnel progress in the SBS as does a Royal Marine? In the event, the vast majority of non-Royal Marines/'green hatted' personnel end up in M Squadron, affectionately now known as Munch, mainly responsible for maritime safety. There are rumours that some of them have been seen wearing Green Berets, despite never having done the commando course. C Squadron remains the repository of traditional SBS skills, like beach reconnaissance and blowing up enemy ships. But there are still men walking around Poole who haven't been commando-trained and so lack the essential *esprit de corps* that characterized the old SBS and all other Royal Marines branches. Like the guy arrested at sea by the SBS for drug smuggling in 1997 – a man who was actually a serving member of the SBS, but only by virtue of Hereford. Non-badged, as they say. 'It wasn't just that a serving Royal Marine, let alone an SC [swimmer/canoeist] would never have done that,' sniffed a former member of the branch. 'But even if a former member of the Corps and branch had gone bad, he'd never have been caught.' But overall, the branch and all Royal Marines felt the disgrace very badly. How do you explain to the world that the drug-smuggler wasn't really one of your own, when he was an official member of the Special Boat Service?

A modest proposal

Of course, one might have thought that if the planners were serious about combining the two Services, and so cutting costs while preserving the best in both, the SAS Boat and Mountain Troops would have been disbanded in favour of the SBS, the Royal Marines Landing Craft Branch/539 Assault Squadron and Brigade Patrol Group (now the home of the former Arctic and Mountain Warfare Cadre). Or at least that the Landing Craft Branch and the BPT were made wholly responsible for training SAS personnel in these skills. Naturally, this hasn't happened yet – at least, not at the moment of writing – for any suggestion that the permanent training cadre at Hereford aren't always the best in the world is often greeted with an outrage verging on the defensive. It really is criminal that because of Whitehall and Westminster bungling, Britain's defence planning has so often been reduced to a contest between separate regiments and Services. As it is, the result in this case appears to be the type of utilitarian solution so beloved of Whitehall and its warring ministries: the ultimate triumph of (illogical) self-interest. There again, if this type of approach is to be the way forward, there can be little argument against disbanding the RAF and apportioning its duties between the Royal Navy Fleet Air Arm, the Army Air Corps and Royal Logistics Corps. Especially as this should also cut the number of MoD civil servants, at all levels – cost accounting can be a double-edged sword. There are descriptions of how the SBS operates later on in this book, in the chapters on the Falklands and Gulf Wars. For the moment they still remain the Corps's special forces – at least, some of them do.

But what do they actually do?

A good question, and with the dearth of any best-selling books or popular films about the SBS, one that the country as a whole has been asking for many years.

(The military approach to security, by the way, can be quite touchingly naive. A classified operation or organization may be seen as still enjoying total secrecy as long as it hasn't officially been declassified; and the average grunt, or infantryman, doesn't seem to know much about it.

The civilian – political and civil service – approach differs slightly. Secrecy is assumed to have been maintained if everyone who's officially been allowed to know is on a list.

In practice, this means that even though the British and foreign media are carrying accurate stories about something very, very secret, and even though Moscow, Washington, Paris, Berlin and Ulan Bator have known all about it for years, the operation or organization will remain an official secret until it's been declassified, or the whole world is on the list. Which means that the government never has to answer any questions.

Security classifications may initially be applied to protect someone or something. But in time all too many are used to prevent embarrassment and extra work, while conferring power and importance on those with access – rather like an up-market company car, or a fitted office carpet. These general comments are made more in anger than sorrow.)

Officially, the SBS is responsible for security at sea; for example, retaking captured oil rigs or ships; pathfinding; sea-based covert operations, such as landing or collecting agents; direct sabotage against maritime targets; wartime intelligence gathering and sabotage at a strategic level; and as always, the catch-all phrase that covers all of Britain's armed forces: aiding the civil power.

Security at sea, as we've seen, is mainly undertaken by M Squadron.

Pathfinding refers specifically to amphibious operations, and concerns beach reconnaissance for landing craft operations, or hinterland reconnaissance for helicopter-borne assaults.

Sea-based covert operations are nearly always run from a submarine, although this may act as a mothership for the high-tech mini-subs the SBS has helped develop over the years. In addition to landing and collecting agents, this area can include pro-active anti-terrorist/piracy operations, i.e. getting the bastards before they get you; the reconnaissance of specific sabotage targets, if a foreign country shows signs of becoming a little frisky; and general intelligence gathering on the basis that one day, what you don't know will undoubtedly hurt you.

Direct sabotage against maritime targets means destroying ships and land installations that could adversely affect maritime operations . . . or anything that is best approached by sea.

Wartime strategic and intelligence gathering will be dealt with in a moment.

Aiding the civil power means doing whatever the politicians want. That said, a system of checks and balances does exist, so that chances of the SBS – or SAS – being used in some totally hare-brained scheme are remote. The really good news is that if they were, the British public would never know about it. But in practice, this means that the SBS has to be extremely flexible and capable of acting like civilians, in a civilian environment. You have been warned.

Wartime strategic and intelligence gathering has been left to the last because it means explaining the difference between strategy and tactics. Astute readers will have noticed that until now this subject has been carefully avoided, mainly because the definitions keep on changing and one does so want to be up to date.

Tactics is the manner in which soldier fights soldier. Strategy is the manner in which armies fight armies . . . and countries fight countries, often without first declaring war. Strategy is the beloved 'big picture'. Tactics is the specific here-and-now, often dirty, cold and wet.

Strategy is what you need to do in order to win a war. Tactics is how you do it. Taken to its logical conclusion, the only true tactic is the actual pressure of a finger on the trigger of a gun.

Strategy, as in strategic, also refers to military action taken against non-military targets. Although it's arguable that there's no such thing as a non-military target, since any target that can affect the enemy's ability actually to fight is by its nature military. Hence strategic nuclear weapons; the firebombing of Dresden; Saddam Hussein's gassing of the Kurds; the Mongol commander, Hulegu, cutting off the right hands of ten thousand Arabs in order to wipe out the Assassins (who were a thirteenth-century version of Hamas); but not the US Army playing loud rock music at General Noriega during the invasion of Panama, which was bad tactics: they should have played Leonard Cohen or *The Birdie Song*.

Is that all clear? Try this: tactics is how military units of any size manoeuvre and fight. Strategy is concerned with what those military units are doing there in the first place.

In terms of the SBS's wartime role, they are usually used to affect the outcome of the war as a whole, rather than a specific action, although their activities might well lead to a victorious battle or ten. In practical terms this means operations against the enemy's command and control infrastructure, taking out an enemy general, for example, far away from the actual fighting, or taking out a communications centre. In theory they will operate up to sixty kilometres beyond the front line. 'In theory' because front lines don't exist any more, and the SBS may well be found far further afield. Officially the SBS is a divisional asset. In reality, they are a 'theatre' asset, where 'theatre' defines any large geographical area of actual or potential military activity. At present, Britain is concerned with the following 'theatres', by virtue of the national interest (trade and political stability) and/or treaty obligations: Europe; the Middle East; West, East and South Africa; South East Asia; the Caribbean; and various useful islands scattered around the world's oceans.

In peace or war, the SBS don't half get around.

Brigade Patrol Troop

This is a formation unique to the Royal Marines, although the Para Pathfinders might well fulfil a similar role – but without the same skills and assets that the BPT can call on. Tucked away within the BPT is the Mountain Leader Training Cadre, which featured on the six-part BBC TV series *Beyond The Front Line*. In fact the Cadre had begun filling the role of a Brigade reconnaissance troop even before the Falklands War. It's now become permanent, but with considerably more responsibility. The BPT is similar to the USMC Force Reconnaissance – when used in conjunction with other Brigade reconnaissance units – but is far better trained.

To quote from the official description: 'The Brigade Patrol Troop Royal Marines provides the Commander 3 Commando Brigade with his dedicated close and deep reconnaissance capability. When used in conjunction with the other elements of the Brigade Reconnaissance

Force (BRF) it supplies a potent and sustainable asset for the acquisition of battlefield intelligence and the attrition of the enemy prior to engagement between ground forces.'

What this means is this: the BPT belongs to the Brigadier. No higher command can take them away from him, as they can with any attached SBS personnel. Usually the BPT operates anywhere within ten to fifty kilometres ahead of the main force. When used in conjunction with the reconnaissance troops of the commando-trained Royal Engineers and Royal Artillery, plus Y Troop (of which more later), BPT becomes the Brigade Reconnaissance Force and can cause the enemy any amount of serious damage. 'Acquiring battlefield intelligence', by the way, means anything from returning with a slightly shocked prisoner . . . to intercepting enemy telecommunications . . . observing enemy troop dispositions . . . capturing special equipment . . . plotting the lie of the land . . . to contacting agents.

The BPT can provide six specialized reconnaissance teams. Each member will be either a Mountain Leader (ML) or Reconnaissance Leader (RL) – highly trained, but hasn't done the ML2's course yet. But they will all be specially trained in climbing and cliff assault; survival in the worst possible conditions; sniping; long range patrolling on ski and by foot; long range communications; high altitude mountaineering; snow and ice climbing; target and route reconnaissance; primary interrogation and resistance to interrogation; and sabotage. Most of them will also have been on the Jungle Long Range Patrol Course in Brunei, and there'll be at least one specialist in desert operations. All of them are trained in HALO (High Altitude, Low Opening) parachute techniques and are strong, SCUBA trained swimmers, meaning that they can arrive at their destination by sea, land or air. One of their main jobs is to provide what's known as Initial Terminal Guidance for the Landing Force, that is, set up the beacons and generally conduct the first wave of troops ashore, before moving off into the hinterland and out on to the flank. What all this gives the Brigade is a reconnaissance asset that can be used in any part of the world, and then in the most hostile conditions imaginable.

But the Mountain Leader Training Cadre (MLTC) still remains the core of the BPT, BRF and indeed all of 3 Commando Brigade's reconnaissance capabilities. A man who's passed the ML2's course – arguably one of the longest and toughest military courses in the world, certainly without equal in Britain – is not only a specialist operative, but also an instructor. In fact, as with all other branches, his future progress will partly depend on his ability to instruct and so pass on the skills he's learned, albeit in modified form.

Like so many other skills within the corps, mountain and Arctic warfare is something the Marines quietly acquired over the years, often contrary to the then popular military wisdom. And when it finally became apparent that there was a real need for those skills, the Corps was ready and waiting in the wings to supply them. Originally, the ML Branch was known as the Cliff Assault Wing, and confined its expertise to getting troops off beaches. And although some members of the CAW were sent to improve their climbing techniques in

Austria, Norway, Canada and the French Alps – and attended snow warfare courses in Scotland and Norway – the accent was still very much on cliff assaults from the beachhead. Once men plus equipment had managed to get up a cliff, the Cliff Leader's (CL) role diminished. But by the early 1960s, the CAW had become more and more involved in cold weather warfare (CWW). By 1962 the CAW had changed its name to the Cliff Assault Troop (providing a permanent fighting nucleus), and had trained various companies from 43 Commando (now defunct) before they went to Norway on Exercise Donald Duck (12–24 October 1962). This exercise marked the beginning of 3 Commando Brigade's present responsibility (together with the Royal Netherlands Marine Corps) of protecting NATO's northern flank. Between 1962 and 1965 the Corps realized that helicopters would change the face of modern warfare. Increased troop mobility resulted in a greater need for accurate long-range reconnaissance. So in 1965 the Cliff Assault Troop were put through a reconnaissance course by the Platoon Weapons Branch at Lympstone, and subsequently renamed the Reconnaissance Leader (RL) Troop. RLs combined advanced climbing skills, cold-weather warfare skills and the reconnaissance skills of survival and sniping. At this time the Norwegians were regarded as being the experts on winter warfare. And yet the Corps found itself a little uneasy about the current Norwegian attitude to a possible Soviet/Warsaw Pact attack on northern Norway (strategically vital since whoever controls northern Norway effectively controls the North Atlantic). Discounting the possibility of battles being fought off the beaten track, the Norwegian plan was basically to guard the E9, the main road that runs the full length of the country. However, it's a foolish commander who plays to his opponent's strengths; Russian commanders were far from foolish and the presence on the Kola Peninsula of large numbers of Mongolian-raised and trained troops suggested that Soviet plans called for a less simplistic approach. So it was that the Corps utilized the RL Troop to become the experts on mountain and Arctic warfare – which they've done to such an extent that in 1986 the Norwegians requested their help in training Norway's own troops.

By 1970, the RL Troop had been renamed yet again, this time as the Mountain and Arctic Warfare Cadre, and moved to its present location in Stonehouse Barracks, Plymouth. Now it's become the MLTC.

(This whole process of naming and renaming conjures up a vision of an increasingly frustrated planner in the Ministry of Defence who discovers that every time he thinks he's managed to persuade the Royal Marines to give up one of their units he discovers, a few months or years later, that the unit continues to exist – but under another name.)

There is no ML3 rate within the MLTC, since it is primarily an instructor's branch, and all instructing in the Corps is done by corporals and above; corporals possess a 2 rating, so the MLTC trains only ML2s and ML1s. Officers take the ML2 course but not the ML1, since they don't have the time. Both courses last for nine months, and a good part of the ML1 course is spent instructing the ML2s.

Climbing can be taught. What can't be taught is an enthusiasm for mountains and wilderness. While MLs don't need to be natural climbers, or fixated mountaineers, they do need to enjoy what they're doing whether in the Arctic, desert or tropical jungle. They also need to be self-confident, assured, totally professional and only interested in the job for the job's sake: glory hunters need not apply.

Y Troop

The members of Y Troop are not, strictly speaking, special forces with a capital S and F. They will all have been trained to Reconnaissance Leader standard. What makes them so special, at least in the author's eyes, is that they're totally unique and do a job that's usually done many miles away from any possibility of fighting. Y Troop are 3 Commando Brigade's electronic warfare specialists. And how they came to be formed is typical of the way the Corps evolves. It all began during the Falklands War. One of the biggest problems facing any force is that of signals security: making sure that your own side aren't giving anything away, are keeping to agreed procedures and avoiding being located by the enemy's own detection gear. This was particularly important during the Falklands War because the Argentinian forces possessed some very sophisticated electronic warfare kit, and the men to operate it. It is the responsibility of the Royal Marines Signals Branch to monitor their own telecommunications at all levels to make sure that everything is as it should be. In the Army, this job is usually done by the Royal Corps of Signals. In the Royal Marines this monitoring takes place as close to the combat area as possible, often bang in the middle of it. One day several Signal Branch NCOs were out doing just that, when it suddenly occurred to them that they could just as easily be monitoring the Argentinian communication systems. It wasn't that the Argentinians weren't being monitored and the results evaluated; they were, but from some considerable distance away. That type of work is usually considered the responsibility of Signal Analysts, junior versions of the types you'd meet at GCHQ, rarely if ever to be found anywhere near a fire-fight. At least, not on purpose. Special forces – the SAS/SBS – will fulfil a similar role, but only at strategic level. What the Signals Branch NCOs proposed was that this could be done in a tactical area, the place where two opposing forces lock horns, looking to gain immediate tactical information. For a problem associated with the usual system is that by the time enemy transmissions had been intercepted, the radiating piece of equipment located and the information analysed, the information gained is often too late to effect the tactical outcome. The branch received the go-ahead and began experimenting. When 3 Commando Brigade returned to Britain, the experiments continued – remember, innovation is the responsibility of each individual branch. The idea made more and more sense, but specialized equipment was needed which the Royal Marines couldn't afford. So the Corps talked to the Army, specifically to the Royal Corps of Signals who became very excited by the idea and, bless them, promised the Corps all the help it needed. So while today's Y Troop is very much a Royal Marines unit, it probably couldn't have happened without Royal Signals help and support. It was that old signallers' freemasonry working again, for professional enthusiasm cuts across all Service boundaries.

Today Y Troop is responsible for advance force electronic warfare, using the type of equipment that's so highly classified they won't even talk about it. They monitor all enemy transmissions and are also capable of decoy or deception operations, working as far in front or on the flank of the main force as necessary. One of their more vital roles is using signal intelligence to ascertain dispositions – and this needs a word of explanation. Once upon a time it was comparatively easy to figure out what sort of battlefield tactics an enemy would use. Generally speaking, all armies either followed the Warsaw Pact or NATO systems, with certain variations thrown in. For example, Julian Thompson suspected that the Argentinians would follow American doctrine during the Falklands War, since so many of them had been trained there. Several Argentinian officers had also been trained by the British, but thankfully their commanders never listened to them. So 3 Commando Brigade did the opposite to what the Argentinians' had been trained to expect, with the well-known result.

It's not as simple as that any more. Potential enemies have either become far more sophisticated, or are very much more basic – even confused – all of which can cause unforeseen problems. And one of the things a commander has to know is the enemy's ORBAT, or order of battle – the manner in which the opposing force will operate in theory, and how troop dispositions have been made in practice. And while it's true that organizations like GCHQ or the NSA can provide a great deal of this information, it's not always in time for it to be of any use. Some of the terminals needed to receive NSA or GCHQ transmissions are so highly classified that there's no chance of one being allowed anywhere near any actual fighting. Some time ago one of these terminals was used on exercise. It had its own little tent, surrounded by razor wire and armed guards. People wondered if it was primed to self-destruct, like the briefing tape in *Mission Impossible*.

It would be stretching the point to say that 3 Commando Brigade now goes into battle carrying its own reconnaissance version of GCHQ. What can be said is that Y Troop fulfils a role previously only supplied by Special Forces, and at a place and time most useful to the Brigade Commander. Which makes Y Troop pretty damn special in anyone's language.

Ordeal by ice

The following is a description of a day and a night on an ML2 Course. It talks of temperatures that we've all heard mentioned on nature programmes – but until you've actually experienced them, you can have no idea how frightening extreme cold can be. One small example. The author spent a night out with the ML2s, under canvas some nine thousand feet up in the Norwegian mountains. A few days beforehand, someone had said that whatever else he did, the author should see the night sky because at that latitude and altitude the stars were awe-inspiring. That night the author managed to cook himself a meal while lying in his sleeping bag, with considerable help from one of the trainees.

Aside from natural courtesy, the course would probably have been marked down if a journalist had gone and died on them. Then came a cup of coffee too hot to drink for the moment. The author remembered the earlier comment about Arctic stars, got out of his bag and into protective clothing then took himself and his coffee outside. The stars blazed down. The author gazed at them entranced for all of two minutes before checking to see if his coffee had cooled down. It had. The coffee had frozen solid. That night the author crawled back into his sleeping bag and wondered if he'd actually wake up in the morning.

No one said it was going to be easy

The exhaustion showed when they packed up their tents one morning – a hard, frustrating business since frozen canvas is one of the most stubborn materials known to man. You could see the trainees check for a minute, summoning up the strength to kick the canvas into shape. You could see it in the way they packed up their gear to go climbing – trying so hard to summon up the will to concentrate on the job in hand. You could see it in the fixed determination on their faces to pass, to survive. A fit man is a relaxed man, and these men were too tired to allow themselves the luxury of relaxing for a single minute.

During the day the temperature had been a comfortable minus twenty degrees Fahrenheit. Comfortable, that is, as long as you stayed out of the shadows and the wind. But as the shadows lengthened and the wind freshened, the temperature plus wind-chill factor dropped to minus forty degrees Fahrenheit – cold enough to freeze bare flesh to metal instantly if anyone were foolish enough to work without gloves.

The ML2s were training at approximately ten thousand feet in the Norwegian mountains. The day had been spent practising the skills of ice climbing: how to use crampons and ice picks to claw one's way up sheet ice pitches; how to avoid grey or white ice as it's usually extremely brittle and will flake off in large chunks that will crash on to the man below. And learning that even blue or green ice, the hardest and most stable, will flake and splinter in the extreme cold.

One of the trainees had slipped on an ice pitch and cut his face open. Since wounds do not heal easily, if at all, in the extreme cold, he'd had to be taken back to base, some sixty kilometres away, hoping against hope that the injury would not prevent him from finishing the course. (Nor did it, and he eventually passed out near the top.)

But there was one particular trainee who was finding the going very difficult indeed. Harry (not his real name) had originally wanted to become an ML as much for a career move as anything else. It rather fitted in with his own image of himself, which was that of a supremely professional Royal Marine officer. And Harry was very conscious of being an officer. That in itself tends to be an un-officer characteristic, particularly among the young lieutenants in the Corps, and particularly on an ML course, where rank plays no part and has no privileges. Nor had Harry managed to develop that particular bloodymindedness that can help to counter a flawed motivation; nor did he appear to be totally at home in the mountains. To counter that, he had his pride, extreme physical fitness and possibly an overdeveloped sense of *noblesse oblige* – Harry was going to pass the ML2 course because officers couldn't fail.

But his fellow trainees had begun to doubt Harry's ability to pass; the instructors had certainly begun to doubt it; and in his heart of hearts, Harry himself had also begun to doubt his ability to pass. Unfortunately, his perceptions of how an officer should behave had prevented him from sharing his self-doubts with his fellow trainees, and even from examining them more closely himself. If only he had done so, he would – paradoxically – have found the course that much easier to take.

Generally speaking, there are two types of people who successfully complete special forces training. There are those who are the supreme naturals, who find it all quite easy. These men are few and far between.

ML2 and ML1 TRAINING PROGRAMME

ML2	ML1
September	
Cornwall – climbing, including free climbing (without ropes) at night	Instructs ML2 course
October	
Wales – climbing	Wales – upgrading own
Isle of Islay – survival training (classified) – resistance to interrogation	standards of climbing

November Mountain training	Detached to commando units for assessment as instructors
December Mountain training and Arctic techniques	Norway preparation
January Norway – snow and ice techniques	Detached to commando units as instructors
February Norway – ski patrol and resistance to interrogation	Continuing instruction
March Norway – final exercise	Rejoin ML2 course for exercise
April Scotland – climb on Ben Nevis	Scotland – climb on Ben Nevis

Men on the ML1 course who are detached to units as instructors are continually assessed as to how good they are at instructing. It doesn't matter how good they are at the skills of their trade, they must also be able to teach those skills to other Marines of all ranks. They must also show a good deal of maturity since in the Arctic, the ML1 – and to a lesser extent the ML2 – is the man to whom everyone else looks for advice, from the CO of a commando on down.

Then there are the others who do find it difficult and are forced to dig deep within themselves for the motivation, the energy to carry on. In the process they are forced to become totally honest with themselves, and by extension, totally honest with each other.

It's often obvious when a man is going through this particular 'dark night of the soul', the time when he comes face to face with himself, with all his weaknesses as well as his strengths. The man becomes a little, often more than a little, introverted as he begins to strip away the barriers built up over the years. At some point he more or less has to make the decision – not whether to carry on, but whether he deserves to carry on. For some people this process is so alarming that they refuse to face it. Possibly there is some dread secret that they can't bear to confront.

The really 'special' thing about special forces personnel is that they have all passed through this process of self-knowledge and learnt to accept themselves as they really are.

But Harry had put off and put off his inner confrontation, still would not admit it openly when he couldn't cope. His clinging so desperately to a self-image born of less trying times had come close to having him thrown off the course. And as the pressure grew, Harry had begun to fall apart. His kit had become totally disorganized. His mess tins – always a good indication of a man's morale – had become filthy, encrusted with the remains of hastily snatched meals. If it hadn't been so cold, Harry would probably have gone down with food poisoning. He had, to an extent, become the butt of the other trainees' humour – yet the ML2 course is the last one in the world that needs a natural class clown.

Ice climbing over, trainees skied back down the valley to where a collection of ten-man conical tents had been pitched directly on to the hard-packed snow. That night the outside temperature was to go down to minus seventy degrees Fahrenheit – including the wind chill – which is cold enough to worry anyone, experiencing it for the first time, that they won't wake up in the morning. But warmed by the trainees and a solitary candle, the temperature inside the tents remained at a comfortable minus fifteen Fahrenheit.

The rule in the Arctic is that one should always be in a sleeping bag at night unless there's a guard duty or some other chore to be done. Men cook from their sleeping bags, repair and pack kit from their sleeping bags – and if they could, they'd urinate from their sleeping bags. As it is, the need to urinate invariably strikes at about 03.00, and the tent becomes noisy with groans followed by curses as someone gets out of his nice, warm sleeping bag, gets dressed and makes his way outside into forty below.

All the trainees in Harry's tent had got into their bags as soon as possible. But Harry was still up, wrestling with a recalcitrant crampon. During the time he'd spent on it, the others had managed to cook themselves an evening meal, prepare a hot drink for the morning, shave, sort out their kit for the next day, and settle down for the night. And Harry still wrestled with his crampon.

It was a measure of the way the other trainees thought of him that no one had offered to help. For the rule is that one only helps a man who can help himself and help you in return. There is no way that the trainees will carry a man on the ML2 course – they haven't the energy and the instructors wouldn't let them. They would – and did – help Harry to the extent that they wouldn't let him die up there, but that's as far as it went. That meant the time was fast approaching when Harry might be faced with two choices: quit of his own accord, or be binned.

Interestingly enough, Marines appear to have more respect for a man who quits of his own accord, recognizing that he's just not up to it, than the man who's binned after it's become apparent that he's not going to finish training. First, it does take a certain moral integrity to be able to face oneself and admit that you've failed – even though it may not be through any fault of your own. Secondly, the man who hangs on and hangs on is usually trying to get his fellow trainees to get him through, giving nothing in return. As we've seen, that's one of the unforgivable sins in the Corps.

Food cooked, every last bit of snow brushed from their sleeping bags (in case it melted, then froze later, forming a cold spot), gear ready for the next day, the trainees settled down for the night. All except Harry, who had only now begun to cook his food. And again tiredness told as he tried to take a short cut in lighting his cooker, the whole thing caught fire and burning fuel covered his hand. A chorus of 'Oh, Harry' was heard in the tent, followed by 'Get you and the effing stove outside before we all go up.'

'Knew you'd give your right arm for me, mate, but you don't have to *flambée* it!'

'Playing at Buddhist monks, Harry?'

Little harm had been done except to Harry's already

damaged self-esteem. Finally, he managed to get to bed.

The next day, the trainees – after packing up their camp – were taken to learn how to traverse a snow slope, and how to use an overhanging snow cornice as a hidden observation post – not by peeping around the corner, but by burrowing inside it – something that requires a good deal of nerve, as well as skill.

Ahead of the trainees was the final exercise, 300 kilometres of escape and evasion finishing with a particularly brutal resistance-to-interrogation session. Somehow, Harry had still been there at the end, and was eventually given a provisional pass. This meant that he would effectively be on probation for the next eighteen months; if the authorities felt that he wasn't up to the job, that his climbing techniques hadn't improved sufficiently, then his rate would be taken away from him. Or if that proved difficult, he would never serve in an operational role with the Brigade Patrol Group.

On the other hand, two men who had been at the top of the course were failed when the instructors discovered that they had slept overnight in one of the huts that dot the Norwegian mountains, totally against orders. The disappointment amongst the instructors when the two men were discovered was real and perplexed. No one knew why they'd done it. The rules were that trainees stay tactical at all times, meaning snowholes and tents. The result was an instant binning. (On the bright side, one of the men applied again for an ML2 course the next year. At the latest sighting he was doing well again – and sticking to the rules.)

CHAPTER SEVEN

Don't Panic

Survival

Military survival is very different from civilian survival.

Civilian survival is essentially a matter of staying alive until someone comes to rescue you. Or of making sure you can be seen easily by potential rescuers. Military survival teaches how to stay hidden until you can make your own way back to friendly troops. Or to man an OP without being seen. Either way, you do not want to attract attention to yourself. This means that the 'hunter and gatherer' role so beloved of various textbooks has little or no place in military survival – unless you're lost in peacetime, in which case the rules for civilian survival apply.

The first rule, in either case, is *don't panic*. It's not easy to say when you're stuck out in the middle of nowhere, with nothing to eat, and with maybe an injured companion to worry about – or even a broken bone in your own body. But panic saps energy and makes you do silly things. Panic also saps the will to survive. The next rule is to use your *common sense* – and remember the difference between theory and practice.

Or, as a Marine survival instructor said:

'I often wonder why people buy all those books about living off the land, or how to survive in the jungle. There's not one person I know who can tell what an edible plant looks like after only seeing a drawing or a picture – no matter how accurate it is. You have to be shown the plant, in the flesh as it were. There's no other way.'

It's a wonderful idea, that there's enough 'natural' food out there to support one – and it totally disregards the fact that all but the most primitive peoples are farmers and herders. Nor do the majority of those who survive purely by hunting and gathering live a particularly fulfilling life, even by their own standards. The small percentage who have managed to attain a reasonably comfortable way of life have usually done so by adding trading to their skills – that and by playing host to a seemingly inexhaustible supply of scientists, explorers and journalists, all of whom provide an extra source of revenue, medicines and transistor radios. None the less, the legend has grown up that survival in the wild is possible, and without using any of civilization's tools – like guns or even fish hooks. It's not. It's the quickest way to dying unnecessarily. Probably a painful death, too.

The third rule is *take stock of your situation*. Figure out your assets – including human assets. There does appear to be such a character as a born survivor; and this person should become leader. According to the Cadre, he will be a person with common sense, imagination and stubbornness – and one who's prepared to do anything at all to stay alive. Not baulking at cannibalism if that's what it takes.

The Corps doesn't actually teach the best way of cooking human flesh. (Similar to any kind of meat really, although it does tend to 'go off' in temperate climates sooner than, say, beef or goat.) What the Corps would do is to hold up as examples of the 'natural' survivor those men in the Andean plane crash who survived by eating the flesh of their dead comrades. Of those survivors, the man who finally struggled through to get help was such a one, and even those survivors who initially baulked at the idea were, eventually, saved by the practice of cannibalism.

Hunting for your own food is, of course, a happier alternative, but unfortunately takes time and energy. And if it takes more energy to actually catch, say, a rabbit (high in protein, low in carbohydrate – not to be recommended as an exclusive diet) than you will get from *eating* it, the exercise becomes rather pointless. Similarly, while there are many edible plants around, it often does take an inordinate amount of time (and energy) to gather them. For example, nettles (boiled or dried and used as tea) may be one of the commonest plants in most parts of the country, but they seem to vanish in the more isolated areas. Fat hen, a plant that enjoyed a wide amount of publicity a year or so ago, is extremely difficult to identify. It also prefers growing close to civilization, which is irritating for potential survivors. Rosehips are a valuable source of vitamin C. But they're usually found in hedgerows, not in the wilds of Scotland. Certainly not in the Arctic during winter. Fungi may abound – but their season is fairly limited. They can also be pretty damn dangerous – and it only takes a fraction of the more virulent varieties to kill.

The Corps teaches a number of ways of testing wild plants. You can take a small amount – a very small amount – of the plant and put it between your front gums and lips. Leave it there for at least an hour, trying not to swallow too much, and if there's no stinging, or blistering, then you can reasonably assume that the plant is okay to eat. Quite how nutritious it'll be is another matter. Or you can crush a leaf or a stalk and tape it to a sensitive part of the body, say inside the armpit or in the crook of the elbow. Again, if after some time (at least twelve hours for this method) there are no unpleasant side effects, then you can be reasonably happy about eating it.

One of the Royal Marine survival experts was happy to explode a few myths:

'You know all those Japanese survivors left over from the last war that kept on being discovered in the jungles of Borneo or the Philippines? Guys who were doing their duty to the Emperor by staying alive and hidden from the enemy, who hadn't realized the war was over? Well, the papers made a big thing about how those guys had survived for so long in the ulu [jungle]. But in every case it turned out that they'd survived largely by scavenging from isolated villages, or from abandoned slash-and-burn plantations. No way could they, did they, live off the land as I understand the term.

'By and large, the only people who can truly live off the land are the people who were born to do it. Have you ever examined the upbringing of a Bushman, say? You'll find that his first twelve or thirteen years are mainly devoted to learning just how to survive, and the process carries on throughout the rest of his short life.

Now, he's got a natural aptitude for it – certainly he's born acclimatized – and he's surrounded by teachers, got nothing else to do with his time. But it does take a hell of a long time to learn those skills – and even with the Bushmen there are some guys who are never as good as the rest.

'Same goes for the Inuit [Eskimos] – and you don't find many of them using only harpoons these days. It's all rifles and snowmobiles. Again, the majority of so-called primitive tribes survive by a mixture of hunting, gathering and primitive farming – usually slash and burn. Where the hell the public gets the idea that anyone can learn, in a matter of months, to be able to survive totally unaided in the wild, any wild, beats me. They must have been reading too many books about it.'

It's unlikely that the average reader will ever have to survive in the Arctic, desert or jungle, it's unlikely that the average reader *could* survive in those areas for any great length of time – and certainly not on the basis of having read a few books on the subject. But every year, people are caught out in *temperate* wildernesses; some of them die because they don't know the basic rules of survival. Here, then, is an example of how you can survive if you followed Royal Marines teaching – with the proviso that most survival techniques are standard throughout the British armed forces.

The scenario is that you and three other civilians have been shipwrecked somewhere on the Scottish west coast. Two of your companions are injured – one with a broken leg, the other with possible broken ribs. Nothing of any note has been saved from the shipwreck. It's late autumn and the weather is atrocious – almost continual rain, often gale-force winds. The area you're in is totally deserted. There are signs that an attempt has been made recently to develop it for forestry, but those workers are long gone. You have found a single track that leads into the mainland – but you can see that it passes over the mountains that stand between you and the nearest settlement some forty or fifty miles away. You have only one set of oilskins between the four of you – and even if you had wanted to follow the track inland, early snow on the mountains has made you think twice. The most sensible course appears to be to wait where you are until you can attract the attention of a passing ship. But as few ships sail in those waters, and you won't be reported missing for at least another ten days, you have to be prepared for a long wait. What happens next? (This scenario is similar to one given Royal Marine officer candidates at a recent Admiralty Interview Board. Not many of them got it right, either.)

What doesn't happen is that one of the two fit people immediately sets off up the track on a rescue mission. The nearest main road is at least two day's walking away, which will mean spending a night in the open. Just because you go walking every weekend won't necessarily qualify you for the job of going for help. In order to make it, whoever does go has to be both fit and mature. Anyone hoping to be a hero, or simply get themselves out of trouble, should be left languishing on the beach.

More to the point, in order to make it, given the weather conditions, the walker will have to take the only set of oilskins. Whoever is left to look after the injured will spend all their time soaking wet. If an attempt is to be made, better to wait for a break in the weather – and better to be a little more prepared than you are at the moment.

The first thing you do is to move the injured people into the shelter of the trees – get off the beach as quickly as possible because beaches are rocky and slippery and if you're not careful, you'll end up with another broken leg. Once under the trees, you roughly splint the broken leg – making sure than the splint ties are not so tight as to restrict circulation, so causing gangrene, and you tape the suspected broken ribs as lightly as possible, using torn strips of cloth from the victim's own clothing. Don't use panty hose, because that can stretch or chafe. Besides, panty hose can be used as a water filter, a fish trap, string or simply to keep someone warm.

NB *Everyone who takes part in some form of outdoor activity should know basic first aid.*

Casualties reasonably well bandaged, your next problem is to keep them comparatively warm and dry while the two fit members of the party build a more permanent home. Dig down into the forest floor. Chances are that under several inches, even a foot or so, of leaves and pine needles you'll find that it's reasonably dry. Scrape out a depression, and line it with any dry foliage you can find. If necessary, tear a few live branches off the trees and beat them against a tree trunk to get rid of most of the moisture. Line the scrape with them, pile on a layer of dry – or dryish – pine needles, lay the injured on that and cover them in turn with more dry(ish) branches, pine needles and leaves. Now to look for a more permanent home. (You have, incidentally, got one working cigarette lighter with you. Which is just as well because without it you would be in very serious trouble indeed. Always carry a lighter or waterproof matches on your person when you are walking in the wild – or sailing inshore.)

The site of your home is going to be determined by a number of factors: proximity to a water supply; proximity to firewood; proximity to the beach – your most obvious source of food; and somewhere which allows easy access. Don't choose a cave high on a hill, because someone's bound to fall down it at night and you'll have three casualties on your hands.

So you look for and find a stream running down to the beach, through the forest – and through a part of the forest where there are many fallen branches. You also find a deadfall – a tree blown down by the wind with its top caught in the lower branches of another tree. It's ideal, because it's lying on a north-south axis and the prevailing wind is coming from the west. You now scavenge, remembering that there are signs that foresters or loggers have been in that location fairly recently.

Nature lovers the world over bemoan the fact that plastic and corrugated iron turn up in the most surprising places. Remember that and begin to look for them. (Plastic and metal, not nature lovers!) They'll help save your life. You're out of luck with the corrugated iron, but you do find a couple of discarded plastic sacks and some thin-gauge plastic sheeting. Fine – the sacks will make sets of waterproofs, the sheeting insulation for your new home.

Stripping away the downside branches of the deadfall, you produce a very basic tent shape. Again, you scrape out a depression on the floor, trying to slope the sides gently down to a central point. Here you dig a hole two feet deep and measuring about six inches across, which you fill with stones. *Voilà,* one drain pit. You then fill the depression with more dry(ish) branches and leaves, remembering that you're going to have to sleep on it. Drape some of the plastic sheeting over the deadfall, sandwiching it between layers of more branches and leaves. Top the whole thing off with earth and grass taken from the sides of the stream – not too soggy, but damp enough to bond to the rest of the construction. The rest of the sheeting is hung up inside the shelter so that all the water on it can drain off. Do not put it on to the ground yet.

Now for the fire. Build a raised fireplace, or fire base, with stones. Shelter it from the prevailing wind with more stones. Don't build it inside the shelter, otherwise you'll smoke yourselves out. Try to give it as much protection from the rain as possible – make it its own little tent if necessary from large branches – and build a wall around it with more branches, small logs, etc., closed on all sides except the one facing the shelter entrance. This will reflect the heat into the shelter once the fire has started. Remember to leave a space on two sides of the fire base for drying out firewood. Now light your fire.

You can always find dry tinder *somewhere* in a forest. You might have to dig for it, you might have to break up rotten trees for it, but find it you can. Kindling you can usually get from the dead lower branches of trees, particularly conifers. The most important thing is to get a big blaze going as soon as you can – aside from the physical advantages of keeping you all warm and drying out clothes, it is a great psychological boost. Once it's going well, you can think about bringing the casualties to the shelter.

Incidentally, the casualties will not have spent the past few hours lying totally alone and wondering what the hell's going on. If they haven't been in a position to see what progress you've been making, you will have taken the time to check on them and give them a progress report – loss of morale will kill them more quickly than their injuries. So when you do bring them to the shelter – waterproofed and with a fire blazing – it'll be a tremendous boost. Arrange them as comfortably as possible in the shelter entrance – don't touch the spare sheeting yet – and consider the next stage. The first thing is to dry as much clothing as possible – but don't you, the fit ones, hang around the camp site while you're doing so. Get used to the idea that you're going to spend a large part of the time feeling damp and miserable. The important thing is to have warm clothes to sleep in. So take off most of your clothes and arrange them to dry in front of the fire – make this the responsibility of the injured. Again, injured people should always be given some task to do. It helps boost their morale as well as taking some of the load off your own back. You now make holes in the sacks for your head and arms (using your teeth if you don't have a knife, since teeth are more capable of precise work than a blunt stick or jagged stone) and set off on more foraging. Check out the stream – work your way upstream for at least a hundred yards to make sure that there are no dead sheep in it. The basic rule is that you should not take water from a stream within at least a hundred yards in either direction of a dead animal, and even then you're running a major risk. If there is an animal there, and you can't safely get water from higher up, move the carcass out – using sticks, not your hands. And then, at least a hundred yards up or down stream, dig a hole some three or more feet from the river bank, the bottom three feet below the stream level. Line it with charcoal taken from the fire. The water you finally get from this mini-well won't taste particularly pure, but it will have been filtered.

Even if there is no dead animal in sight, always make sure that you take water from the fast-moving part of the stream – where the water bubbles as it moves over the little rapids. Don't drink from the deeper and more still pools.

Next you'll need some sort of water container. Well, you're lucky enough to have an extra plastic sack. Failing that, you could make one out of plastic sheeting – a circular piece can obviously be made into a hollow cone. But you must wash the sack or sheeting first as it could have contained insecticide or fertilizer, either of which can harm you. The same applies to the sacks you're wearing.

If you don't have the plastic for a water container make one out of bark and mud or clay. Don't worry what it looks like, and don't worry if it falls to pieces after a few goes. You can always make another one – it's something else the casualties can do.

By now you've earned a hot drink. You take the filled container back to the camp site. The fire's blazing merrily – and you feel thankful that you had the foresight to put several loose stones between the fire and its base. By now, they've become red hot. You're also glad that you had the foresight to gather a few nettles, which you found in a sheltered part of the stream bank. These have been dried over the fire to the point that they crumble to the touch. The stones are placed as gently as possible into the container and naturally the water begins to heat up. You put the stones in one at a time, taking each one out as soon as it's transferred its heat to the water. Natually, you'll have chosen stones that are easy to pick up using two pieces of stick as tongs. If you don't take the stones out, chances are that their weight will break your container. Certainly by the time the water boils, you'll have more stones than liquid. As the water begins to warm up, crumble the dried nettle leaves into it – you'll need a biggish handful for the four of you. Alternatively, you can boil up fresh nettles, eat them and drink the liquid.

However, man cannot live on nettle tea or nettle soup alone. Nor, with the sea so close, will you need to. Limpets scraped or smashed from the rocks can be boiled or eaten raw. When the tide goes out, search rock pools for tiny crabs and shrimps – if nothing else, they'll flavour the nettle soup. There are all sorts of edible shellfish available – any doubts, and apply the taste test (a small bit held between the front gum and lower lip for an hour or so – no blistering or stinging, and it's reasonably safe to eat).

Aside from the seashore, in the ground, you've got worms. The preferred Royal Marine way of eating a worm is to first dip it into a glass of good brandy. Assuming that you don't have one, dry them out over the fire first and then add them to your soup.

And then there may be fish in the stream. Don't waste your time trying to fashion fish hooks or fish spears out of wood or thorns. You haven't got the time or the skill. What you should have done is fashion a basic stone knife by chipping an edge on it, much as your ancestors once did. Failing that, look for broken glass washed up on the shore, or razor shells. You should also check the shore for bits of nylon netting, plastic containers and driftwood.

Armed with some sort of knife, you move to the stream. Try to pick an area where fast-moving rapids empty into a fairly shallow broad area. If you've found some nylon netting, fix it across the stream at the downstream end of the still water, making sure the base is anchored firmly to the bottom. The top should be clear of the water level. If you couldn't find any nylon netting, you've got a little bit of construction work to do. Dam the area of the rapids – not completely, but enough to restrict the water flow by at least eighty per cent. Dig out the bottom of the stream so that there's a clear channel running downstream. Then you wedge branches at the furthest end of the channel so that the water can get out but nothing else. Or build a loose dam across the stream, with small spaces for the water to escape. Now go upstream beyond the first dam and move towards it, in the water, making as much noise and movement as you can. The idea is to drive the fish before you, to channel them into the current caused by the small gap in the first dam. (Ideally, that gap should result in a small waterfall so that the fish find it difficult to get back upstream.) Work the same stretch of water at least half a dozen times – starting a little higher up on each new approach. Finally, plug the gap in the first dam. The water in the stream below should now drain away through the channel you've dug. And if there are any fish there, they'll either be stranded on the bottom, or caught against the net if you had one. But do search the bottom of the stream very carefully – some fish will burrow into the mud, others will hide under stones. Fresh-water crayfish are fine to eat, but it's best to stay away from fresh-water mussels.

Small fish can be cooked whole – just be sure to cut off the fins and tail. A larger fish can be killed quite easily by simply putting your finger – or two fingers – into its mouth and jerking its head back, so breaking its neck. Cut off the head, fins and tail – these can be used for soup, but don't eat them: too bony. Now you can either scale the fish or not – if you haven't scaled it, you can't eat the skin. Cleaning it's no problem – a quick cut along the bottom of the body, running from the anal opening to the gills, and scoop out the contents. Your fish can now be grilled or wrapped in damp leaves and mud and baked in the fire embers. Or it can be boiled in the ubiquitous nettle soup – but first it should be wrapped in a piece of cloth. When it's done, unwrap the fish, which will fall apart, pick out the bones and put the fish back into the soup. And don't boil unscaled fish, even in a cloth.

Any food remains should be buried in a gash pit you've dug at least thirty feet away from the shelter. Site it near, but not next to, the latrine you will also have dug. This should be as far away from the camp site as possible and nowhere near the stream. Have two separate areas, one for urinating and one for defecating.

Everyone uses them, even the person with a broken leg. Hygiene is vital – damp moss, large leaves can make an acceptable substitute for lavatory paper, but you should still wash your nether regions at least once a day – downstream from the water point, using sand from the stream bottom or seashore. If you do wash in sea water, make sure you rinse in fresh water afterwards to avoid salt sores. Incidentally, sea water is an excellent cure for many fungal infections like athlete's foot. Similarly, if someone is cut and it looks like turning septic, a poultice of boiled seaweed will help – there's a good chance that some of the seaweed will contain iodine.

And now for bed. Everybody bar none goes to the latrine before settling down for the night. The fire is then banked down – dry wood with dampish wood on top. A supply of kindling is handy to produce a blaze from the coals in the morning. If you have any doubts at all about your collective ability to keep the fire going, someone must always stay awake to make sure it doesn't go out. Work on the premise that you only have the one match or the one go with the lighter. Next, the two of you who have been doing all the work get into your dry clothes. Take the plastic sheeting and put it over the branches and leaves covering the floor. Use just enough to cover the floor only. Position the two injured in the middle, and the two fit ones on the outsides. Then wrap the remainder of the plastic sheet around all of you, but not so tightly as to prevent sweat vapour from escaping. The combined heat from your bodies should keep you all warm.

So far so good – you've all survived maybe your first two days in the wild. But the injured are causing concern – one of you has to go for help. Spend the day before you go reconnoitring the track you're going to use. Start at first light, go as far as you can until midday and then come back. This is because when you do go, you're going to leave at night – hopefully a clear, bright night – in order to let you cross the mountains by daylight.

So you need to know as much of the track as possible since you'll be using it in the dark – remember the old military maxim: time spent in reconnaissance is seldom wasted. The day before you set off, dead grass has been gathered and dried before the fire. This you'll stuff inside your clothing, next to your skin. If it's possible, swap your shoes for a pair a size larger, and stuff those with dried grass as well. It'll probably itch, but it should keep you warm. Take the oilskins, but don't wear them unless you absolutely must – again, your sweat vapour will condense inside and you'll get damp. If someone has a pair of thick woollen socks, you take them. Either you can use them as gloves, or – more importantly – if it suddenly freezes and you find yourself struggling over ice, you can put them over your shoes and they'll help to stop you slipping. Get a good stout stick and set off.

The plan is for you to follow the track. And you'll do just that. Even if it looks like going in the wrong direction, you stay with it. The only possible reason you can have for leaving it is if you see a house or an obvious road in the distance. If you do leave the track, you will leave some indication of the direction you've gone in – preferably a cairn of stones. Certainly it will be a sign that everyone back at the camp knows about. Similarly, as you go along the track, try to blaze some sort of trail every half mile or so – a few stones in arrow formation, say, pointing in the direction you've come from. The reasons for all this are fairly straightforward.

First, it may well be that your companions are rescued within a few hours of you setting off – and the rescuers will want to set off up the track after you. So if you have left it, they'll want to know in what direction – in case you've fallen into a gulley, or got trapped in a marsh. Similarly, if you're discovered by rescuers coming from the other direction – or even a passing shepherd – it'll be important to know what direction you've come from. Particularly if you're dead or unconscious when found – from exposure or from a fall. If you have any writing materials on you, make a note of where your companions are and put it into a dry pocket.

One final point. If you do go off the track and on to rough moorland, stay away from the edges of pools or surface streams – that's where the marshes are. Overall, don't travel unless you can see at least ten feet in front of you on the track and at least a quarter of a mile in front of you in open country – enough so you can recognize landmarks. And the next time you're sailing in rough weather, make sure you have a waterproof survival pack always handy. Similarly, never go hiking unless you're prepared to spend the night in the open – take a survival bag, chocolate, nuts and raisins, a lightweight portable stove, metal cup, tea bags and sugar, torch, waterproof matches, compass and map. At the most you're looking at possibly three extra pounds to carry. It could save your life.

Minimizing the risks

There is a deal of difference between military and civilian survival. But some of the lessons taught by the Royal Marines do have particular relevance to civilians, particularly those involved in outdoor activities like walking, climbing or skiing. And while it's true that many walkers, climbers or skiers can take care of themselves, a surprisingly large number can't – especially the 'amateurs', those who are possibly trying it for the first time. Or even experienced people who think that they don't have to worry too much because nothing bad will ever happen to them. Well it can, and it does. Every year, people suffer injury because what was intended as a gentle stroll in the foothills or across the moors turned into a nightmare when a sudden mist came down. Or a rain squall blew up out of nowhere. Or someone slipped, twisted an ankle – and a two-hour stroll turned into an eight-hour slog.

In Britain, many people die every year from exposure and some may even suffer frostbite, quite needlessly. Another big killer is avalanches. Reading this chapter will not necessarily save your life in these situations, but if it succeeds in making you more aware of the dangers, and how to overcome them, it'll prove well worthwhile. Aside from anything else, understanding the dangers gives you much more freedom to enjoy the wilderness. Before looking at exposure, frostbite and avalanches in some detail, a word of warning: don't try to do anything that's beyond your capabilities. Not many people can walk a straight ten or fifteen miles across open moorland without experiencing some difficulty, so don't take on too much. And always be prepared for the worst. It might be a beautiful day, but carry a pack containing at least waterproofs and a survival bag – plus spare compass and a map – if you're planning a long trek.

This chapter is based on the teaching of the Mountain Leader Training Cadre. However, not all their rules have been given, for the simple reason that too much knowledge could encourage a false sense of security. For example, the Cadre teaches a 'safe' way of crossing an avalanche slope – simply because that type of action is sometimes necessary in time of war. But there is no safe way of crossing an avalanche slope. The MLTC's method isn't so much safe as a way of trying to minimize the risks. Again, much of this teaching presupposes a high degree of physical fitness, together with a basic knowledge of first aid and already well-honed survival skills. It's unreasonable, and probably downright dangerous, to expect the average reader to possess those attributes. The last thing one wants to do is give anyone a false sense of security – the feeling that 'now I've read the book, I can go and climb the nearest mountain'. Or disappear into the wilds for weeks on end. Or ski away from the accepted trails and runs. There is a world of difference between knowing something in theory and being able to do it in practice – in a way it's similar to the problem of being able to recognize an edible plant from a book illustration.

So don't, please, rush out and make like Royal Marines in the wilderness on the basis of reading this chapter. If you're that keen, join a recognized club. Or there's always your local Royal Marine Reserve. . . .

Exposure

Exposure is when the 'core' of your body cools down below the level at which your brain and muscular system can operate. It's caused by a combination of: cold; wind; moisture in the air (rain, snow, sleet, fog, spray, etc.); wet clothing; tiredness; anxiety; illness or injury; overexertion (carrying too heavy a load, trying to walk/climb too far, etc.); not enough food or water; bad planning and simply trying to do far too much.

The symptoms are easily recognizable. First of all the victim feels chilly and his skin feels numb. He will start to shiver and find that his muscular co-ordination has begun to suffer, particularly in the hands. Next, he'll begin to feel weak, the lack of muscular co-ordination will intensify, he'll begin to stumble and show signs of mild confusion.

The next stage sees him stumble even more, to the point of falling over. Both his thoughts and speech will appear slow and halting. Then he stops shivering. However, he's unable to walk or stand and appears both incoherent and irrational. From there he lapses into semi-consciousness, with dilated pupils and a weak heart-beat or pulse. Finally he lapses into complete unconsciousness and will probably die due to heart failure.

The only way to prevent exposure is to fully understand and be able to recognize all its symptoms – and to realize that you don't have to be caught out in an Arctic blizzard to die from it. You should also make sure that when you're out in the wilds you always carry the right equipment; that you eat and drink enough, remembering that salt reduces dehydration, so use it; that you're properly dressed and that you understand the wind-chill factor: that the wind can produce the effect of freezing temperatures even though the actual temperature is well above freezing.

Treatment is reasonably straightforward, but you must be able to recognize the early symptoms, as the body temperature continues to fall for one to two hours after treatment has begun. If someone is showing the first-stage symptoms, get them to the nearest shelter as soon as possible, get them into warm, dry clothing – build a fire if at all possible – and give them warm but not hot drinks, since too hot a drink will cause tissue damage. This is assuming that the nearest shelter is reachable before the second-stage symptoms occur. If it's not, you go right into the second-stage treatment.

You stop and provide some sort of shelter – even if it's just a large survival bag. Get the casualty into dry clothes and zip two sleeping bags together if you have them. Then get the casualty into the bags with a companion who's also dressed in dry clothes. Give the casualty any sugary food you have and a warm drink. When they recover, continue to treat them as injured and get them back to civilization – preferably on a stretcher if it can be arranged – as soon as possible. Never, ever give alcohol to someone suffering from exposure, since it will only worsen their condition. (If a friendly St Bernard appears with a keg of brandy use the brandy to light a fire and put the dog into the sleeping bag with the casualty.)

Do remember to cover the casualty's hands, feet, ears and nose, as anyone suffering from exposure is very susceptible to frostbite – and remember that ten per cent of your body heat is lost through your head: don't wait for really bad conditions before putting on a hat.

Frostbite

Frostbite occurs when parts of your body either freeze or partially freeze. It usually attacks the face, hands and feet. There are three degrees of frostbite. First, frostnip or localized frostbite, showing itself as dead white areas on the skin. Second, the skin ultimately blisters but doesn't die. Third, the flesh under the blisters dies.

Frostbite is obviously caused by cold temperatures. But the combination of cold plus wind plus moisture is the most dangerous – and the moisture can even be your own perspiration. The first symptom you'll be aware of is a feeling of cold and pain. Then comes the change of colour – white spots – in the skin, followed by total insensitivity in the afflicted part. Finally, you'll find it difficult to move your hand, foot or whatever.

The problem is that the insensitivity associated with second- and third-degree frostbite is very similar to the 'dead' feeling associated with frostnip. And the blisters from second-degree frostbite or the wounds from third-degree frostbite show only after the limb has thawed out. Many people have lost a finger, a toe and more simply because they thought it was only frostnip. So if you're in conditions that can cause frostbite, you must be particularly observant regarding yourself and your companions.

You can avoid frostbite reasonably easily. Make sure you always dress according to the weather conditions and what you expect to be doing. Try to avoid sweating (sweat=moisture=frostbite). If you have sweated, try to keep going until your clothes are dried out – and then put on extra clothing when you stop for a rest. Keep as active as you can, even down to exercising your face muscles, fingers and toes every now and then. This will help to keep them warm – and help you to detect any numb areas, i.e. the onset of frostbite. Make sure you get into shelter before you're exhausted. If you're camping out, brush all the loose snow from your clothes before you get into your tent – and make doubly sure that there's no loose snow inside your sleeping bag. The snow will melt, your clothing will get damp and you'll probably get frostbite the following day. Always make sure you've a spare pair of dry socks and mittens – and that they're both clean and dry. Eat as often as you can and take a warm drink as often as you can since this helps to keep your body temperature up.

Immediate treatment for frostnip or frostbite is fairly basic. Get out of the wind and put a warm hand on the part of your face – or that of a companion – that is frozen. If your hands are affected, put them under your armpits. If your feet are affected, you have to wait until you get back to proper shelter. Then take off your boots and socks and put your feet against the warm skin of a friend (which is when you discover who your friends really are). Whatever you do, don't rub the affected part – with snow or anything else. Don't use any ointment on it and don't expose it to any direct heat like a stove or a fire, since chilled flesh is very easily damaged.

The Royal Marines have a little mnemonic to teach the principles of keeping warm in extreme conditions:

Keep clothing	Clean
Avoid	Overheating
Dress loosely and in	Layers
Keep clothing	Dry

Avalanches

Every year, hundreds of people die needlessly in avalanches – needlessly, because if they'd followed basic safety rules they'd never have been caught in an avalanche in the first place. Or if they had, they'd know how to have the best chance of surviving. By virtue of their long experience in Northern Norway, the Royal Marines have become somewhat expert about avalanches – here, then, are their basic rules for survival:

- Keep as high up the slope as possible, since most avalanches are triggered by their very victims.
- Stay away from snow accumulation areas during and immediately after a snow storm.
- Remember that lee slopes are particularly prone to 'soft-slab' avalanches.
- Never travel alone and never expose more than one person in your party to an avalanche risk at any one time. And don't assume that just because someone else has successfully crossed a risk area that it's safe.
- Stay well away from snow cornices and the slopes beneath them.
- Remember that snow fractures take place on the convex part of the slope, and that the most dan-

gerous slopes are those between thirty and forty-five degrees.

- If you do cross beneath a potential avalanche slope, keep well below the tree line – and listen to what the local experts have to tell you.

- Watch out for avalanche warning signs, like snow booming, heavy snow balling, fresh avalanche tracks, cracks appearing in the snow when you stand on it or even mini avalanches from your boots or skis. Remember that the deeper the snow, the greater the danger. Snow settling at more than one inch an hour means avalanche danger.

- Remember also that snow takes up to three days to settle properly, longer in cold weather and if it's out of the sun.

If you are caught in an avalanche there are a few things you can do other than offering up a quick prayer and wishing that you had been a better person. Get rid of your rucksack and skis (if you're wearing them) as soon as possible, although if you're a good skier you may be able to ski out of trouble. Then take the time to assess the avalanche and where you are in relation to it – at the top, bottom or middle, or to one side, and where your best escape route is. But don't try to escape immediately. Wait as long as you can, because the more snow that goes past you in the beginning, the less there'll be to bury you at the finish. If you are caught up in it, and swimming movements are possible, don't try the breaststroke or crawl. Apparently the most effective is the double back stroke with your back to the force of the avalanche. But overall, just try to ride it out as best you can, conserving your strength for the last few minutes. Keep your mouth closed and if you're in a powder-snow avalanche, cover your face with clothing to help you to breathe.

You'll feel the avalanche begin to lose momentum and settle. At this point don't try to fight towards the surface, just make an air space around your head so that you can breathe. When everything comes to a stop, don't immediately dig upwards. You may be digging downwards. There are two ways of finding out which direction is up. You can spit and see which way the saliva flows, or you can urinate and feel which way the urine goes. Whichever method, you dig in the opposite direction – and don't panic, because the greater the panic the greater the chance of developing exposure and indeed tiring yourself out. Dig slowly and sensibly, resting whenever you feel tired, to conserve your strength.

CHAPTER EIGHT

First Draft

Leaving Lympstone is a joyous time for YO and recruit alike: the end to a very difficult year or six months, the right to be called Royal Marine Commandos – and the feeling that they've earned that right. But the joy is often tinged with a little apprehension, for as trained Marines their standards will be expected to be that much higher. No excuses, or rather allowances, are made for the fact that the man's still only a beginner (not that many allowances ever were made). Life in a troop will be altogether harsher and more unforgiving for the newcomer until he begins to show signs of coming to grips with his job.

The young officer who goes to a troop for the first time will be left under no illusion by his OC or commanding officer that his studies are still continuing. The Corps's attitude on this is best illustrated by the Company Commander (a major) who called a new troop sergeant into his office to explain his duties as he, the OC, saw them.

The sergeant was there to run the troop and train the new troop officer. If the sergeant had any problems with the new officer, he was to let the OC know via the sergeant major, and the OC would sort them out instantly. But this approach does not mean that a sergeant can take liberties with a new officer; the troop sergeant's job is to train that young man up to the point where he could run the troop himself. Unfortunately, young officers never have long enough with a troop to fully learn this specific aspect of soldiering as well as they – and their men – would like.

The relationship that develops, or should develop, between officer and sergeant is one of the most important in the officer's life. It must be based on mutual trust and respect. And since the sergeant will often be several years older than the officer, a certain fatherly – or rather, big brotherly – attitude is bound to creep in.

In describing this, one senior officer remembered the time that his troop first invited him out for a drink with the lads. This is a time-honoured Corps custom which lets an officer know that he's been accepted – and on this one occasion ended with the sergeant throwing the officer over his shoulder and carrying him back to the Officers' Mess. A slightly extreme example, perhaps, but it does emphasize that a troop sergeant does have a responsibility for a new officer – a responsibility to keep him out of trouble as much as teach him his trade.

The other major problem for YO and young Marine alike is discovering how little they do actually know, no matter that they've passed out of Lympstone. Time was that Marines first sent to a unit were put in the charge of an experienced Marine, whom they had to refer to as 'Trained Soldier' for at least the first year. Things are a little bit more relaxed these days, but a sprog Marine is still a sprog Marine – and if he's spared the annoyance of being told what to do by someone without any rank, he has to work that much harder on his own, has to accept that much more responsibility since he's very much thrown in at the deep end.

Suddenly, he discovers that the thirty-miler is nothing in comparison to what he'll be expected to do in Norway. The three-week Arctic Warfare Course is not too bad, and the accent is very much on the practical, so it can be an absorbing, though tiring, time. But when he gets to a unit and discovers that he's expected to be able to ski (cross country) fifty kilometres, carrying anything up to a hundred and twenty pounds, that's when it really begins to hurt. It probably takes at least two years to build up the stamina needed to operate effectively as a Royal Marine in Northern Norway, and at least that long to learn how to ski cross country properly. After all, with over a hundred pounds on one's back, it's that much easier to fall over – and that much harder to get up and get started again.

But there again, there is considerable criticism within the Corps that Marines do carry so much weight on their backs, since it often leads to knee and back problems at quite an early age. Part of the problem is that young Marines tend to go out with more kit than they really need. But the major problem is that military equipment is traditionally heavy and bulky and is often developed by people without any real practical experience. It also takes far too long for the latest technology to filter through, and the military research and development departments often appear to be stubborn in their refusal to buy direct from an outside source without spending time and money on their own development procedures. The simple truth is that many companies do manufacture kit for the civilian market (admittedly the civilian specialized market of mountaineering or trekking) that is usable by the military, albeit with a few minor changes. This is one reason why the supremely professional units, like the Royal Marines or Paras, turn a blind eye to unofficial equipment as long as it's being used for practical reasons and not because it's become fashionable – an attitude that is intensely disliked in many military research and development circles, since every non-issue pair of boots worn, for example, points out their own failure to provide the right equipment.

Two classic examples are the boot, combat, high, responsible for so much trench foot and shin splints – and the 'new' SA 80 rifle. Great sight, excellent sling but the rest is garbage. Not only does it break too easily, but it needs far too much maintenance. There are times when it simply isn't possible or practical to clean your rifle. Imagine, for example, that you're in the jungle and lying up in close observation position, which could mean only a scant few metres away from an enemy position. You can't strip and clean your weapon because you might need it any moment. With the SA 80 this means risking a jam, as does not continually cleaning the little blighter in the desert. What's required in all types of warfare is a rugged, simple and very forgiving weapon which will fire under the worst conditions – the old SLR was a classic example of the genre, as was/is the Kalashnikov. In fact the Corps wanted the American AR 16 system, as did many Army regiments, but the SA 80 it had to be. Even after the MoD had ironed out various problems – like a plastic stock that tended to splinter in extreme cold, or any left-handed shot risking the loss of an eye – the weapon was nowhere as good as its rivals. But at least it was cheaper – on paper.

However, the Royal Marines take comfort from the fact that the USMC is in a far worse position, particularly vis-à-vis Norway. Not only do they suffer from the 'it must be American' proviso that affects the use of all kit by US forces, the USMC also forbids any non-issue kit. So whereas a Royal Marine in the field in Northern Norway will be wearing Norwegian Army roll-top shirts and thick sweaters, possibly British civilian climbing boots, even Finnish cross-country ski boots – all kit designed to keep a man safe in those conditions – the US Marine will be suffering from the issue of cold-weather gear that might be effective in the High Sierras, New England or even the Yukon, but has little or no relevance to weather conditions in Norway – where it can be minus forty Fahrenheit one day with driving blizzards, and plus two the next with driving rain, followed by a sudden freeze back down to minus forty.

One of the more stimulating aspects of Arctic training for the novice YO or Marine is the ice swim. Its origins lie in the supposition that at any time, any man may break through the ice into the water below – and that he'd better know how to get himself out of it. The technique is fairly simple.

For demonstration purposes, a Mountain Leader has already cut a hole in the ice with a chain saw (they used to use explosives but it all got out of hand. . .). Then, the same Mountain Leader demonstrates the technique.

He skis towards the hole in the ice, fully equipped,

and into the water. (Not leaping in while holding his nose and crying 'For the honour of the Regiment!' as one British soldier did recently.) He then kicks off his skis, shrugs his way out of his bergen – which he tries to put on to the safe ice around him – and then uses his ski-poles (which must never be let go) to lever his way out of the water and on to the ice.

Depending on the weather conditions, his mates then have up to two minutes to get him out of his wet clothes (which will probably freeze solid as soon as he's in the open air) and into a dry set.

But breaking through the ice on a river or lake is not the worst danger. At least you have a reasonably good chance of getting out, assuming that the current isn't so strong that it will sweep you away; that you're fit enough and well trained enough to withstand the sudden shock of falling into extremely cold water; that your companions have the presence of mind to be getting dry clothing out of their bergens while you're still struggling to get out of the water; or if you're alone, and have managed to get your own bergen to safety, that you've had the forethought to have a dry change of clothes safely wrapped in a waterproof bag. Assuming all that, falling in shouldn't pose too much of a problem.

As a Mountain Leader explained: 'There's no real way of knowing if river or lake ice is safe or not – although after a time, you do develop a sixth sense about it. But breaking through into the water isn't the worst thing. Up in the mountains there are a lot of reservoirs or small lakes that go on draining away long after an ice crust has formed. So you get an ice roof and nothing beneath it. Break through that, and it's a long drop to the rocky floor below.

'And you also get the situation where the weight of the snow has pressed the ice surface down below the waterline, and the water has seeped on to the surface from the edges of a lake. So there's maybe six or seven feet of snow and beneath that several feet of slush before you reach the ice. It's possible to drown in that slush, or at the best get wet feet, which can be pretty dangerous.

'Basically, if you're not on skis you should be on snowshoes outside the camp, unless you know the area very, very well. Even then, you can be walking on what you think is hard-packed snow and suddenly you'll hit a soft spot – easy to sprain a knee or an ankle that way.'

Snowholes are dug into a deep bank of snow and there is a strict procedure for digging them. First of all the troop leader finds an area with enough snow by using his avalanche probe. Then the men who're going to do the actual digging take off as many clothes as they can – on a bright day, they'll strip down to trousers and boots. This is because they'll sweat while digging and it's very hard to dry clothes in minus temperatures. Two shovels are always used, although only one is ever inside the snowhole at any one time – you'll see why in a moment. Two men carve out a doorway, usually about six feet high by three feet wide. The size doesn't matter because it can be filled in later. One man then digs straight into the side of the bank for some ten to fifteen feet, depending on how many men are going to be living there. When he's got as far as he needs to, he turns to his right and begins to dig out a shelf, starting at about waist level. This will be expanded, and will form the living quarters. The roof will be arched and ribbed, so that any melt water will run down the ribs, rather than drip on to the men. He'll probably also carve a niche for a candle and finally poke a ski pole through the roof into the open air to provide ventilation.

Obviously, the same man or men don't do all the digging. But someone always stays outside with a spare shovel in case the hole collapses and buries the digger in snow. Similarly, a shovel is always left outside in case the hole collapses when it's being used, and the sentries can then dig out the occupants. Finally, the main doorway will be partially blocked off from the top, making a tunnel through which you have to crawl to get inside.

The living accommodation – the shelf – is higher than the actual floor of the snowhole and since warm air rises, the coldest air remains below the shelf. The candle must be lit whenever the snowhole's being used. At night, there will always be a minimum of two sentries who will check the snowholes together, making sure that there hasn't been a cave-in or that the occupants aren't suffocating because of cooker fumes or a blocked ventilation shaft. When the sentries do check the snowholes, one of them always waits outside – again, in case of a cave-in. Survival in the Arctic is an infinite capacity for taking pains.

Cooking is done with naphtha-fuelled stoves, since paraffin will turn to jelly at very low temperatures. Arctic ration packs feature freeze-dried food, lots of coffee and tea, the ubiquitous packet of Rolos – someone in the MoD must have shares in the company that makes them – the ever-present five pieces of hard lavatory paper, plus the usual assortment of glucose tablets, matches, etc. There can be an awful sameness about Arctic ration packs, but for all that, the food ain't bad – in fact, the rolled oatmeal flakes mixed with dried apple flakes can be warmly recommended for breakfast, particularly since they can be cooked in the bag, as it were – boiling water poured directly into the packet, rather than mixing everything together in a mess tin, which only means more washing up.

There is a set procedure for cooking in the field, designed to save time and fuel. The main meal is always at night. Using the buddy system, one man cooks for two, both usually sharing the same mess tin, which saves washing up (i.e. saves fuel and time). While the meal is being eaten, water will also be boiled – and that will be used to make a hot drink which will be put in a Thermos flask for breakfast. So come breakfast, all the men have to do is prepare their oatmeal and apple flakes, and make another hot drink in the Thermos to be carried with them for use during the day. Hot water is never used for shaving – 'wet' razors should never be used in the Arctic since nicks and scrapes do not heal properly in low temperatures. Battery razors are the rule, and every man must shave – not because beards are illegal, but because a beard disguises the telltale signs of frostbite.

The camp itself will either be a snowhole, a bivvie made from tentsheets (lozenge-shaped pieces of canvas, carried one per man, which clip together in a variety of configurations depending on the size of 'tent' required), or possibly a brushwood bivvie, constructed so that the heat from the fire burning outside is reflected back into the bivvy by an improvised windbreak.

Norway is a tough few months – as an officer explained: 'People at home [civilians] don't realize quite how hard the boys work out here, or what the conditions are like. Look at 42 Commando – very few of those guys will see a woman for the whole three or so months they're out here. It's one continual slog, with only Saturday night – and not always then – to relax in the NAAFI bar. Sunday, they're getting ready to go back out in the field again. 45 Commando have it a little bit easier because they're nearer a major town [Narvik] but even then the opportunities for rest and relaxation are extremely limited. It's the equivalent of mounting a major polar expedition year after year. The pressures on the Corps are so great that we don't have the time to make it easier for the lads.'

This brings us to the subject of Royal Marines misbehaving when they get amongst the innocent Norwegian civilians. Every year there's at least one horror story, usually wildly inaccurate, which has the unfortunate result of breeding a very defensive attitude on the part of the Corps. As witness the legend that Royal Marines from 45 Commando had once taken part in a homosexual orgy in a Narvik bar – and without charging admission, too. The story was first run by a local, left-wing newspaper and picked up six weeks later by the British tabloid press who did actually call the Royal Marines PR office, but quickly realized that the explanation given was an obvious cover-up. It had to be a cover-up. If it wasn't a cover-up, there wouldn't be any story.

What actually happened is that a group of Royal Marines, admittedly in a, well, happy frame of mind, treated other drinkers to a rendition of 'Old MacDonald had a Farm' and 'Zulu Warrior', two Corps favourites which, as any rugby player will tell you, for some reason result in someone stripping off all his clothes. Slightly crude maybe, but a homosexual orgy it's not.

Certainly the local Norwegian authorities do go to some lengths to protect their womenfolk from the invading barbarian hordes. On one – perhaps apocryphal – occasion, the mayor of a town complained to the Marines that girls younger than the legal age of eighteen were drinking in the Royal Marines bar.

'Well,' said an ever-helpful Marine, 'maybe you should give us a list of all the girls who are old enough to drink in our bars, that way we'll be able to double check their ID.'

The mayor thought this a great idea and produced a list of names and addresses. Within twenty-four hours every woman on it had been issued a personal invitation to a Marines party the following weekend.

'I don't know why the mayor got so upset about it,' said one of the Marines, 'we were only trying to be helpful. . . .'

The basic kit

For those of you who are interested, here's the basic kit that a Royal Marine will carry in his bergen (actually a Crusader-pattern rucksack) in the Arctic:

Minimum one day's rations
Duvet boots

Quilted suit (known as a Mao suit)
Waterproof outers
Sleeping bag
Waterproof bivvie bag
Sleeping mat
Mess tin
Metal mug ('gaffer' or masking tape applied to the mug edge to avoid burning the lips)
Spoon (preferably strong plastic to avoid heat or cold burns)
Fuel can (naphtha)
Cooker
Funnel
Snowbrush (hard-bristled, used to brush snow off equipment, clothes, sleeping mat, etc.)
Unbreakable Thermos flask
Battery shaver
Toothbrush and paste
Candles (used to provide basic heat and light inside a snowhole or other bivvie)
Meta-tabs (to light stove)
Moon boots
Six pairs of spare socks
Spare shirt
Camouflage outers
Tent or tent sheets
Toe caps

Some words of explanation:

Duvet boots are ankle-height padded bootees, used when the Marine is inside his snowhole or bivvie – he'll probably also wear them for sleeping, as he will the quilted Mao suit, although this can also be worn under his outer clothes if he's on sentry duty. Moon boots are very large boot covers, made from canvas and an insulating material. They can be worn over regular boots or duvet boots. For example, if a man needs to use the latrine in the middle of the night, rather than go to all the trouble of putting his regular boots back on, he can simply slip on the moon boots over his duvet boots. Toe caps are canvas and rubber 'slip overs', and are worn when the man is fairly stationary outside, since the foot loses heat from the toe area more quickly than from the heel.

There is, naturally, an optimum way of packing a bergen:

To begin with, all spare clothing is rolled up tight and secured with masking tape – this makes it considerably easier to pack. The sleeping bag plus waterproof outer is carried at the base of the pack – duvet boots rolled up inside.

Starting from the bottom of the bergen, the man will pack his spare clothing, then his windproof bottoms (he wears the windproof jacket), then a spare shirt, spare socks, moon boots, Mao suit, and his flask on top – in other words, all items accessible in the order they're most likely to be needed. In the large pocket on the back of the bergen will be packed a snowbrush, battery shaver, toothbrush and paste and tomorrow's breakfast meal – items that won't be needed until last thing at night. In the left-hand side pocket will be the fuel can, cooker, funnel, Meta-tabs and candles – all inflammable items together. His sleeping mat goes under the hood of the bergen, and if he's carrying a tent or tentsheet(s), they'll be secured on top. Finally, inside the top pocket will be his spare hat and gloves, in plastic. All the clothing items will also be carefully waterproofed.

Now, as to how he's dressed:

First, he'll be wearing thermal underwear. Then, at least two pairs of thermal socks. Then, standard trousers, probably a Norwegian-style, roll-neck shirt, a pullover, windproof jacket with hood (hood rolled down inside the collar when not in use), boots with a special welt for cross-country skiing, Gortex gaiters from boot to knee, inner gloves, outer wool gloves and windproof glove covers. He'll also be carrying special gloves used when filling the stove or touching bare metal. He may also be using camouflage mittens.

Obviously, not all this clothing will be worn at the same time – he'll discard this or that layer, depending on how hard he's working. When gloves are not being worn, they're always tucked inside the top of his jacket – they're never put on to the ground, nor is the hat.

Finally, one other piece of kit which for all its simplicity is probably one of the finest inventions ever – the headover. Essentially a wide woollen sleeve, the headover is worn around the neck as a scarf. It can also be worn over the neck and head, or twisted and worn around the ears. It's extremely versatile and whoever thought of it deserves a medal.

The Marine will also be carrying a shovel, his personal weapon, spare ammunition, probably spare ammunition for the section weapon or spare batteries for the radio, snowshoes and any other little creature comforts that he feels like carrying. Altogether, he'll be carrying on his back and on his person well over a hundred pounds in weight. And incidentally, the total cost of his Arctic kit is well over £1,000 – which makes losing it an expensive business.

The total weight of all his equipment – official issue plus personal items – is likely to exceed one hundred and twenty pounds – probably nearer a hundred and thirty. That's approximately nine stone to be carried, on skis, up and down hill, day in day out for three months in weather conditions ranging from freezing rain to blizzards, from plus seven degrees to minus twenty or thirty Fahrenheit. It's hardly surprising that the average age of a Royal Marine rifleman is twenty.

CHAPTER NINE

Royal at War

The Royal Marines have never been found wanting in bravery. They do not, however, believe in the pointless death – the *folie de grandeur* of the death-or-glory charge against insurmountable odds that tends to obscure the fact that something has gone seriously wrong.

The Royal Marines do not believe that dying well is the point of war. They believe in winning; in achieving their objectives as safely as possible, by using every means at their disposal. Not least of those means are the courage and aggression of the men who fight – but never in isolation, never divorced from intellect and imagination.

A senior Royal Navy officer who served 'down South' found himself extremely impressed by 'Royal's caution': when the Marines were faced with an enemy strong point, they'd assess the problem before rushing off to attack it. They always considered how to take an objective with the minimum of their own casualties. Interestingly enough, this rarely if ever slowed up the Marines, since there was less chance of them becoming bogged down by enemy fire. A Royal Marine officer remembered watching his men fighting along the top of Mount Harriet, and being amused by the way, whenever they reached an Argentinian fortified position, they'd duck round behind the nearest rock, maybe have a quick puff at a cigarette, think about the problem for a few minutes – and then suddenly swing into action with tremendous speed, efficiency and even ferocity.

This almost surgical approach, this recognition that war is really about destroying the enemy and that the Marines were there to take back the Falklands by destroying the Argentinians, did not always sit well with those at home who were unwilling to accept the reality that fighting a war means killing.

Nor, for that matter, does the style of the Royal Marines always sit well with soldiers from elsewhere in the British armed forces (who often complain of Royal's arrogance) since the Marine approach requires great independence and initiative – sometimes bloodyminded independence and initiative – on the part of the most junior Marine. This does not always please those accustomed to a more docile type of soldier – nor indeed those accustomed to a more docile type of officer. Not that this applied to relations between the Marines and the Paras – one of the more gratifying results from the Falklands was the recognition of the respect that existed between the Royal Marines and the Parachute Regiment.

As a Marine senior NCO said at the time: 'The Paras are pretty much like us, really. Very professional and simply wanting to get the job done as quickly as possible. There'll always be rivalry of some sort – it's only natural, particularly amongst the young soldiers and

Marines. But the relationship between the older guys is excellent. I know that there's no one else I'd rather go into battle alongside. If there is a difference, it's that we probably think a little bit more about a problem at troop and even section level. But that reflects the training and the different roles – Paras have to go for broke because you can't really disguise a Para drop, whereas we're trained as much to infiltrate – to be that little more sneaky. But I don't like to hear anyone slagging the Paras off, even a Marine. They're good soldiers and our guys'll fight alongside them any time.'

Royal Marines like to characterize themselves as 'the thinking man's infantry'. Add to this their ability to improve – their flexibility – and their discipline plus their endurance, and you have many of the reasons why the Falklands were recaptured when all academic military logic suggested that the Argentinians could have performed far better – or even possibly won.

Of course, the effectiveness of the Royal Marines as a fighting force had been demonstrated when Argentina invaded South Georgia and the Falkland Islands. On South Georgia, the Royal Marines shot down one troop-carrying helicopter and one Alouette helicopter, and crippled one corvette. On the Falklands, Royal Marines had taken out one Amtrak (armoured, tracked personnel carrier), captured three prisoners (Argentinian special forces who'd broken into Government House) and wounded seventeen and marked three known kills – excluding those men in the Amtrak. All this without losing a single man.

During the planning for the Falklands War, 3 Commando Brigade were promised that the air battle would be won before the landings were to take place. This didn't mean that the entire Argentinian Air Force would be wiped out, merely that casualties due to air attacks could be kept to manageable proportions. As a result, it had been planned that the Task Force ships would be kept in close logistical support and that *Canberra,* in particular, would be used as a field dressing station. Unless they remain secret, amphibious landings require air parity if not superiority. In the event, this was not the case.

For a variety of reasons, notably the fear of submarine attacks which kept ships at sea, it hadn't been possible to test-fire Rapier (anti-aircraft missile system) during April 1982 at Ascension Island where the Task Force had gathered to restow, to train and to wait for intelligence being gathered on South Georgia and the Falklands by the SBS and SAS (who, officially, began operating in the Falklands on 2 May). Not only that, but Rapier had been crammed into the ships' holds, with people scrambling all over it, and experiencing temperatures that ranged from 120 degrees to 0 degrees Fahrenheit on the trip from Ascension to the Falklands. This is not the best way of treating sensitive electronic equipment.

As a result, when Rapier was finally deployed following the landings on 21 May, out of the ten Rapiers on shore, only six were actually ready to fire, in spite of the almost heroic efforts of their crews to get them into position and into commission. It was estimated afterwards that it would have needed at least twenty Rapiers to do a proper job – still not totally denying air space to the Argentinians, but certainly not incurring the losses that the task force did. And then there was the bravery and skill of the Argentinian pilots themselves.

As one of the Rapier officers said: 'We'd trained for a war in Germany, with aircraft coming in at 250 feet doing a maximum 350 knots. And there were those guys coming in at 100 feet doing 450 knots. It took us a little time to work out how to handle them.'

Eventually the Rapier crews and the Harrier pilots did work out how to handle the Argentinian aircraft. But not until the *Atlantic Conveyor* (among others) had been sunk. And not until Task Force ships like the *Canberra* had been sent away to the edge of the Total Exclusion Zone, well out of Exocet range. Sunk with the *Atlantic Conveyor* were three Chinook and five Wessex helicopters – vital for moving stores and equipment. Sailed away with the *Canberra* were all the unit stores of 40 Commando, 42 Commando and 3 Para, plus the equivalent of 90,000 man days of rations. The *Canberra* was not to make its reappearance until hostilities were over – which obviously denied its use as a field dressing station.

It's bad enough to lose so many stores, so much vital equipment at the best of times – when you're in a position to be easily resupplied. In the South Atlantic, thousands of miles away from any resupply base, it could have been, probably should have been, fatal. That it wasn't was as much due to a little-known Royal Marine unit as it was to the fighting qualities of the Royal Marines or the Paras themselves. And this unit's very existence emphasizes how different the Marines are.

LOGISTICIANS – according to Cdo Log Regt
The role of the logistician in war is appreciated by very few. The Commando Logistic Regiment Royal Marines explain it in this way (without claiming original authorship):

'Logisticians are a sad, embittered race of men, very much in demand in war [but] who sink resentfully into obscurity in peace.

'They deal only with facts but must work for men who merchant in theories. They emerge in war because war is very much fact. They disappear in peace because in peace, war is mostly theory. Generals are the people who merchant in theories, who employ logisticians in war and ignore them in peace. Logisticians hate generals. Generals are a happily blessed race who radiate confidence and power, feeding only on ambrosia and drinking only nectar. They stride confidently forward in peace, invading countries simply by sweeping their hands over a map. In war they must stride more slowly because each general then has a logistician on his back who may, at any moment, lean forward and whisper: "No, you can't do that." Generals fear logisticians in war and try to forget about them in peace.

'Romping happily alongside generals are strategists and tacticians. Logisticians despise strategists and tacticians – who in turn do not know about logisticians, until they grow up and become generals. This they usually do.

'Sometimes a logistician gets to become a general. And then he must associate with other generals

> whom he hates, while listening to tacticians and strategists whom he despises, while on his own back he now has another logistician whom he fears. This is why logisticians who get stars on their shoulders also get ulcers and cannot eat their ambrosia.'

Commando Logistical Regiment Royal Marines

Based at Chivenor, North Devon, Commando Logs is a truly unique formation. Nothing else like it exists anywhere in the world. It was formed between July 1971 and January 1972, when the logistical elements from 3 Commando Brigade and administrative elements from HQ Commando Forces were gathered together and given their own separate identity.

Commando Logs exists to supply second-line medical, transport, ordnance and workshop support. Once landed, it can keep the Brigade operating without resupply for at least a month. It's composed of Royal Marines, plus Army personnel from the Royal Engineers, REME and Royal Logistics Corps who've all been 'green-hatted' – and all of whom bar none are among the most enthusiastic soldiers you could hope to find.

'First it's because the lads have all won a green lid,' explained a RLC officer. 'Which means they've done something the average infantry grunt in the Army will never do. And then it's because they get so much more responsibility. They also get an enormous kick out of working with the Brigade. There are a few Army sergeants around who've spent their entire service career with Commando Logs, only going back to their own Corps for promotion and skills upgrading courses.'

For most of the Royal Marines, Commando Logs was the obvious choice when their knees began complaining and they wanted to develop skills useful in civilian life. Generally speaking they tend to be older than their Army counterparts, and a little more laid back. But once again, the morale is as high as you'll find anywhere.

Commando Logs exists to supply 3 Commando Brigade. But it can also produce – at literally a moment's notice – a smaller version of itself to support an individual commando that's operating independently or some distance away from its parent formation. And there can be no doubt that much of the success of the Falklands was due to the fact that Commando Logs coped brilliantly with disaster after disaster.

Soldiers – and Marines – in the front line are usually aware of the logistics units supplying them only when something doesn't turn up. Or the wrong thing turns up. Otherwise, they tend to treat resupply as a matter of course. In the Falklands, in the vast majority of cases supplies did turn up when and where they were needed. Considering that the Brigade was spread out over the islands and that the lines of communication were harassed by Argentinian aircraft, and that Commando Logs had to supply all the units on the islands, and that transport was at a minimum as were supplies themselves, this was nothing short of miraculous. Except that a Marine would say that it was just another example of a unit doing the job they were trained for – no big deal, that's how they earn their pay.

Commando Logs works by first establishing a Beach Support Area (BSA), where stocks are held close to the beach landing area or port. Then, as the Brigade moves forward, Commando Logs follows and sets up a secondary supply area – the Brigade Maintenance Area or BMA. If the forward unit gets very far forward, Commando Logs establishes a third supply area – the Forward Brigade Maintenance Area (FBMA). In the Falklands, the FBMA had been set up at Teal Inlet to support the final attack for Port Stanley – a distance of some thirty-four kilometres from San Carlos, over some of the worst terrain in the world. And all the while the BSA was under attack from Argentinian aircraft. Again, it was the flexibility of Commando Logs that allowed them to cope with the situation, that and the ability to stay cool at a moment of disaster, and immediately start figuring out a change in plan. In fact these are the same characteristics that you would find amongst all Marine units – but without Commando Logs those units wouldn't have been able to survive a day, let alone take Port Stanley.

Royal in action

From Commando Logs to the commando himself – and a couple of examples of why a Royal Marine has the reputation that he does:

It's difficult and extremely dangerous to attack an enemy machine-gun position. Theoretically, it needs at least one troop (about thirty men) in three sections. One section provides covering fire while the other two attack.

These are odds of thirty against three or four – and even then victory cannot be guaranteed. Certainly the troop will suffer casualties.

The Argentinians were well supplied with machine-guns. And the Royal Marines decided not to use troop attacks on them, but simply to take them out using anti-tank rockets.

'It was', as a Marine senior NCO said, 'something that the boys decided very quickly. It didn't come down from on high as a new piece of tactical thinking, it originated with the average Marine in a rifle section who didn't see why he should get shot up because that's what the book said. To me it's a good example of Royal using his imagination and initiative. And of course, being set up the way we are, it was dead easy for the guys to get the sixty-sixes or eighty-fours they needed [66 mm Light Anti-Tank Weapon and 84 mm Medium Anti-Tank Weapon, used at section level]. Like, I would imagine that in an army regiment, it wouldn't be so easy. But with us, all the guys had to do was go and ask for the kit, and there it was. And then we had crateloads of rockets being sent down from the UK. With never a tank in sight.'

42 Commando used anti-tank rockets against Argentinian machine-guns in its attack on Mount Harriet – except in this instance, MILAN anti-tank missiles were chosen. J Company, 42 Commando, set up a diversionary attack, hoping that the Argentinians would reply with all their machine-guns, thus pinpointing the enemy positions. And, since MILAN did not have night sights at that time, 42 Commando would use mortar illumination to aid the MILAN crews' aim at their

targets. It was a superb piece of tactical improvisation and worked like a charm. J Company started firing, the Argentinians replied with everything they had, up went the illumination shells, in went the MILAN rockets, and heavy-machine-gun post after heavy-machine-gun post disappeared in fragments. Meanwhile, K and L Companies were also attacking Mount Harriet – but from a totally unexpected direction. Here again, they fought the classic 'thinking Marine's battle' – no senseless charging, taking their time to work out how to destroy an enemy position and then doing so with tremendous speed and aggression.

'The thing I'll always remember about Royal down South,' said one of the Navy attached personnel, 'was coming across the lads in 42 one day, up in the mountains, sitting down and having a laugh and a joke with their CO. And it was absolutely pissing down and freezing cold. No one liked it, of course – but it wasn't the CO's fault and it wasn't the brigadier's fault that the weather was so lousy – so why bitch about it? They just took whatever was thrown at them and went on and did their job.'

When the Falklands had been won and the British forces were on their way home, a check was made on the Royal Marines who had been up in the mountains. It was found that in each unit, between seventy-five and ninety per cent of all men had developed trench foot to a greater or lesser extent. Trench foot is one of the most painful injuries imaginable . . . the Royal Marines had proved once again that it's the ability to endure that wins battles as much as anything else.

Knowing the enemy

Once again, rumours are circulating about Argentinian soldiers being killed after they had surrendered. This is what really happened:

British forces would fight forward against Argentinian fortified positions. As they advanced, at least one Argentinian trench would fly a white flag. This would be ignored, as bitter experience taught that a white flag simply meant that a single trench – often a single man in a single trench – had surrendered, and that the other Argentinians did not consider that white flag binding on the rest of them. Not even for the few minutes it would take to clear up the matter.

Again, the Argentinian forces had an unfortunate tendency to fight until the very last moment, trying to kill as many British troops as they could, until their opponents were literally at the edge of their trenches. At which point they would immediately try to give up – would either throw their hands in the air, or cower at the bottom of the trench. Too little too late, and very few survived.

You cannot expect a man to suddenly rein in his aggressions, particularly in the confusion of a firefight, particularly if that firefight was at night as so many were. And when you think about it, the Argentinian attitude was either incomprehensibly naive – or totally arrogant. In effect they were saying, 'It's OK for us to kill as many of you as we can, but the moment we can't kill any more, you must stop trying to kill us.' That, with a little admixture of Latin pride that demands a man make a gesture before giving in – never mind that the gesture involved the killing of other people.

War is not a place for immature, adolescent fantasies. It is a place where each man is judged by his actions, not his intentions. And the moral for any future enemy of this country is that the time to surrender to the Royal Marines or the Paras is before you kill any of them, not afterwards. Either that, or run away. That said, the Royals were impressed by certain Argentinian troops, especially the Special Forces captured at Top Malo. Argentinian pilots, too, were considered extremely brave and skilled.

CHAPTER TEN

3 Commando Brigade

There's only one principle in war, me lad, and that's this. Hit the
other fellow, as quick as you can, and as hard as you can, where
it hurts him most, when he ain't looking!
**Advice from a Sergeant-Major to Officer Cadet, later
Field Marshal, William Slim**

One of the main advantages the Commander of 3
Commando Brigade has over his Army counterparts is
the control of all his own assets. The Brigade is a totally
self-sufficient fighting force, which means that everything comes under one roof. For example, 29 Commando Regiment Royal Artillery is not part of a
divisional artillery formation. Nor is 59 Independent
Squadron Royal Engineers (reinforced in wartime by
131 Independant Commando Squadron RE) independently answerable to any higher Engineers organization.
It makes for an extremely flexible Brigade. It also calls
for enormous skill on the part of the men who run
Brigade headquarters.

The image of the slightly thick soldier or Royal
Marine is one still religiously believed by many civilians.
The fact is that there are few civilian jobs that carry the

same amount of responsibility as leading a platoon or troop in wartime. When it comes to ensuring that an entire brigade runs smoothly, often in the most appalling conditions, the people responsible need to be highly intelligent, imaginative and determined. You can double that for an amphibious brigade, as often as not operating thousands of miles from home. This is a point recently discovered by Wall Street, of all places, where two manuals quoted in the opening chapter have taken over from the rather esoteric, *A Book Of Five Rings,* written in 1645 by the Samurai warrior Miyamoto Musashi, and long beloved as a source of strategy and tactics by Japanese executives. So it is that many American executive briefcases now hold copies of the warfighting and campaigning manuals produced by General A. M. Gray USMC, along with the obligatory copy of Sun Tzu. How much more switched-on, then, must be those men who've studied Musashi, Sun Tzu and Gray for real, and learned how to apply the concepts as a matter of life and death. Which leads into the inescapable fact that there are more Staff-trained officers to be found at 3 Commando Brigade's head-quarters than is comfortable for a journalist asking questions.

A brief word of explanation. Staff College is where all officers go if they want to move up the promotion pole to at least major. There are further courses for more exalted beings, but the initial one is roughly the equivalent of doing a year's MA in a complex subject. Staff College is not for the dumb or the faint-hearted. It's where an officer learns the business side of war, and how to control larger formations of men and material than are found at troop or company level, as well as theory, large-scale tactics, military doctrine and so on. And 3 Commando Brigade really does have more Staff-trained officers than its Army equivalent, if only because it's larger than an Army Brigade and necessarily more complex. Nor will these officers all have been to Staff College in the UK. Just as long as another country teaches standard NATO doctrine, and its staff college is an acceptable standard – and the officer in question has learned the language, if necessary – then the Royal Marines are perfectly happy to see someone go off to Norway, the Netherlands, Malaya or America. It all helps add to the collective wisdom of the Corps. Naturally, anyone going abroad is expected to do as well as if he'd stayed at home. Similarly, there are always foreign officers to be found attached to HQ 3 Commando Brigade, where they're expected to do a real job. There is nearly always a member of the Royal Netherlands Marines, because 3 Commando Brigade is also the major unit of the UK/Netherlands Landing Force when reinforced by Dutch Marines and shipping. Often a member of the USMC is present and, nowadays, an officer from the French Marines since Britain and France are now the European leading defence players. The Corps will unashamedly learn from anyone.

Here is a diagram of how 3 Commando Brigade Royal Marines is organized. A few points to note are:

As mentioned earlier, in time of war the Brigade is reinforced by units from the Royal Netherlands Marines Corps, of which Whisky Company is permanently attached to 45 Commando. The Brigade would also be reinforced by men from the Royal Marines Reserve, plus Territorial Army gunners, engineers and logistics personnel, all of whom have been commando-trained. Royal Marine Reservists also serve with the Brigade in peacetime. 45 Commando also has Sphinx Battery, 29 Commando Regiment Royal Artillery attached permanently to it, which developed out of 45's primary role as spearhead guardian of NATO's northern flank.

HQ and Signal Squadron is the Brigade Commanders' C2 (Command and Control) unit. Borrowing a phrase well known in military circles, the concept of Command and Control can be likened to 'managing chaos'. For as everyone knows, no plan survives contact with the enemy. Or anything very much else, come to that. It was said earlier that speed and flexibility are two hallmarks of commando operations. Without a highly professional HQ and Signal Squadron, neither of these is obtainable. The Brigade uses four electronic communications systems:

Combat Net Radio (CNR), which operates in HF, VHF and UHF bands, and is how all units within the Brigade communicate with each other. Currently represented by CLANSMAN, to be superseded by BOWMAN before 2000.

Data Communications, mostly used for transmitting blocks of tabulated data via modems fitted to CNR. Used mainly for transmitting logistics information.

Satellite Communications, which allows the Brigade to communicate with the UK from anywhere in the world.

The Organization of
3 Commando Brigade Royal Marines

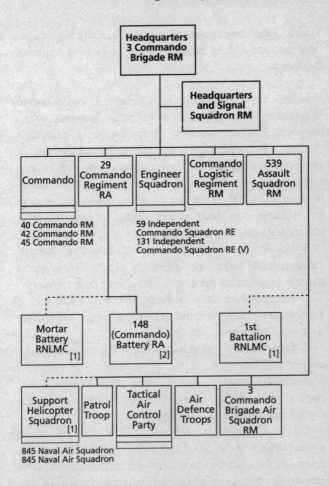

```
┌─────────────────────┐
│ Headquarters        │
│ 3 Commando          │
│ Brigade RM          │
└─────────────────────┘
        ┌────────────────────┐
        │ Headquarters       │
        │ and Signal         │
        │ Squadron RM        │
        └────────────────────┘
```

| Commando | 29 Commando Regiment RA | Engineer Squadron | Commando Logistic Regiment RM | 539 Assault Squadron RM |

40 Commando RM
42 Commando RM
45 Commando RM

59 Independent
Commando Squadron RE
131 Independent
Commando Squadron RE (V)

| Mortar Battery RNLMC [1] | 148 (Commando) Battery RA [2] | 1st Battalion RNLMC [1] |

| Support Helicopter Squadron [1] | Patrol Troop | Tactical Air Control Party | Air Defence Troops | 3 Commando Brigade Air Squadron RM |

845 Naval Air Squadron
845 Naval Air Squadron

1. For operations and exercises only.
2. Naval Gunfire Forward Observers.

Also used to communicate with long-range reconnaissance units and/or special forces.

Trunk Communications, which are basically high capacity, flexible and extremely secure links to a superior formation.

Which leads inescapably to **Command and Control Warfare** (C2W). We all know what happens when telephones aren't working properly, or a computer crashes, or traffic lights on a main road develop a nervous breakdown. If a communications failure can affect civilian life to such an extent, imagine what it does in warfare. C2W is the art of making sure the enemy can't do to you what you're doing to him. C2W is concerned with four main areas:

1 Psychological operations, for example, broadcasting information designed to affect the enemy's morale or question the sanity of his own commanders.

2 Deception, such as making the enemy think you're somewhere you're not, or are either larger or smaller than you really are.

3 Operational security, defending against the enemy's C2W.

4 Physical attacks against the enemy's command and control assets, such as a headquarters or communications complex; landlines; or intelligence sensors.

In 3 Commando Brigade, C2W is the main responsibility of the SO (Staff Officer) 3 C2W who will normally be a captain from the Signals Branch and who effectively fights an electronic war on behalf of the Brigade Commander.

Tactical Air Control Parties co-ordinate and direct close air support aircraft. At the moment of writing, two TACPs are operating in Bosnia.

Royal Marines Police Troop is, as the name suggests, the Corps's own cops. The branch was originally formed in 1964 when 3 Commando Brigade RM was stationed at HMS Simbang in Singapore. Initially this was little more than a Provost section, equivalent to the Army's Regimental Police system. Naturally, Royal Marines being what they are, the branch developed new skills and with them, new responsibilities. Yet another example of the Corps ethos: adapt and improve – or die. Nowadays the branch operates wherever Royal Marines are to be found in any large number, and several places where they aren't – it also works on occasion for the Foreign and Commonwealth Office, especially in terms of close protection – that is, body-guarding. In its garrison police role, the branch acts much like the Royal Military Police, which includes both criminal investigation and patrolling hot spots on a Saturday night – plus obtaining and organizing evidence for use in Courts Martial. On exercise or in time of war, the role expands to include the traditional route reconnaissance and signing; advising on the control of PoWs, refugees and stragglers; security advice and assistance; liaising with local, civilian police and other military police organizations; and of course, close protection. The branch trains at the Royal Military Police school in Chichester, also with civilian police agencies for advanced or specialized subjects, such as Scenes of Crime or Advanced Investigation. It's one of the smallest branches in the

Corps, is for Royal Marines NCOs only, and is usually commanded by a 'green-hatted' Royal Military Police officer. To say that the branch enjoys the affection of the average Royal Marine is stretching things a bit far. But it sure as hell enjoys his respect. And why does the Corps need its own police in the first instance? First, there's the requirement that all men serving permanently with the Brigade should be 'green-hatted'. Second, the Brigade is designed to be as self-sufficient as possible. Third, the Corps in general is expected to operate in various far-flung corners of the globe, which requires a certain degree of expertise that can only be acquired by experience.

Medium reconnaissance is provided by the Army, currently B Squadron The Household Cavalry, operating SCIMITAR and STRIKER armoured vehicles. It is the only unit within the Brigade not to be commando-trained. But such is the cavalry charm – and, it must be said, sheer professionalism – that no one seems to mind. Or even notice. It's to be noted that the cavalry are among the most enthusiastic of all attached Army personnel. Aside from the challenge of negotiating an armoured reconnaissance vehicle into an LCU or on to a Mexeflote, and thence landing on a beach, the cavalry adapt extremely well to commando doctrine and tactics. As witness Operation Dragon Hammer in the early Nineties, which was a series of NATO amphibious exercises conducted in the Mediterranean. A squadron of Household Cavalry infiltrated high into the French hills and managed to ambush – and for exercise purposes, destroy – an entire battalion of United States Marines.

Elements of Special Forces usually refers to the SBS, although the SAS also operates with the Brigade, as it did during the Falklands. However, special forces are always considered to be at least a divisional asset, may find themselves being tasked by a higher formation, or directly from the Permanent Joint Headquarters at Northwood.

Weapons. Aside from personal weapons, each Commando unit – 40, 42 and 45 – is equipped with:

24 x MILAN anti-armour missiles, range 1,950 metres.

9 x 8lmm mortars, range 5,650 metres.

9 x 51mm mortars, range 1,000 metres.

100 x 94mm anti-tank weapons.

13 x sustained fire machine-guns.

16 snipers armed with the L96, 7.62 rifle.

18 x 0.5 Browning machine-guns.

12 x 0.5 infantry support weapons.

It's to be remembered that all these will probably have to be carried on someone's back, although the 0.5 Browning machine-gun can be mounted on top of an ATV. Contrary to popular myth, this weapon cannot be hand-held and fired from the hip without spraying bullets everywhere – mostly into the sky.

Even in peacetime, there are over 4,000 personnel attached to 3 Commando Brigade; twenty-eight helicopters, four hovercraft, six landing craft, eighteen raiding craft, two hundred and thirty-six tracked vehicles, one thousand and twenty-five wheeled vehicles; heavy plant equipment and armoured recce vehicles; twenty-four 105mm guns, fifty-four light and medium mortars, twelve anti-aircraft weapons systems. And it all has to be ready to go at a moment's notice. So the next time you hear a business fat cat justify yet another bonus on the grounds of hard work and wonderful professionalism, spare a thought for 3 Commando Brigade Royal Marines' staff officers. Most businessmen couldn't even begin to cope with the job.

Royal Marines Reserve

The Royal Marines Reserve belongs in this chapter because its members can and do play an active role within 3 Commando Brigade.

Do you run five miles in under thirty-eight minutes, twice a week? Can you do a circuit of forty press-ups, followed by sixty sit-ups in two minutes, followed by thirty-five burpees in one minute, followed by seven pull-ups, and a five times sixty-metre sprint in sixty-two seconds? (But you are allowed to rest for a full minute between each exercise.) You can? Good. You are now at the necessary fitness level to join the Royal Marines Reserve. Assuming you can also swim. And assuming that they want you in the first instance.

There are harder Territorial units to join. There's the SAS, for a start. And the . . . and of course the . . . let's not forget the . . . and what was its name? Seriously, the Commando Gunners and Engineers work towards a similar level of fitness. It's just that the Royal Marines Reserve have this theory that really, they should be some sort of standard bearer. Why? Not to lord it over their pongo cousins, that's for sure. Like all members of the

Corps, the RMR is quietly proud that any non-Marine should want to win a Green Beret. No, the reason is that the RMR measure themselves against the regulars. And actually, it's far harder to win a Green Beret as a Reservist. They have to pass the same commando tests in the same times as the recruits at Lympstone. They have to be able to demonstrate a similar competence in field craft and other military skills. True, their drill might not be to the same standard as the Kings Squad – at least, not at first. But it will be in time. A member of the RMR has to do most if not all of his fitness training on his own, without a kind PTI or PW corporal offering encouragement every step, or heave, on the way. Which is one reason Royal Marines Reservists can be slotted into a fighting company as a matter of course on exercises, or even on active duty. Royal Marines Reservists are not expected to hang around Brigade headquarters making the tea. Like regular Marines they can and do join specific branches. Like the SBS. Or Landing Craft – 2 Raiding Troop is an RMR unit – Drivers, Signals, Platoon Weapons, Assault Engineers, PTIs, Mountain Leaders and even Tactical Air Control Parties. A few years back, during a NATO exercise, the Norwegian Army was zealously guarding a bridge over a fjord. They'd been told the SBS planned an attack, and so concentrated on every possible clandestine approach. So much so that they ignored the battered old Ford Transit van with three unshaven, scruffy Brits who seemed to be making for Sweden. RMR SBS one, Norwegian Army nil. They never saw the Reservists place the dummy charges, either. True, most Territorial soldiers and

Reservists take their duties seriously. But the RMR are expected to be able to do the job of a regular Marine.

All Reservists start out as recruits, and it takes them on average a year to gain a Green Beret. All promotion is through the ranks – an average eight years to be commissioned, and a Reservist officer has to pass both the POC and AIB, unless he's a former RM officer. Former officers from the rest of the Armed Forces may also keep their commissions – assuming they gain a Green Beret and demonstrate a sufficiently high standard in all other areas. There is no easy ride. In fact, the Reserve will tell you that they look for a civilian who's a cut above the regular Recruit or Young Officer. Well, they would, wouldn't they? Except they mean it. In how many other Reserve units would you find a biologist serving alongside a traffic engineer alongside a doctor alongside an unemployed scaffolder alongside a man who's steadfastly refused all promotion over the past twenty years – possibly because in his day job, he's a civil servant with the equivalent rank of a lieutenant colonel? Which only goes to prove that the Civil Service can't be all bad.

At present, the RMR has a theoretical strength of nine hundred and fifty, all ranks. In fact there are nine hundred serving Reservists, of whom sixty per cent are fully trained. In real terms this makes the RMR one of the most successful units in the Armed Forces in terms of recruitment and retention. In London alone there are two hundred Reservists out of a possible two hundred and twenty, with only twenty-five per cent under training – a success rate that would be envied by many regular units in the Armed Forces, let alone the Reserves.

So why do they do it? What makes a man take on a

commitment that will eat into so much of his spare time? Fair enough, he gets paid for it, and at the same rate as a regular Marine. He'll even get a bounty if he completes one hundred training periods plus two weeks' continuation training in a year. (An evening counts as two training periods, and a weekend as eight.)

Royal Marine Reservists are men far more attracted by the challenge than the glamour. The Corps has always disliked the idea of becoming glamorous, or even fashionable, since the desire for either won't help anyone complete the training. There's also the sense of comradeship, and the fact that the RMR offers such a broad range of skills. Most other Territorial or Reserve units are comparatively limited, single skills organizations. But the RMR has to reflect as many branches, and skills, found within the Brigade as possible. Yet overall, it appears that the opportunity to face as many continual challenges as one wants remains the prime motivation.

CHAPTER ELEVEN

The Feminine Angle

Very few Royal Marines could finish their initial training at Lympstone without the support of their families. Similarly, very few Royal Marines could carry on with their job without the support of their wives. And just as it takes someone out of the ordinary to be a Royal Marine, so too are their wives really rather special

One of the Corps clichés is that Royal Marines tend to marry nurses or teachers. Like most clichés, it contains more than a grain of truth.

'I suppose the reason is that nurses and Royal Marines have a similar sense of humour,' said one woman, herself a nurse and married to a Royal Marine sergeant. 'Plus they're both used to coping with enormous pressure, so they've got a lot in common.'

Another possible reason occurs – that the jobs of a Royal Marine, or a nurse or a teacher, all require some sense of vocation, of service. Certainly most women married to Royal Marines tend to be far removed from the stereotyped domestic, regimented, dependent service wife – a semi-fictitious character in any event.

Most women married to Royal Marines show a

refreshing independence. Most pursue their own careers and have a far greater say in the running of the household, have far greater responsibility within the relationship than most of their civilian sisters – if only because of the amount of time their husbands spend away.

'I had to deal with selling and buying a new home, and arrange the move all on my own,' remembers one wife, 'and I'm sure that in the early years of our marriage I knew more about handling domestic problems than my husband did – things like mending plugs and fixing a leaking pipe.'

Sudden responsibility can come as a shock. As another woman said: 'The very day we were due to move to our new house, he was sent off to the Falklands. And that was very shortly after we were married. I'd always lived with my parents before – very cosy and safe – and suddenly I had to cope with my husband disappearing and the move to a new home, and it was a bit difficult. But I think it was good for me, it made me far more self-sufficient.'

The Corps encourages Marines to buy their own houses – there are fewer married quarters available than in the Army, and wives cannot normally accompany their husbands on a posting of a year or less. This, plus the Corps's overseas training commitments, does result in a great deal of separation, and encourages wives to develop their own careers – as well as encouraging Royal Marines to look for wives who will be able to cope on their own.

One woman had been very impressed that her husband had been prepared to leave the Corps because he hadn't wanted to subject her to the pressures of separation when they were first married. But after thinking about it, she'd decided that since the job was so important to her husband – and since she agreed with what he did – it would be totally unfair to ask him to quit.

Which raises the question of how much do wives understand about their husbands' jobs? Much of what the Royal Marines do is classified. Nor do Royal Marines as a body particularly enjoy taking their work home with them. But they are aware that leaving families in total ignorance can have an absolutely devastating effect.

'The policy in this branch', explained a member of the SBS, 'is that we should tell our wives as much as we possibly can without breaching security. We do try to involve them in our work, as much as they want to be involved and as much as we legitimately can.'

However, not every Marine is in the SBS – and the fact that they are both trained for and capable of legitimate violence is not always immediately apparent within a relationship.

'All the Royal Marines I know are really gentle, caring people at home. They never go over the top, as you might expect.'

'I look at my husband sometimes, when he's bimbling around the house, and think, "Can you really be a Royal Marine, you're just so relaxed – how can you do your job!" He'll switch on the aggression sometimes, usually when he's talking to an insurance salesman, but mostly he's just very quiet, very content to stay in the house.'

'One of the biggest shocks I ever had in our marriage was the day I drove him up to his unit when he was leaving for Northern Ireland – and suddenly I saw him with a gun in his hand for the very first time. That's when it really struck home. I knew about it in theory of course, but that side of his life is something you try not to think too much about because if you do you'll begin to worry about him.'

'Yes, of course I've thought about the possibility of him killing someone, specially when he was in the Falklands. All I can say, if it's a choice between him and the other guy, I only hope it's him.'

Royal Marines themselves, particularly the men and NCOs, tend to be more intelligent and better educated than their army equivalents. Their wives reflect this fact, which has resulted in a lessening of the traditional class barriers between wives of officers and other ranks. But not altogether.

'I think the problem is that many of the women don't actually know how to behave with one another,' said one highly successful (working) wife of a Royal Marine senior NCO, 'and so you get a degree of snobbery that the men themselves don't show. It's all very silly really, but I do think that if there's a problem it's more of the wives' own making.'

Another wife of a senior NCO said that she'd found far more snobbery in the sergeants' mess than she ever had from officers' wives:

'I went to two major functions there and then told my husband "never again". Too many women sitting around claiming that they were better than someone else, for whatever reason. I don't know why they should be like that – I only know I don't want to be involved. But on the whole I find that outside the mess, all the wives take you pretty much as they find you. Not that I know many – a few in my husband's own branch, a few married to his close friends. But because we've got our own house and live some distance away from his work, most of our friends are civilians, most of mine are from work.'

This attitude runs very strongly counter to traditional military practice, which saw the families of a soldier effectively as part of the same regiment or corps, to the extent that wives often appeared to be given the same (honorary) rank as their husbands – and were expected to take part in the regimental life. Yet it appears to be the norm nowadays that wives not only don't want to be treated in that way, but that their husbands prefer a complete separation of job and family: they need an antidote to the highly pressurized, intensely masculine life that they lead when on duty.

'The nice thing is', said the wife of an officer, 'that they don't seem to have to prove themselves at home, don't have to strut around saying "I'm a big tough Marine", because of course they've already proved how tough they are in their training. If you look in our village on a Saturday morning, you'll find that most of the men who are out shopping with their wives or pushing a pram are Royal Marines. I notice that my husband seems to enjoy the simple domestic things – like going shopping.'

But not all is sweetness and light, particularly when the men have to go away. Fairly obviously, the problem times are just before and just after a trip.

'It's always the same. We know he'll be going away for a month or even longer, and we tell each other we'll have a really nice few days before he goes off. But it never happens that way – we find ourselves snapping at each other, both becoming very tense. So we never do get to have those candlelit farewell dinners!'

'I find that just before he's off I get very edgy and lose my temper for no apparent reason. We've both got used to the idea that we'll have at least one major row before he goes. I think it's as much due to the anxiety I'm feeling as anything else. After he's gone, the first two weeks are the worst, and then you get into your own routine and life gets back to normal.'

Returning home brings its own problems.

'Of course you're pleased to see him come home. But you've also established your own way of doing things and you frankly resent this other person who demands to be considered too! The biggest thing with me is meal times. I never have set ones when I'm on my own, except when the children are home, but he insists that we do!'

'Dirty laundry. Suddenly there's piles of it scattered around, bits of military kit that he hasn't got round to cleaning yet.'

'I find that I also have to remind him to be considerate to his family when he's been away for any great length of time. We'll be out for a walk with the children and he'll be striding off in front, and I have to say: "Look, remember they're still very small and can't actually keep up." Mind you, I'm not saying that he wouldn't set off at a near run anyway. It's just that that lack of thought is more marked when he's been away for any length of time. It takes him a few weeks to adapt to us as individuals again.'

A series of absences obviously has some effect on the role of the man as the head of the household. It seems that Royal Marines – and possibly many other service marriages – concur far more with the partnership ideal than many civilian relationships. As one wife put it:

'I suppose he is "head of the household" in one sense – but there's never any question of suddenly reasserting his authority when he gets back home. He's quite happy to let me go on making the decisions I've done in the past. In fact, he won't let me push any of them on to him, says it's good for me to carry on as before. All he – and most of his friends – appear to want to do when they get back is just become involved. In a way, it would be easier if they did take over completely, because then you wouldn't have to continually remind yourself that there's another person involved and that you *should* discuss things with them, no matter how well you've coped when they haven't been there. Of course, there are some wives who just never cope when their husbands are away. You hear stories about some women suffering breakdowns. But how much of that is due to the increased responsibility, and how much to just worrying about them, I don't know. Personally, I can usually handle any separation up to three months. After that I begin to ask myself have I really got a husband, or is he a figment of my imagination?'

Long separations also call for a high degree of trust from husband and wife alike, particularly since Royal Marines don't spend all their time away in a theatre of war like the Falklands or Northern Ireland.

'You have to learn to trust one another,' explained one woman, 'because if you didn't, the marriage couldn't work. Oh, I'll go out with friends and enjoy myself when he's not here, but I'd never dream of having an affair. I don't want to, aside from anything else. But that element of trust is absolutely vital, on both sides. We couldn't exist without it.'

The picture that begins to build up is of a relationship that exists almost independently of the husband's job. One wife said that she felt it was unhealthy for both husband and wife to be too strongly wrapped up in the same organization – if for no other reason than that the husband will find it all the more traumatic when he retires. She thought that a family life away from the Corps would help him make the inevitable adjustment to civilian life much more easily. However, it's not quite that simple. Even the most independent wives are aware of the fact that the Corps is there, as a potential cushion, and can take comfort in the fact. As one said:

'I suppose it is always nice to know that if you do have any problem, there's always someone who'll come round and help. And I do think that the Corps looks after, or cares, more about the families than a lot of other services. But on the other hand, I think too much of that can be a bad thing, makes not only the man but also his wife too dependent. I tell some of the guys that they don't know how spoilt they are – if they live in the mess, they never have to worry about a thing, everything's taken care of for them.'

The other part of the picture is that the wife is largely responsible for developing and maintaining the family unit. She has to compensate for the fact that her husband may miss a good part of the growing up of their children. In effect, she often becomes both father and mother – but has to be able to help her husband take over the father's role when he's at home. In some ways, the father's absences appear to affect daughters the most. Sons usually find it far easier to identify with their father's job, to gain vicarious pleasure from the fact that he's doing so many things that they themselves would like to do. But daughters may find it more difficult to appreciate the fact that their father's a soldier, doing something that they will never be able to do themselves.

And as an extremely personal observation, it might be that this is the reason why many service fathers make such an effort to get close to their daughters – even more so than to their sons. It's not that they don't love their sons, simply that they're aware that their daughters find it more difficult to comprehend and identify with their father's job.

The divorce rate is as high in the Royal Marines as it is elsewhere, possibly a little higher. But for the most part it appears to affect those marriages made when the man himself was still comparatively young – not long out of training – and when the woman herself was correspondingly young: neither totally aware of how difficult it is to be married to a Royal Marine, because of the separations, because of the demands of the job. Besides, not all Marines marry nurses or teachers and it appears to be difficult for many young women to comprehend or appreciate the dedication required to be a Royal Marine. They feel, perhaps naturally, perhaps not, that all a husband's energies should be focused upon his wife and family. Certainly those women, married in their mid-twenties and beyond to Royal Marines who had been in the Corps for several years, were struck by the way their husbands-to-be explained exactly how difficult being married to a Royal Marine would be – that no attempt was made to gloss over the problems. It is almost as if Royal Marines decide to get married, and then search for a woman who they think will be able to cope – that the need is as much for a domestic environment as it is for the 'one true love' in their life.

Certainly those marriages that work appear to do so extremely well. And in spite of their independence, many wives positively enjoy the very 'Royal Marinish' aspects of their husbands' characters – even down to the unique slang that Marines talk.

'I don't think I understood one word in three when we first met,' remembered one wife, 'and it took me some time to get used to words like "scran", "drip", "prof", "threaders" and all their other little expressions. Now I don't give it a moment's thought, often find myself using the same slang when I'm at work – much to the surprise of the people I work with.'

The one thing that all wives have to do is get used to the sardonic Marine sense of humour. It was characterized by one woman as the ability to laugh at anything, including themselves. Another woman said that she still found it a little bit too savage, even hurtful on occasions. But by and large she'd learnt not to fall for the bite, the deliberate wind-up, which only works if the recipient reacts to it.

But ask them what qualities make their husbands unique in their wives' eyes, and most women find it difficult to express their feelings.

'I think that if you walk into any room, you can usually tell who's the serviceman there,' said one, 'and not just because he's the one with the short hair. It's something about him – more relaxed, more confident perhaps, more at ease with everyone. Well, Marines are like that, but more so.

'They are an elite force,' explained another woman, 'and I know that because my husband's always telling me so! But seriously, they do have this sense that they're that much better than other soldiers – better trained, better able to look after themselves, better able to do the job – and I suppose this confidence just shows through.'

'To me it's that he's always so relaxed about everything, to the point that he won't argue or quarrel about trivial things – nor will I, for that matter, because we don't have that much time together as it is.'

'I think it's just that he can get on with absolutely everyone, doesn't matter who they are.'

'You always hear about macho Marines, but honestly I don't think I've ever met more than two who thought they were God's gift – and you'll always get one bad apple. If anything, the surprising thing about my husband is that he is so quiet. But at the end of the day you are aware that he *is* a little bit special – and God forbid that I should be married to a nine-to-five bank clerk – can't imagine anything more boring.'

'I suppose the thing is, I'm aware that no matter how laid back he appears, he always likes to feel independent and in control. He doesn't miss very much, you know.'

The sum of all this appears to be that the wives of Royal Marines, like Royal Marines themselves, are 'naturals' for the job.

What is true is that Royal Marines themselves couldn't operate a fraction as efficiently as they do without the support of their wives and families.

CHAPTER TWELVE

East of Suez

Royal Marines in the Far East, in the jungle and at sea – and some indication of how they differ in operational effectiveness from the United States Marine Corps

The USMC gunnery sergeant had been happily surprised to discover how similar his own corps was to the Royal Marines. Sent as an observer to Bravo Company, 40 Commando Royal Marines, as they trained in jungle warfare in Brunei, he'd been struck by the similarity of many Royal Marine techniques to those practised by the USMC – but with the proviso that the Royal Marine techniques were perhaps a little too basic.

For example, 'harbouring-up' techniques are among the most vital practised by any military formation in the jungle. They're used when a unit establishes camp for the night or a permanent or semi-permanent camp by day. The Royal Marines always try to work on the principle of a triangular perimeter, with a fire-support team at each angle and the headquarters somewhere in the middle. The first fire-support unit moves in to secure the perimeter's apex, then the other two teams secure the two base positions, always one at a time so that two teams can cover the one moving. A similar technique is used, say, for river crossings. First one team will cross, supported by the two on the original river bank. Then one more crosses, and the two teams set up the base of a pyramid. Then comes headquarters (if there is one), finally followed by the third fire-support team who will complete the triangle's perimeter. Then, having established via scouts that the area is safe, the entire unit will move out. By and large, this triangular technique holds good for all Royal Marine formations in the jungle, from section to full-company level – although the Royal Marines would be loath to move a full company in the jungle as this invariably causes problems. This demonstrates the Corps's belief that in order to fight successfully – and survive – in the jungle, you must follow that well-known Corps acronym KISS, otherwise known as Keep It Simple, Stupid.

The USMC on the other hand will use a variety of harbouring-up techniques, including an oval perimeter formation and one known as the doughnut – essentially two ovals one inside the other. But then, the USMC tends to operate in slightly larger fighting units than the Royal Marines, with subsequently greater firepower at its disposal. And often, extra men and extra firepower don't so much allow for different tactics as dictate them.

The basic fighting unit within the Royal Marines is undoubtedly the ten-man section led by a corporal. That's ten in theory, because the section often numbers considerably less, which means that a tremendous amount of responsibility is given to and expected from a Royal Marine corporal – far more so than from his equivalent in the USMC, where the basic fighting unit tends to be the platoon, or troop, numbering at least thirty.

In part this is dictated by the sheer size of the USMC (although, proportionate to the population of the United States, the USMC is the same size as the Royal Marines) – a size that allows for wholesale battalion, regimental and divisional manoeuvring. The Royal Marines can usually expect no more than two Commandos (that is, two battalions) to be deployed together, and then strung out over a large land area. Small wonder that the Royal Marines have had to develop the art of fighting in small units – as indeed has the British Army, although not to quite the same extent – tactics which are in any case more suited both to the modern battlefield and the Royal Marines' role as commando troops.

This difference between the USMC and the Royal Marines has also been partly dictated by the basic American belief that superior firepower will conquer all. It is a theory that was once described by a US military attaché in London as the 'wagon train' tactic, owing its origins to the old pioneer technique of closing ranks and bringing as much firepower as possible to bear on attacking Indian tribes. It is primarily defensive in nature and tends to assume that the enemy will always attack first. Translated into modern warfare – particularly jungle warfare – it explains the thirty-man patrols that the American forces tended to use in Vietnam. (But not all American forces did this – their Long Range Reconnaissance Patrols, for example, borrowed and improved on tactics used by the British during the Malayan Emergency.)

However, the jungle warfare techniques the Royal

Marines now teach are not based so much on the Malayan Emergency, or the Confrontation with Indonesia, as on the Australian and New Zealand experiences in Vietnam. It was generally accepted that the Australian contingent in Vietnam were among the most effective troops there. They used the four- or six-man-patrol technique: men going out into the jungle for weeks at a time (living off the land wherever possible), both to gather intelligence and to deny the ground to the Vietcong or the North Vietnamese Army (NVA). It was far harder for either the Vietcong or the NVA to discover such small patrols – which in turn were plenty large enough to mount hit-and-run ambushes at night, particularly on couriers or supply columns.

The point is that a pitched battle between large opposing forces in the jungle is often a waste of time. Visibility is at best fifteen metres, often only five. It's too easy to be either outmanoeuvred, or to discover that you've spent an hour or so pouring fire in on an enemy who simply isn't there. It's also far too easy for a large unit to be tied down by a much smaller enemy force. In other words, the best counter to guerrilla tactics is . . . guerrilla tactics. It is those tactics that the Royal Marines teach their men – and again, the only reason they're able to do so is because their basic fighting unit is so comparatively small.

It's in the jungle, too, that the basic difference between USMC and Royal Marine recruit training techniques shows itself. The USMC breaks a man down to rebuild him in its own image. The Royal Marines challenge – and help – a man to develop those abilities that will make him a competent rifleman in a troop –

and all subsequent Royal Marine training is of the same pattern. It's almost brainwashing versus high-pressure education, and means that the young Royal Marine tends to be far more self-reliant (and with far more to say for himself) than his USMC equivalent. Far more is also expected of him in terms of initiative and self-discipline – and in the jungle especially, these qualities are invaluable.

Overall, the major difference between the USMC and the Royal Marines is their countries' different cultures. It's a great mistake to assume that a common language means a similar culture, a similar way of looking at things. It's often a source of puzzlement that a country like the United States, overall far less formal than Britain, should have developed a military system that relies so much on imposed discipline. It's particularly strange when you consider that the earliest military traditions in the US were those of commando-type formations – George Washington's sharpshooters who played such havoc with British and German mercenary forces. In many ways today's USMC has as much, if not more, in common with the French Foreign Legion – a very formal, imposed discipline – than with the Royal Marines.

A world of difference

By way of a slight detour, there's another area which highlights one of the differences between US and British military thinking – the way each country uses its special forces. While the US Navy's SEAL (SEA Air Land) and

UDT (Underwater Demolition Teams) are quite close in concept and activity to Britain's SBS and Royal Navy Clearance Divers, there is a world of difference between the SAS and SBS on the one hand, and the US Special Forces on the other. It's a difference that goes as far back as the Second World War, and briefly it is this: US Special Forces are intended, where possible, to work closely with and train 'friendly' local forces, such as the Montignards in Vietnam, or the Resistance in Occupied France. The SAS and SBS are expected to operate as independently as possible, coming into contact with local resistance groups or potential allies only if absolutely necessary, or possibly for a one-off operation.

In many ways it's a contrast between extreme pragmatism on the one hand and idealism on the other. It's not that idealism is lacking in the British armed forces, merely that it has little or no place tactically. Nor would the SAS or SBS assume, because a local guerrilla force was fighting the same enemy, that they all shared the same motivations or objectives. With that, both the SAS and SBS always operate in conditions of extreme secrecy, in peacetime as well as war, and neither group is expected to be as regimental as, say, the Brigade of Guards. On the other hand, the US Special Forces appear to be expected to fulfil an unconventional role while looking, and operating, as conventional military forces – to the point that Pentagon-applied bullshit has on many occasions definitely baffled US Special Forces' brains. It may well be that the new independent US Special Forces' unified command will free its units to operate more effectively – but the thought still remains that until the Pentagon radically rethinks its approach to modern warfare, and realizes that image is less important than ability, it will not be able to develop its armed forces to their best potential.

CHAPTER THIRTEEN

Royal Marines in the Middle East

While few Royal Marines served in the Iraq War, the Corps made its presence felt when 3 Commando Brigade spearheaded the Allies' plans to bring the Kurds home and to safety.

It was rumoured that the Special Boat Service began operating in Kuwait within days of the Iraqi invasion. Like all rumours to do with British special forces it was neither confirmed nor denied – officially, that is: unofficially, numerous 'spokesmen' and other trustworthy sources confided to favoured journalists that this was to be an American show, therefore no British special force units would be involved. Which is every reason to believe that they were, and the superb role played by the SAS is – for once – common knowledge. Or what passes for common knowledge with anything to do with the SAS.

Still, the SBS have been active in the Gulf for many years, operating from one of several friendly countries, concerned with both oil rig protection and training. If they were involved in the Gulf War, one would imagine it would have been in the role of long-range reconnaissance and sabotage . . . together with their standard role of beach reconnaissance as preparation for an amphibious landing. In fact, their supposed presence in the area would have confirmed to the Iraqis that an amphibious landing was planned – as indeed appeared to be the case. Convinced that the United States Marine Corps were planning to land on the beaches, Saddam Hussein totally ignored the possibility of an armoured thrust deep into Iraqi, let alone Kuwaiti, territory.

In fact, the SBS were active and especially in one of the special forces' prime roles: operations against the enemy's command and control assets, or C2W as explained in Chapter Ten. Battlefield information relayed between relatively fixed positions will, if at all possible, be done via buried landlines since these are impervious to jamming; are next to impossible to intercept; and very difficult to destroy. Fibre-optic landlines, that can carry vast amounts of information, say between heavily defended SCUD or anti-aircraft batteries and their tactical headquarters. Or simply between formations at different levels. One such operation took place at the time that Bravo Two Zero was setting off into the desert. One American source has claimed that the two missions were identical, that is, as much aimed at the SCUD command and control systems as the SCUDs themselves. Whatever the truth of it, a small SBS patrol was fast-inserted by Royal Navy helicopter at night deep into Kuwait, accompanied by two US Air Force Special Forces soldiers whose job it was to call down tactical air support if ever necessary. The helicopter's pilot was afterwards heard to observe that he'd never known a man could dig so fast. The cables themselves were buried between four and five feet below the sand, and there was more than one. In different places. Without very much cover, and even if there had been, a helicopter will tend to attract attention. The overall point being that there are some missions in which you simply have to go for broke. There's no other way of achieving the objective. But if there were any goatherds or itinerant souvenir-sellers around that night, they very wisely kept their heads down. It took less than twenty minutes to expose and destroy the landlines, and then fill in the holes. No point in showing the Iraqis exactly where the damage had been done. The operation, a complete success. The SCs later presented General Schwarzkopf with a special souvenir: a length of fibre-optic cable mounted on a nicely varnished board.

Aside from CHOSC – and more about that later – the Royal Marines presence in the Gulf was otherwise limited to Royal Navy Ships Detachments.

Most ships within the Royal Navy bigger than a patrol boat, or perhaps a frigate, have a Royal Marines Detachment on board. Not always submarines, of course, and even patrol boats or frigates can find themselves the proud possessors of a few Royals, both often wondering what exactly they're doing there. Traditionally and in the days of sail, ships' detachments were used as snipers, as land raiders – and to keep the crew away from the officers. This latter possibly explaining why many rank and file members of the Royal Navy still regard Royal Marines with a certain amount of suspicion.

In the Gulf, ships' detachments had two main roles. First, to provide the manpower for maritime stop-and-search missions. Second, to provide heavy weapons (machine-guns and even anti-tank rockets, both effective against armed speed boats, and more cost effective) since many of the Royal Navy's ships were better equipped for fighting a more conventional sea battle.

'I left [Britain] on September the tenth', remembered one corporal, 'on board HMS *London*, came back the following March. Like all Ships' Detachments we were part of the crew, like we had to work watches same as everyone else. Six hours on and six off, and never less than ten or fifteen seconds away from your gun (or rocket). It was good that we always knew what was happening on land, 'cause the skipper gave regular briefing and then we watched CNN, listened to the BBC World Service whenever we could. Far as I can make out, we knew a hell of a sight more than the boys on the ground who were doing the hard fighting!'

As it happened, the only rocket the corporal saw fired in anger – or self-defence – was the Sea Dart from HMS *Gloucester* that took out an Exocet aimed at a nearby US warship.

'First we had the warning that they [the Iraqis] had fired a missile. So then you begin to wonder who it was aimed at! Then an almighty bang and flash as *Gloucester* fired her Sea Dart and took the Iraqis' out. I was in the Ops Room so I could hear all the radio traffic, knew that *Gloucester* had pinged the Iraqis' missile, knew – at least, we all guessed – which ship it was going for. Anyways, after that we all felt a bit safer. I'll tell you, though – those guys on *Gloucester* operated as smooth as you'd like, real textbook stuff. No question but they saved a lot of American lives. And like I said, made us feel a damn sight safer, too!'

Ships in the Allied fleet in the Gulf tended to work eight days at sea and four ashore. You have to remember that for those eight days – and it could be longer – the tension was continual. Undoubtedly they could have spent longer before 'going alongside', but that would have impaired their efficiency as well as being more expensive, since a RAS (Replenishment At Sea, that is, stores and fuel transferred from one ship to another at sea) is expensive. It also makes the two ships concerned sitting ducks for any on-shore missile battery, is not recommended close to land. Also, given the size of the Allied fleet, the sheer logistics of RASing them all would have been impossible.

All aboard

For the most part, Royal Marines Ships' Detachments were involved in boarding suspect freighters bound for Iraq. Or bound anywhere near Iraq, that is sailing anywhere in the Gulf. Although US led, the fleet was multinational and the US authorities were keen that it should be seen to be so. While the French or Italians, for example, were given their own sector to patrol, as was the case when British ships were involved, the whole operation was designed to be as multinational as possible. Presumably to prevent either a case of pique because some country or another wasn't involved . . . or to prevent one or two countries being held mainly responsible for any damage or death. Either way, it made for good public relations, even if the command was a trifle confused at times.

For example, as far as the Ships' Detachment on *London* was concerned, they were part of a boarding party that included USA SEALs and Australian sailors.

'We'd get the message that a ship had been stopped. Then chopper over to her, abseil down on to the deck and find a bunch of US SEALs waiting there . . . all geared up, like. We were a bit confused (!) at first because the SEALs always wore their personal radio call signs on their helmets. Remember there was one guy with 'T-BAR' stencilled on his, which we thought was maybe a bit over the top.' (A 'T-BAR' is an American issue fighting knife, not something produced by Cadburys.)

'OK, what had happened was that the Yanks had radio'd the freighter to stop, then sent over SEALs initially to secure it, which I guess meant taking over the wheelhouse. Then we'd arrive, take over from the SEALs who'd vanish off somewhere, and then the Aussies would show up to do the actual searching. We were guarding the Aussies while they searched and generally stopping the crew from getting too excited . . . there was one Iraqi I remember who'd spent a few years in Middlesbrough of all places, kept on wanting to talk football to us. We never actually found anything, at least the Aussies didn't, but I suppose we were as much a deterrent as anything else. Maybe the Navy guys who deserve the real credit for what went on in the Gulf were the minesweepers?'

Chop-chop

CHOSC (pronounced 'chosk') stands for Commando Helicopter Support Cell. Not many people know that.

It's one of those units that the Royal Marines

invented – although in this case, the Royal Navy also has to take a great deal of the credit. Or blame. But then, the Royal Navy is equally adept at inventing units for a specific task, only telling the MoD when it's too late to do anything about it, as are the Royal Marines.

CHOSC is essentially a child of the doctrine of amphibiosity, which was mentioned in Chapter One. It answers the problem of how to control helicopter support once the Marines have landed from their commando carriers. Or it did – nowadays, it's grown a little. The problem was that while the Marines are at sea, and during the landing itself, helicopter support is organized from sea. That includes maintenance, traffic control, resource allocation etc. But when the Royals have landed and perhaps moved inshore several miles, the problem of command and control becomes complex. At that point, the Brigadier or senior Royal Marines' officer in charge of the landing/task force takes control. Obviously he can't allow 'his' helicopters to be controlled from a ship somewhere off in the wide blue yonder. The answer was and is a fully air portable support unit that detaches itself from whatever ship it's based on, and effectively follows the Brigadier around as part of his own headquarters. They won't necessarily be in the same place, of course, but the intention is clear.

What has happened is that this basic, common-sense approach has developed into a unit that's unique within the British forces (possibly explaining why few people know what the letters stand for), and has taken the concept of helicopter mobility almost, but not quite, to its logical conclusion. (Not quite because the chances are that CHOSC will change even more in the years to come as both the Royal Marines and the Royal Navy discover ever more interesting things for it to do.)

At the moment of writing, CHOSC provides direct support to whatever helicopter Naval Air Squadron has been allocated to the Royal Marines for a specific operation. Squadrons 845 and 846 are permanently attached to 3 Commando Brigade, but others can be and are attached as the situation demands. CHOSC numbers some 110 personnel, all ranks, of which fifty-five are Royal Marines. For once the Navy and the Corps are being scrupulous in the division of labour. It's commanded by a naval officer – a pilot, naturally – and among other duties, supplies MAOTs (Mobile Air Operations Teams) of between four and five men each to work directly with individual Commandos. MAOTs provide an air traffic in the field service and because they are part of CHOSC are ideally placed to provide whatever heli-support the CO of a Commando wants . . . or explain in simple terms why he can't have it.

Have a nice day

CHOSC arrived in the Gulf as part of the Royal Navy's contribution. It found itself controlling three squadrons – 845 and 846 as standard, plus 848 – under the overall control of the US military – Army, not the United States Marine Corps. Very few US Army officers had had any experience of working with either the Royal Navy or Royal Marines. But something must have been said to them, for as far as the Royals at CHOSC were concerned, they could do no wrong.

'There's no doubt that the Americans were magic to us', stated a senior NCO, 'because whatever we wanted, we got and then in double quick time. I found out very early on that the Green Beret meant something to the Yanks . . . if I had to go and get supplies, any kind of supplies, I used to bimble over to the American colonel in charge and simply go directly into his office – ignoring all the other bods waiting to see him, and always wearing the green lid. And you could feel everyone else's eyes pinging your headgear as you went in! But that guy was ace, whatever we wanted we got and never any questions asked.'

(That was also to be the experience of the Royal Marines later in Kurdistan: whatever the need, if it could be supplied the American Army would supply it and then as quickly as possible. Very few Marines, if any, have come back from the Middle East without mixed feelings of amazement and gratitude for US military logistics.)

Initially CHOSC and its squadrons were used for normal men and material missions. Then it was realized by the US military that Royal Marines and Royal Navy pilots had certain other skills. Specifically, they were trained for, and extremely adept at, flying low-level insertion missions. A perhaps slightly unfortunate expression that describes flying at a very, very low level at very high speeds in order to deposit or pick up special forces. Which they did with a high degree of success – but remain obstinately close mouthed as to who, what and where. Although it is likely that any British special forces (if they were operating in the area!) would find it easier to work with CHOSC than anyone else.

Hostilities over, CHOSC spent a little time ferrying PoWs back and forth. A time made memorable only by *someone* giving a bunch of Iraqi prisoners, who hadn't eaten for days, chocolate yoghurt just before a chopper took off in slightly bumpy conditions.

'I'm sure that to this day those Iraqis are convinced it was done on purpose,' said one member of CHOSC, 'but it wasn't – I mean, would you like to spend hours cleaning out the inside of a helicopter?'

A cunning plan

If CHOSC thought that they would be going home after the cease-fire they were sadly mistaken. Although as it turned out, they and 3 Commando Brigade were to become involved in an operation that, at the time, many felt to be the most worthwhile of their service careers: Operation Safe Haven.

When it was announced that 'safe havens' were to be set up in Kurdistan, and that the Kurds were to be taken back into their (de-militarized) homeland, many people breathed a sigh of relief. There was only one minor problem: no one knew what a safe haven was, or how to set it up, or how to administer it.

Possibly, that was one reason why 3 Commando Brigade was chosen to spearhead British activity in this area. For as any Royal will tell you, a good deal of their time is spent trying to make some sort of sense out of a politician's more wishful thinking. That and just making things happen more or less the way they should happen. On the other hand, it's also true that imagination and flexibility are two qualities that both the Marines and the British Army hold dear. Well, perhaps not quite all the British Army, some of whose units would still form squares on the battlefield given half a chance . . . but certainly the Paras, who were also in line for the job, have very similar qualities of imagination, etc., as the Royal Marines.

Two factors appear to have swung it in the Corps's favour. First, the fact a deal of work had to be done in the Kurdish mountains and the Royal Marines have extensive mountain experience, courtesy of Norway.

Secondly, even with US back-up, logistics were going to be a nightmare – and that could only mean using Commando Logistics Regiment RM, who had performed so brilliantly in the Falklands. As Commando Logs tell it, the rest of the Brigade really only got to Kurdistan on their back – but they would say that, wouldn't they? Although few if any personnel in 3 Commando Brigade would ever deny quite how efficient Cdo Logs is . . . or adaptable, or flexible, or mobile.

Whatever the reasons, 3 Cdo Bde got the job. Then had to figure out what they were supposed to be doing and how they were going to do it.

Terror is as terror does

45 Commando, fresh from Northern Ireland (and in the words of an officer 'still with a little pent up frustration that's always the hallmark of a tour [across the water]') were given the job, in co-operation with the USMC, of clearing the Iraqi military and secret police out of

Kurdistan itself . . . or rather, south of the border that had been designated as Kurdistan's southern-most boundary. 40 Commando were given the job of getting the Kurds down from the mountains, temporarily feeding and housing them, attending to their medical needs and then sending them back to their towns and villages. The only fly in the ointment being that whatever the Iraqis had agreed to originally, Saddam Hussein was certainly not going to keep his word. Not that anyone on the ground expected him to, lacking that faith in human nature then being shown in Washington.

The plan of 3 Cdo Bde's deployment, incidentally, was established in about three days by Brigade HQ. Royal Marines' staff work can be pretty impressive at times, too.

From the very beginning it was clearly understood that the Western forces were not going to be in Kurdistan for ever. Therefore, 3 Cdo Bde saw its job as not only bringing the Kurds down from the mountains and eventually into their homes now clean of Iraqi soldiers, secret police, minefields and booby traps (a very high percentage of abandoned Kurdish houses were booby-trapped by departing Iraqi personnel. As is well known, Kurdish women and children pose a very serious threat to Baghdad's continued existence), but also trying to ensure that the Kurds would be able to fend for themselves after the Alliance had gone home.

'The problem is', explained a senior officer, 'that while the Kurds are a fine people, one of the finest I've ever been privileged to meet, they've been conditioned over the years by the Iraqis. That's to say, not only did Saddam Hussein deliberately attempt to break the

Kurdish nation up by destroying their clan and family structures, but thousands of other Iraqis also saw the Kurds as being fair game – theirs to do with what they willed. The Kurds were seen as being a totally subject race, inferior in every way to the Southern Iraqis and I feel that there was a good deal of genuine – if wholly deplorable – amazement on the part of the Iraqis that the West should care about such people in the first instance.

'Not that the West has cared about them to any great extent, until recently. After all, if various governments, including Britain, had kept their word at the end of both world wars, then the Kurds would have had their own country and this situation would never have happened in the first instance.

'The other problem is that this part of the world can be extremely fatalistic, at least by our standards . . . there was almost a discernible attitude on the part of many Kurds that it was somehow their lot in life to be bullied by the Iraqis in the first place.'

The problem here was that a Kurdish organization, the Pesh Murga did and does exist, that believes in fighting back: but that none of the Allied troops could run the risk of being seen to be in collusion with the Pesh Murga in any way. Not so much because of Saddam Hussein's tender sensibilities, but because the Turks, too, are extremely sensitive about their own Kurdish population (even more so about the possibility of an independent Kurdistan, and Turkey is an ally . . .).

When 45 Commando arrived in their area of operations they were disgusted by what they found. Dead Kurds only half buried by departing Iraqis, so that their hands, feet and sometimes heads protruded from the ground: not carelessness, but applied terror. Bloodstained rooms in what had been Iraqi secret police headquarters, graphic testimony to the type and frequency of torture used. Mass graves, one containing only women and children whose menfolk had been forced to watch while their loved ones were shot.

'When the guys said that they felt like going straight into Baghdad', remembered an officer, 'and finishing off Saddam once and for all, I knew exactly how they felt. But it also made it difficult in dealing with the other Iraqis, for how could you have any respect for a man who had been part of that . . . given that most if not all Iraqis we had to deal with were the most arrogant sons-of-bitches you could ever not want to meet. But then, if you've spent your life beating up defenceless people, I expect a certain arrogance would develop.'

The problem was that the withdrawal of Iraqi troops from Kurdistan was taking far longer than anyone in high places had apparently expected. Simply put, the Iraqis didn't want to go, didn't see why they should go (many believed that Iraq had won the war) and certainly didn't want to be seen by Saddam Hussein as being involved in any sort of face-losing retreat.

'You see', explained the same officer, 'if you're trying to negotiate with an Iraqi officer, telling him that he has to take his men south, so far as he's concerned if he doesn't, the worst thing that will happen is that you'll shoot him dead. Or maybe he'll escape in the ensuing fire-fight, who knows?

'But what he also knows is that in Baghdad there's a man called Saddam Hussein who's looking for someone, anyone, to blame for his own mistakes. And if he, the

Iraqi officer, goes along with what you want, then his family back home will probably be shot, if not tortured into the bargain. As will he if he gets back alive. Bottom line being that the Iraqis were a damn sight more scared of Saddam and his secret police than they were of us. Having seen what had happened, you could understand why.'

So it was that all negotiations had to be cleared directly with Baghdad, and in many cases, with Saddam Hussein himself. No one wanted to take the responsibility, on the Iraqi side, of retreating from Iraqi territory. In fact, the Iraqis did have one extremely able negotiator, a brigadier, who appeared to have more of a handle on the situation than the rest of his colleagues. He it was who managed to persuade the Americans that Iraqi armed guards could be left in Saddam Hussein's many palaces in the area to prevent looting. All the Allies agreed that this man did an exceptionally able job and many even came to respect him for it. Certainly he wrung concessions from the Allies for his master in Baghdad that were quite remarkable. True to form, he was recalled to Baghdad before the Allies left Kurdistan . . . and if he was expecting gratitude or even a medal, he was sadly disappointed: Saddam Hussein had him shot.

One of the main problems 45 Cdo encountered was keeping the Kurds away from the remaining Iraqis who were legitimately in the area. An act not always appreciated by the Iraqis themselves, who on one occasion fired at a sub-unit from inside a palace they were guarding. It's public knowledge that the Marines fired back with a little more accuracy . . . certainly after that incident, the

Iraqis kept themselves to themselves. Although initially, they had to be politely dissuaded from coming out of their fastnesses to indulge in a little Kurd-bashing whenever the mood took them. The story that, in order to teach the Iraqis what the military pecking order really was, a palace was very quietly raided while its guards were asleep and their weapons 'borrowed' for a while is just that: an unsubstantiated story. As is the aftermath, that when a band of Pesh Murga drove past the following morning, firing their own weapons in the air and the Iraqi guards suddenly realized they didn't have any – weapons – they were extremely pleased when a Royal Marines patrol hove into sight. And thereafter, kept inside the palace they were guarding.

3 Cdo Bde had decided that the Kurds had to be taught a measure of self-sufficiency. Had in fact, to be enabled to regain their self-respect. So it was that various committees were formed, to handle problems with reconstruction – fresh water, engineering, health, etc. – in which the Kurds were expected, encouraged (and occasionally told they bloody well had) to play a full role.

'We kept on telling them that we wouldn't be there for ever . . . that was the hardest part, because they obviously thought, wanted, us to be their guardians long into the future . . . but it just wasn't on. First we knew we couldn't stay, anyway. Secondly, that type of paternalistic approach wouldn't have been good for them – is it good for anybody? – and also would have sold the Kurds very short indeed. Given half a chance they're an extraordinarily capable people – given their history – who would have defeated most other nations I can think of.

'All the same, one would have liked to stay perhaps a little longer. As it is, one only hopes that we did manage to put them back onto the right road.'

As 45 Cdo were 'escorting' Iraqis out of Kurdish territory, 40 Cdo had been landed with the job of getting Kurds down from the mountains and establishing 'way-stations'. Naturally, no one was quite sure what a 'way-station' should be – the idea was simple enough, but there weren't any MoD blue-prints.

It's always invidious to single out any particular unit (and is the surest way of ensuring that at some time in the future, you'll be approached by someone saying, 'Why mention them? Didn't you know what we did?'), but even so in this instance one unit is going to be singled out: Support Company, 40 Cdo, Royal Marines. So with apologies to the Arctic and Mountain Warfare Cadre who were active in the mountains, not to mention the rifle companies and everyone else, Support Company it is.

Kani Masi

A support company comprises all those sub-units that operate directly to Cdo HQ – reconnaissance, heavy weapons, anti-tank, etc. – and that can be used any-where within a Commando's area of operations.

So it is that a support company contains a great number of highly specialized, highly experienced troops. They were to need those skills, plus large amounts of flexibility, imagination, discipline, etc. (not forgetting a sense of humour) during Safe Haven itself.

Support Company arrived at Silopi in Turkey on 30 May in time to see the rest of 40 Cdo leaving for Kurdistan/Iraq), closely followed by Reconnaissance Troop which then provided various sub-units to work with US Special Forces in the temporary refugee camps high in the mountains. Recce Troop's main tasks were to help clean up; arrange food supplies; and liaise with both the local leaders and the Pesh Murga, with the latter having to realize that the Allies were friends but not allies, weren't there to fight the Pesh Murga's battles for it, or to train or arm the Pesh Murga. There was also the slight difficulty posed by certain Iraqi secret police who'd infiltrated the refugee camps (possibly in an attempt to get as far away from Saddam Hussein as possible), but when it was explained to them how awkward life could be if the Kurds knew who they really were . . . and that the Kurds did know who they were, since they'd supplied the information in the first instance . . . then all things considered, the secret policeman would be better off far, far away, since no Allied soldier felt disposed to guard him.

The main body of Support Company deployed to Kani Masi on 3 May to set up a 'way-station'. This was intended to facilitate the movement of some 210,000 Kurds from the mountains back to their towns and villages. In the process, a transit camp that held 30,000 people at any one time had to be established.

Remember that nothing on this sort of scale had been attempted since the end of the Second World War. The situation wasn't helped by the Turks refusing to allow British vehicles to cross the border into Iraq – something wrong with the paperwork, probably – which a Royal Marine senior NCO finally successfully countered by stripping all British identity markings from the vehicles and smuggling them across hidden in US convoys, one at a time.

A base camp site was selected – people still wondering what a 'way-station' was, but reports coming from the mountains gave some indication what to expect. Then the scavenging began, for the logistics weren't yet up to scratch. By all accounts the assault engineers fulfilled all expectations and became scavengers par excellence, more than earned their keep until there appeared a US Army general.

General Potter is destined to go down in Royal Marine folklore as one of the most sympathetic, efficient and switched-on officers the Corps has ever worked with. Whatever Support Company wanted, they got if it was available – and if it wasn't then, it soon would be. Interesting because few if any of the Royals had ever worked with the US Army before, didn't know quite what to expect ... and towards the end appeared to believe that General Potter was as much Royal Marine as anything else. Whether he knew it or not, General Potter helped to raise not only the Corps's morale, but also the reputation of his own service.

All together . . .

One of the major problems that faced Support Company – aside from the obvious ones to do with the refugees themselves – was the number of charity and refugee organizations operating in the area. There was no co-ordination, which meant that a certain amount of the considerable effort made was wasted or duplicated. It's not totally clear whether Support Company deliberately set out to be the main co-ordinator in the area, or whether it just happened . . . the suspicion is that seeing something needed organizing, Support Company went ahead and did it, yet gave the impression it was the civilians' own ideas.

Certainly within a matter of weeks, if not days, the Support Company compound was joined by a team from Médecins Sans Frontières (the first time that organization had ever worked directly with the military, anywhere); a team from the Overseas Development Agency (medics, engineers and firemen); a single nurse from Great Ormond Street hospital who ran a medical unit caring for sick babies, and who appears to have won the heart and mind of every Royal Marine who came into contact with her; a small Irish charity called GOAL; plus a wide variety of military personnel from Luxembourg, Holland (Marines), America (USMC) and Canada. The US even provided a two-man air traffic control unit from the US Air Force Special Forces, who endeared themselves to their hosts by insisting that RAF helicopters landed where they said and not where the RAF wanted.

Shortly before Support Company left, a party of Buddhist monks also turned up – all the way from Korea – were slightly disappointed to learn that it was all over bar the shouting.

With thousands of refugees expected hourly, accommodation had to be built for them. Based on hastily acquired local knowledge, the huts were arranged to reflect Kurdish society: family, then clan. So it became a series of villages within villages which in turn made life easier for both Kurds and Allies alike. Similarly, Support Company built both a mosque and a Christian church as soon as possible . . . not seen as a hearts and minds operation, but a project indispensable with a people for whom religion played such a major role in their lives.

Keeping order in the camp posed certain problems as there were not enough military personnel to do the job, nor was it felt that it was their place to do so (except when it came to food distribution, when even the hungriest Kurd learnt to recoil from the bellow of a Royal senior NCO, and patiently wait their turn). The answer was to organize their own police force, their own Kurdish police force, with proportionately equal representation from all religious groups and all political groups.

'I don't know if it would have worked for ever,' commented a member of Support Company, 'but it did then . . . and it was rather nice to see Muslims, Christians, Communists, Royalists, Democrats, Islamic Fundamentalists or whatever all co-operating together as cops. We gave them their own ID cards with their photos on them, too . . . and it wasn't just window dressing, because those guys really took it seriously . . . they didn't manage to stamp out all the black marketeering, mind, but it never got out of hand.'

Then, too, Support Company showed a degree of initiative in direct dealings with the Kurds in the camp. Essentially, the camp was divided into sectors – based on clan affiliations when possible – and each sector was given its own Royal NCO as a liaison officer. If anyone from outside – journalist, medical team or whoever – needed to talk to that 'sector', it had to be arranged through the NCO. Similarly the Kurds made their representations also through the NCOs . . . well, most of the time, at least. As a system it worked extremely well, for it was an extension of the family or clan system itself: the Kurds had one person whom they could totally rely on.

Co-ordinating all the different agencies, groups or whoever who'd set up shop with Support Company was solved by a nightly relaxed, informal meeting. Everyone sat round in a circle, each would give a brief report of what they'd done that day and raise any problems or specific needs. These were dealt with on the spot if possible – an assault engineer, for example, saying 'sure, he could provide the Irish nuns with a few angle-irons or corrugated iron sheets' . . . perhaps a quiet lesson in good military order and discipline.

In fact there's some indication that the civilians did realize they were ever-so-softly being organized. Not that they could have avoided that conclusion, really, as any parcel of 'goodies' from home was firmly shared among everyone. But when a vague rumour surfaced that Support Company might have to arrange the disarming of several thousand Pesh Murga fighters close by, Support Company promptly named their camp 'Rorke's Drift', in memory of the time when a handful of Welsh Borderers held out against many thousand Zulu.

'I mean, I hope it was only a rumour, because there was no way on God's earth that we could have disarmed the Pesh Murga . . . and good as the relations were between us, I think they'd have been a little resentful of any attempt on our part to try!'

The civilians obviously saw the sign, made no comment . . . but the next day a sign appeared outside their mini-compound that read 'Greenham Common'.

'Good sense of humour, that,' was one Royal comment, 'and we had some good discussions afterwards!' In fact, relations were excellent – it was probably one of the best examples of ad hoc organization that really works, with good will on all sides, in Corps history.

Support Company left Kani Masi on 10 May. In that short space of time they had helped transport 210,000 Kurds; had housed 30,000 at any one time; had set up a water supply for over 40,000 people; educated the refugees in basic hygiene; did not lose a single person to cholera; drastically reduced the infant mortality rate; set up health clinics, schools, mosques, food distribution systems throughout the surrounding countryside . . . and generally helped give back to the Kurds not only their homes, but also their self-respect.

'It was one of the more, if not the most, rewarding times I've spent in the Corps. The only sadness, and I guess we all feel it, is knowing that given half a chance, the Iraqis will start trying to dominate and terrorize the Kurds again. And although we were successful, I worry if it was only up to a point.'

APPENDIX

The Band of the Royal Marines

. . . is probably the best military band in the world.

Bar none.

In the first edition of this book no mention of the Band was made. This was because the book is, was, essentially about Royal Marines Commandos, training and deployment. Since the Bandsmen aren't 'green-hatted', don't do the same intensive military training, it was felt that somehow the Band didn't 'belong'.

Hell hath no fury like a Royal Marine who feels his Band has been scorned. Whatever Royal might say about the Band – and a degree of mickey-taking does take place – he is intensely proud of it. Even if Royal knows next to nothing about the Band or Bandsmen. So with a brief apology for leaving them out originally, we are proud to present the Band of the Royal Marines.

Actually, it's also the Band of the Royal Navy for, except for some enthusiastic and gifted amateurs, the Royal Navy doesn't have its own Band. Therefore the Band of the Royal Marines is the Royal Navy's own band. There are those who say the only reason the Navy has supported the Royal Marines' continuance is that without them, the Navy wouldn't have a band. Certainly Royal Marine bandsmen themselves are quite definite on that very point.

Naturally, being part of the Royal Marines, the Band itself is not quite as straightforward an organization as its role would suggest. First there is a greater emphasis placed on basic military training than would normally be expected. This begins with an eight-week basic training course and will, in one way or another, be extended throughout a man's career. No way that they're expected to be as efficient as a 'green-hatted' commando – but they are expected to be able to look after themselves under fire, on the battlefield, when acting as stretcher bearer, runner or POW guard.

Secondly, there are two types of bandsmen: Musician or Bugler. Musicians play a wide variety of instruments ranging from the oboe/cor anglais to the euphonium/violoncello. Most musicians have to be 'double-handed', i.e. play at least two instruments. But instruments like the bassoon or bass appear to require a single-handed devotion.

Buglers were originally drummers. When the Admiral's Regiment was formed in 1664 (the Duke of York and Albany's Maritime Regiment of Foot, and the forerunner of today's Royal Marines) drums were used to give orders on the field of battle. Not just the sound of the drum, either: modern day 'stick-drill', with drumsticks flashing in precise and complex patterns, was originally a primitive form of semaphore. In 1859 the bugle replaced the drum to pass routine and tactical orders – at least, within the Army. The Navy had been using a trumpet to do much the same for some time before that, and in fact switched to the bugle in 1865. As always, the Navy had its own way of doing things. But the drum still remained, along with a regiment's colours, the central rallying point during combat. Even today, and with the exception of the bugle call, *The Last Post*, there are few more emotive sounds than the massed drums of the Royal Marines Beating Retreat. Usually it's a Drum Major from the Buglers' Branch who's resposible for ceremonial matters – it's also the Drum Major who carries the staff at the head of the Band.

All officers within the Band are promoted from the ranks. It's the only way to ensure that the necessary musical abilities are developed. Certainly senior NCOs and officers are expected not only to play to a very high standard, but also to conduct and compose for a full orchestra. One would be hard put to think of any other military band where the musical standard is so high.

Glossary

Royal Marine jargon

Part of the mystique of the Royal Marines possibly derives from the fact that they speak a different language. It sounds like English; it even sounds frustratingly familiar – but is none the less totally incomprehensible to ninety per cent of the population in Britain, and only adds to the confusion when Royal goes abroad. Loosely based on Royal Navy slang, Royal Marinespeak comprises well over five hundred words and about half that number of phrases or expressions – which is a larger vocabulary than used by some recently discovered tribes in the interior of New Guinea. Thanks to the invaluable fieldwork conducted by Captain David Tong and Sergeant Rick Haynes (both Royal Marines), and thanks to the Corps magazine, *The Globe and Laurel*, here are just a few of the more common words and expressions used.

Ace	Good, excellent
Animal run	To really let one's hair down on a run ashore
Banjo	Broken down, as in 'banjoed'
Banyan	Picnic on a beach

Glossary

Bimble	To wander around casually with one's mind in neutral
Bite	To be drawn into an argument; to accept an untruth
Bootneck/Bootie	Royal Marine. Possibly derived from the leather uniform stock worn around the neck during the Nelsonian era (USMC term 'leatherneck' may have same derivation)
Bombed out	Crazy
Boss	Respectful but casual way of referring to the officer in command
Brill/Brills	Brilliant, magnificent (pre-dates modern teenage slang by several decades)
Brammer	Outstandingly good
Bronzy	Sun tan
Bug-out	To conduct a military withdrawal
Buzz	A rumour; or a general description of the situation
Cheese-down	To laugh uncontrollably
Chuck one up	Salute
Cloggie	A Dutchman
Common dog	Common sense
Crab/Crab Air	Member of the RAF/the RAF
Crack	To achieve
Crappers	To be very drunk
Cream in	Collide
Crimbo	Yule-tide
Dig out (blind)	To make supreme effort
Dip-out/dip	To come off worse in any situation
Dischuffed	To take offence
Drip	To complain

Drop a sprog	To give birth
Earwigging	Eavesdropping
Essence	Beautiful, usually applied to one's 'pash' or 'party'
Flakers	Exhausted
Foo foo	Talcum powder
Gen	The truth
Glimp	To peer or peep
Glop	To slurp or drink hurriedly
Glophead	A drunkard
Goffer	a) Wave b) Cold drink c) Punch
Gonk	To sleep
Greenie	Saltwater wave
Grolly	Something unpleasant
Gronk	An unattractive woman
Hand	Trustworthy, efficient man ('he's a good hand')
Ickies	Money
Ish (the)	To be equipped with everything possible; to be the best
Kag kaggage	Unwanted, useless equipment
Knacker/ fat knacker	Someone unfit or overweight
Limers	Soft drink with high vitamin C
Loopy looney juice	Alcohol
Maskers	Masking tape. Invaluable to the Corps. When combined with a hammer is known as the 'Royal Marines tool kit'
Mankey	Filthy
Minging	a) Drunk b) Dirty
Mod Plod	Ministry of Defence police

Nause	Inconvenience
Nod/noddy	RM recruit
Nutty	Confectionery
Nutty fiend	Someone with a sweet tooth
Party	A female
Pash	A female with whom a Royal Marine has formed a more than casual relationship. A fiancee
Percy pongo	A soldier in the Army. Derived from the RM belief that soldiers don't wash very often
Picturize	To give an explanation
Ping	Recognize or identify
Piso	Careful with money
Plums	To gain nothing against expectations (see 'trap')
Plums rating	Someone who's always unsuccessful with women
Prof	a) To do well b) Legitimate perks
Pussers	Relating to anything (stores, equipment, regulations) to do with the Corps and/or Royal Navy. Anything done unimaginatively or by the book is done in a 'Pussers manner'
Puzzle Palace	Headquarters building
Rice	Effort
Rock-all	Nothing
Run ashore	Rest and relaxation away from ship, barracks, office or camp
Rock-ape	Member of the Mountain Leader ranch; also member of the RAF Regiment
Rug rat	A baby

Sad-on	Unhappy
SB	Special Boat Service. One who joins the SBS is said to have 'gone SB'
Scran	Food
Shave off	Expression of annoyance or to speak out of turn
Shoot-through	Someone who fails an undertaking
Skeg	To observe or conduct a reconnaissance
Skin	Immature/inexperienced young man
Sneaky beaky	Intelligence staff and their operations
Snurgle	Advance cautiously or crawl
Sprog	Baby or anyone lacking experience
Stacks	Opposite of 'plums', especially in relation to success with women
Thin-out	Depart
Threaders	Fed up
Trap	To attract successully a member of the opposite sex
Trough	Eat
Twitter	Talk aimlessly
Up homers	Invited into a home
Up the line	Travel away from base
Wet	A drink of any description
Wrap	To stop or give up
Yaffle	Eat hurriedly
Yeti	Spectacular fall on skis
Yomp	Force march with a heavy load
Yo-yo	Young Officer under training at Lympstone
Zap	To shoot or be shot
Zeds	Sleep

Annexes

Annex A: United States Marine Corps Military Doctrine

For Britain, the Dardanelles campaign in 1915 spelt the (temporary) end of large-scale amphibious operations. For the United States Marine Corps, it was only the beginning. In 1921, a Major Earl Ellis USMC published a paper entitled *Advanced Base Operations in Micronesia* which among other things advocated the use of amphibious assaults to secure naval bases. The rest of the US armed forces laughed. The USMC made the concept a cornerstone of their operations – even though they didn't yet have the equipment, obviously the experience, nor the trained men to make this a reality. In fact the first Fleet Exercise, at Calebra in 1924, that tested this new concept was an overwhelming victory – for the defenders, even though their commander, a Colonel Dion Williams, wholeheartedly wanted the concept to succeed. All the new, specialized equipment broke down; Navy coxswains were unable to reach the right beaches at the right time; off-loading stores and equipment was utterly shambolic; there was no air support worthy of the name and the naval gunfire would, in real life, have done little more than frighten the seabirds. Fine, said the

USMC, in a typical display of American thinking, now we know what we have to do and spend in order to make the idea work. By the time Pearl Harbor came round, the USMC had developed the doctrine of amphibiosity to the point that it could be translated into effective operations. Although, as was earlier pointed out, it still had its detractors until MacArthur proved at Inchon the greater flexibility amphibiosity gave to an invading force. In a sense, the Americans and the British had been approaching the same subject from different ends of the spectrum. The British, especially the Royal Navy, had always seen amphibious operations as being extremely flexible, but as underlined by the disaster of Gallipoli, essentially small-scale. Whereas the USMC saw them as relatively inflexible, large-scale methods of achieving major objectives. The Second World War only emphasized both these approaches. During the Pacific War, the Americans had little choice but to retake islands lost to the Japanese: their options were necessarily limited. The same could be said of the Normandy landings – an invasion had to take place somewhere and the sheer scale of the operation again led to a limited choice in terms of location and methods.

After the Korean War, the USMC began looking at amphibious operations in terms of smaller-scale and far more flexible operations, just as the British began looking at them as something more than raiding parties or, at the most, diversionary attacks. Improved techniques and equipment allowed a large amphibious force to land, do whatever was needed, then re-embark and move rapidly down the coast: fluid situations require fluid responses.

Then, too, within the Cold War context it was obviously much easier and safer to use the world's oceans as the main troop highway. Which ultimately led to the concept of amphibious power-projection: making your presence felt anywhere in the world without actually attacking anyone.

This leads to the basic difference between the USMC and the Royal Marines, which in turn explains why some of the doctrines developed by the USMC don't always apply to the Corps, and vice versa. Both are Marines, but the Royals are also commandos to be used in a commando role. In practical terms this means that 3 Commando Brigade and its attendant shipping lacks the firepower and equipment of its American equivalent. For commando troops are by their nature lightly equipped, since they rely so heavily on the elements of speed and surprise.

None the less, USMC amphibious thinking continued to point the way forward, leading to the current doctrine that a beachhead is not the focal point of an amphibious attack, but just another obstacle. This admittedly is easy to say when you're blessed with so many hover-craft and large-lift helicopters, but the point is well made. Today most if not all USMC future thinking is developed by a unit called the Commandant's War Fighting Laboratory, which investigates and develops the techniques and equipment needed to facilitate Sea Dragon: the programme to develop and improve sea-based joint warfare. Actually, after the first British wry smile, the name sums up the overall concept extremely well. The best dragons could always fly as well as swim, and enjoyed a reputation for both extreme ferocity and cunning. They also had a penchant for attractive women – doubtless the Politically Correct Police will shortly demand the name be changed. The War Fighting Laboratory looks at a specific area of amphibious operations for five years, which culminates in an Advanced Warfighting Experiment – known as 'not another goddam/bloody exercise' by American or British bootnecks. But actually one of the fruits of Sea Dragon is to emphasize to the USMC how much better trained and equipped the average US Marine will need to be in the future – and also more flexible and capable of independent action. For while USMC strategic thinking might be imaginative and advanced, tactics especially at company level have tended to be fairly obvious and the chain of command too rigid and hierarchical. This is partly explained by the sheer size of the USMC, and the fact that tactics can become dominated by the available equipment: if it's there, use it. Even more than the British Armed Forces, America was an early victim of that management consultant approach to warfare which insists on reducing everything to a simplistic formula hidden behind unnecessarily complex jargon. But the fact is that the USMC is simply too big to be a commando force – the necessary training would place an enormous strain on budgets that, although vast by British standards, are still limited.

The War Fighting Laboratory is also responsible for two other areas: Non-Lethal Weapons and the Chemical/Biological Incident Response Force (CBIRF). Those of us who scoffed when the USMC arrived in Somalia with all manner of esoteric kit – sticky webs, clinging foam, liquids too slippery to stand on, and so on

– should remember that as with Grenada, the USMC sees instances like this as the perfect opportunity to experiment with equipment and techniques that might well prove impractical. But how will you ever know unless you try them out in relatively hostile circumstances? The willingness of the US military in general to experiment and not give a damn what anyone else thinks has always been one of its more endearing and valuable traits.

CBIRF is now a fully fledged and operational unit based at Camp Lejeune, North Carolina. One is tempted to think of those masked, futuristically equipped soldiers that appear in the *X Files* whenever Scully and Mulder discover something that Washington wants hidden. On the other hand, chemical and biological warfare represents the best, if not the only, way a country like Iraq can seriously damage the American mainland.

The overall point to be made is that the USMC possesses the necessary resources to develop amphibious doctrine beyond the year 2000. For example, the War Laboratory also controls an Experimental Special Purpose Marine Air Ground Task Force. In Britain this would be the equivalent of dedicating 45 Commando, plus extra shipping and air support, to a purely experimental role.

However, it is necessary to sound a cautionary note. The United States tends to be obsessed by order and control – which is all perfectly understandable, given their history, polyglot population and extremes of climate. So American military tactics can be a tad inflexible and extremely dangerous for another nation to copy, unless it also possesses similar firepower and logistical support.

Annex B: Royal Marines Non-Commissioned Officers

The British are generally regarded as having the best NCOs in NATO, probably the world, and the USMC for one regards the Royal Marines NCO as the *ne plus ultra* – an NCO's NCO, as it were. In order to be promoted to corporal and above, all Marines have to attend the relevant courses held at the Non-Commissioned Officers' Training Wing at Lympstone. This is a deliberately centralized system, which as with sniper training, ensures that the identical standards and syllabus are maintained throughout the Corps. The NCOTW runs three main courses, the Junior (promotion to corporal), Senior (to sergeant) and Advanced (to Warrant Officer) Command Courses, with the emphasis on the word 'command'. A corporal must be able to command at least ten men, and a sergeant thirty, in battle. This means more than the ability to receive, interpret and pass on orders: it means the ability to make an independent assessment of the situation and assume total responsibility for his own actions. Given the type of operations Royal Marines Commandos undertake, and the very nature of modern warfare, the amount of responsibility a modern-day NCO is expected to assume can be quite awesome, especially since the Royal Marines believe that experts are there to be listened to, no matter what their rank.

Instructional techniques play a major role in the Junior and Senior Command Courses. No one gets promoted without demonstrating that he can help spread his own branch skills throughout the Corps. In fact, the role of a senior NCO is almost as much teacher as leader, reflected in his relationships with both officers and Marines.

It's often been remarked that Royal Marines officers and NCOs are, even by comparison to the best infantry regiments within the British Army, remarkably relaxed with each other. It's noticeable that outside working hours, most officers and senior NCOs will often talk about each other using first and last names. Even if a rank is included, the absent man's first name will still be included. That might sound a trivial point, but in fact it emphasizes the immensely strong family feeling throughout the Corps as a whole – above and beyond the natural bond between all men who've won a Green Beret. None the less, a great deal of self-discipline and sheer professionalism is required to avoid abuse of the Corps's more relaxed approach to rank. This is especially so as young Marines learn how to relate to officers by the example set by their corporals and sergeants – just as Young Officers are taught how to relate to their men by their first troop sergeant. Remember, a Young Officer is still officially under training for a full year after he's left Lympstone, and can be asked to leave at any time. It's up to his troop sergeant to make sure this doesn't happen. Since the sergeant is also responsible for troop administration and logistics, plus training (in practice if not in theory, until the YO begins to learn his job), not to mention overseeing the corporal's professional development, it's easy to see why the job is as much teacher as leader.

Annex C: Junior Command Course

This is the one a Marine takes for promotion to corporal. Note the amount of time given to instructional technique: the concept of the NCO as leader and teacher starts early.

	Subject Heading	Period Allocation	
		0-9	Night
1	Skill at Arms	21	0
2	Drill	9	0
3	Fieldcraft	11	0
4	Field Engineering	2	0
5	Amphibious Operations	1	0
6	Signals	10	0
7	First Aid	2	0
8	Map Reading	14	3
9	Physical Training	10	0
10	Vehicle & Helicopter Operations	1	0
11	Organization & Role	1	0
12	Military Law	2	0
13	Background Knowledge	2	0
14	Instructional Technique	19	0
15	Leadership & Man Management	10	0
16	General	32	0
17	Attack	20	0
18	Defence	5	0
19	Withdrawal	1	0
20	Military Operations Urbanized Terrain	2	0
21	Fighting in Woods & Forests	2	0

22	Ambushes	2	0
23	Protection	6	0
24	Administration	7	0
25	Transit	19	2
26	Course Administration	73	2
27	Test	4	0
28	Exercise	109	13
	Total	**397**	**18**

Annex D: Platoon Weapons Instructor 2nd Class

This is the branch course a Marine must take and which, assuming he passes the Junior Command Course, qualifies him to promotion to corporal within the branch. Note the use of the word 'instructor' and the amount of time that, again, is given to teaching instructional techniques.

	Subject Heading	Period Allocation	
		0-9	Night
1	Skill at Arms	129	3
2	Army Operational Shooting Policy	10	0
3	Coaching	12	1
4	Fieldcraft	28	0
5	Map Reading	14	2
6	Rangework	59	3
7	Field Firing	61	2
8	Physical Fitness	1	0
9	Instructional Technique	40	0

10	General	9	0
11	Test	16	6
12	Course Administration	34	5
13	Transit	39	0
	Total	**452**	**11**

Annex E: Assault Engineers

There are three different branch courses run by the Assault Engineers. AE3 allows entry to the branch; AE2, promotion to corporal; and AE1, to sergeant and above. No apologies for including these AE courses at length, for this branch is a perfect example of what makes the Royal Marines so unique: their self-sufficiency.

Subject Heading		Period Allocation	
		0-9	Night
1	Tools	24	0
2	Field Geometry	8	0
3	Field Machines	32	0
4	Bridge Construction	17	0
5	First Aid	3	0
6	Organization	3	0
7	Roads and Airfields	5	0
8	Water Supply	14	0
9	Camp Structures and Field Sanitation	6	0
10	Field Fortifications	20	0
11	Watermanship	20	0
12	Demolitions	75	0

		0-9	Night
13	Mine Warfare and Booby Traps	44	0
14	Military Aid to the Civil Community	0	0
15	General	0	0
16	Scaffolding	2	0
17	Transit	9	0
18	Test	1	0
19	Course Administration	11	0
	Total	**294**	**0**

	Subject Heading	Period Allocation	
		0-9	Night
1	Tools	22	0
2	Field Geometry	5	0
3	Field Machines	44	0
4	Bridge Construction	35	0
5	First Aid	3	0
6	Roads and Airfields	5	0
7	Water Supply	14	0
8	Camp Structures and Field Sanitation	26	0
9	Field Fortifications	22	0
10	Watermanship	22	0
11	Demolitions	71	0
12	Mine Warfare and Booby Traps	44	0
13	Military Aid to the Civil Community	1	0
14	General	0	0
15	Transit	12	0
16	Test	1	0
17	Course Administration	14	0
	Total	**347**	**0**

Subject Heading	Period Allocation 0-9	Night
1 Tools	19	0
2 Field Geometry	41	0
3 Bridge Construction	90	0
4 Roads and Airfields	14	0
5 Water Supply	20	0
6 Camp Structures and Field Sanitation	5	0
7 Scaffolding	12	0
8 Field Fortifications	17	0
9. Watermanship	18	0
10 Demolitions	99	0
11 Mine Warfare and Booby Traps	42	0
12 Military Aid to the Civil Community	1	0
13. Instructional Technique	14	0
14 General	6	0
15 Administration	3	0
16. Test	2	0
17. Transit	22	0
18 Course Administration	21	0
Total	446	0

Annex F: All-Arms Commando Course

Below is the syllabus for this course. It can't be compared to Royal Marines recruit training, which takes place over a lot longer period and starts from scratch. Points to note – aside from the amount of time allocated to physical fitness – are thirty-four periods for skill at arms; seventy-three for fieldcraft and minor tactics;

thirty-nine for patrolling; and fifteen for amphibious operations. The CTCRM assumes that all candidates for the All-Arms Course are already infantry-trained to a greater or lesser extent, as indeed they should be. The Course aims to add those commando skills that will help a man take his place in 3 Commando Brigade.

	Subject Heading	Period Allocation 0-9	Night
1	Skill at Arms	34	1
2	Fieldcraft & Minor Tactics	73	4
3	Amphibious Operations	15	0
4	Signals	3	0
5	First Aid	2	0
6	Map Reading & Navigation	5	1
7	Physical Fitness	93	0
8	Vehicle and Helicopter Movement	7	0
9	Organization and Role	1	0
10	General	7	0
11	Defence	2	0
12	Patrolling	39	6
13	Administration	1	0
14	Test	49	5
15	Course Administration	33	5
16	Transit	18	0
	Total	382	21

Annex G: How the SBS began

Forerunners of the SBS include: the Combined Operations Assault Pilotage Parties (COPPs) originally comprising Royal Navy navigators and Royal Engineers officers who were tasked with beach reconnaissance prior to a landing; the Small Scale Raiding Force, responsible for landing – and occasionally collecting – SOE agents operating in occupied Europe; the Special Boat Section of 40 Commando, which operated from submarines; 101 Troop, which mounted recce raids from its Dover base; Naval Beach Reconnaissance Parties (Middle East); SB Squadron (Middle East), which was part of the SAS, ultimately absorbed into D Squadron, and disbanded along with the rest of the SAS in 1946; Raiding Forces Middle East, which at various times had under command: the Greek Sacred Squadron; American Office of Strategic Services personnel (forerunner of the CIA); the Corsican Battalion de Choc; a demolition squad of Royal Engineers; men of the RMBPD who were training as coastal-watchers; an SB Squadron; plus assorted saboteurs, assassins and guides. Think of *The Guns of Navarone* and that Sunday afternoon movie where where Dirk Bogarde captures a German general on a Greek island. Then there was 'X' Group, formed in Australia for anti-shipping raids, and which lost thirty-two men killed or captured during Operation Rimau at Singapore in 1944; 'Z' Group comprising ten canoeists and operating in the Mediterranean; Combined Operations Scout Units, which were used to create diversions; 1st Special Raiding Squadron, an SAS unit commanded by Major Paddy Mayne; and last but not least, the Royal Marine Boom Patrol Detachment, of 'Blondie' Hassler and Norwegian fame. All these units amalgamated – in function if not in name – and became the SBS.

That said, the concept wasn't new even in 1939. Clandestine, water-borne military operations were understood by the Ancient Phoenicians, Greeks, Romans and, much later, by the Royal Navy as it developed in Elizabethan times.

Index